Protecting Asia's Heritage Yesterday and Tomorrow

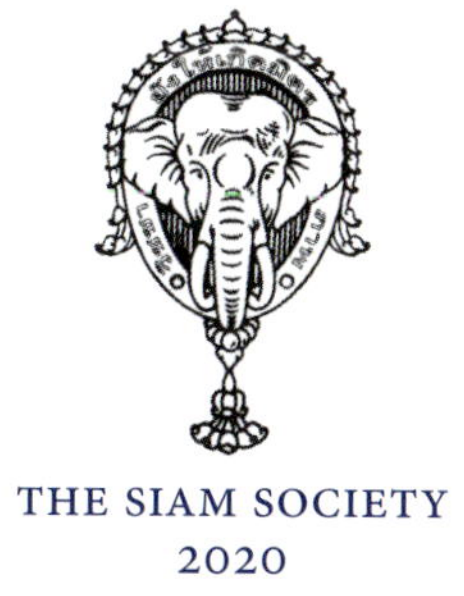

THE SIAM SOCIETY
2020

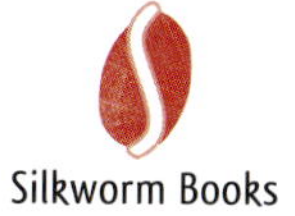

"...we need to be reminded that there is more to heritage than looking out for things that fit a list of cultural criteria. It is also necessary to examine how people relate differently to past experiences and to ideas about their past, whether tangible or not."

Wang Gungwu (*Nanyang: Essays on Heritage*. Singapore: ISEAS-Yusof Ishak Institute, 2018)

Protecting Asia's Heritage Yesterday and Tomorrow

Asia's splendid heritage is at risk. The region's economy has grown faster than anywhere ever. Cities and landscapes are being transformed. Governments are too focused on the future to devote attention and budgets to conserving the past. Tourism is a double-edged sword. But some people have become deeply, passionately, and actively involved in protecting Asia's heritage. In early 2019, a group of them, all Asians, met at a conference in Bangkok. They shared their experience of what they had seen and done in the past. They offered an Asian perspective on the challenges of cultural heritage protection, on what should be done in the future. This book is a record of that meeting.

The twelve chapters showcase the enormous variety of Asia's heritage. The principal authors hail from eleven of the region's countries. They include activists, organizers, critics, teachers, artists, and entrepreneurs. Their interests range across the temples of old Siam, religious murals in Korea, hutong neighborhoods of Beijing, traditional textile art of multiethnic Laos, the ruins of Majapahit Java, traditional performance art in Cambodia, the old quarters of Bangkok and George Town, creative arts of the Philippines, Calcutta's legacy of colonial architecture, China's historic salt industry, and the Burmese cat.

Despite this variety, the contributors to this book agree on many themes. The Western experience with managing heritage has been hugely valuable, but needs now to be extended with concepts and practices relevant to Asia. The legal framework is vital for protecting heritage, but lags behind the pace of change and urgently needs attention. Intangible heritage must be accorded more attention and respect. Heritage management has often failed because it has been driven down from the top. Citizens and local communities are often the best guardians of heritage. Organizations and campaigns that draw on both public and private resources often score success. The heritage and environmental movements can gain from cooperation. Protecting heritage can be good for business, but it requires discipline and vision.

This book records the start of a conversation which promises to transform the protection of Asia's heritage tomorrow.

ISBN 978-616-215-156-9

First published in 2020 by
The Siam Society Under Royal Patronage
131 Sukhumwit Soi 21 (Asoke-Montri Road),
Bangkok 10110, Thailand
Tel. (662) 661 6470–7 Fax. (662) 258 3491
E-mail: info@siam-society.org
www.siam-society.org

and

Silkworm Books
430/58 M. 7, T. Mae Hia, Chiang Mai 50100, Thailand
info@silkwormbooks.com
http://www.silkwormbooks.com

Cover: Nork Airnyvone dancing the peacock dance on the Cambodian Living Arts Stage at the National Museum of Cambodia in April 2018 (Photo © Cambodian Living Arts / Lamo).

Printed and bound in Singapore

Contents

Introduction

James Stent

Definitions of culture are legion, but, until recently, almost all defintions were global and expected to serve equally well wherever applied. The United Nations Educational, Scientific and Cultural Organization (UNESCO) laid down authoritative guidelines on how cultural heritage should be managed.

In today's world, however, the universality of many social, economic, and political concepts, considered axiomatic in the West, are being challenged. Is it not time to also re-examine the concepts of "culture" and "cultural heritage" from new perspectives? Global approaches are no doubt useful to make global best practice universally accessible, but is there now a need to draw on differing local experiences and social contexts to adapt cultural heritage to different cultural contexts? In this collection of essays, *Protecting Asia's Heritage Yesterday and Tomorrow*, Asian practitioners and experts in cultural heritage protection look at cultural heritage from an Asian perspective with focus on the local rather than the global.

During the 19th century, largely in Europe, cultural heritage was first recognized to be deserving of preservation as a nation's patrimony, a link to its past, and a definer of its identity as a people. Inspired by the romantic movement's fascination with the ruins of classical antiquity, Europeans began to recognize that the physical and social transformations brought about by the Industrial Revolution put much important architecture and art of cultural significance at risk of neglect or destruction. In Britain, this resulted in the founding in 1895 of the National Trust, which over its 124 years of existence has preserved an enormous number of properties of cultural importance. On the continent of Europe, governments and private bodies established institutions to successfully define and conserve their nations' cultural heritages. In the Americas, the National Trust of the United States, as well as federal, state, and local bodies, moved actively to conserve cultural heritage.

In Europe and America, citizens took great interest in their nations' cultural heritage, seeing cultural heritage as not only part of national identity, but as part of their own personal identity as well. As one UNESCO officer put it, "The success of French and Italian cultural heritage protection is based on each French and Italian citizen seeing himself as the owner of his or her national cultural heritage." The successful experience of cultural heritage protection in Europe and America has led to that experience being enshrined as a standard of best practice for cultural heritage protection globally.

National and popular commitment to preservation of national cultural heritage in Europe and the Americas ed, in the post-war era, to the formulation, by Paris-based UNESCO, of guiding principles and global best practice, codified in a number of treaties and protocols issued over the years, starting with the Venice Charter of 1964. The Venice Charter focused on proper methods of physical conservation, emphasizing the "authenticity" of any restoration undertaken. Later UNESCO charters and protocols broadened the scope of UNESCO guidance to include intangible heritage, community heritage, greater attention to local and national identity in restoration, and more latitude for responsible reconstruction.

UNESCO also initiated the inscribing of World Heritage Sites. UNESCO formulated well-defined criteria under which a nation could apply for a site being inscribed as a World Heritage Site, developed a transparent mechanism for screening and approving the applications, and monitored the management of inscribed heritage sites. For many nations, World Heritage Sites are coveted recognition at a global level of the value of their own cultural heritage. World Heritage Sites are believed to enhance national prestige and bring in tourist revenue. Notwithstanding the success of the World Heritage Site program, the sites have been criticized for bringing about commercialization, overcrowding, physical degradation, and loss of the original significance they had for local community culture.

In the sphere of economics and politics, the universal validity and applicability of the neoliberal orthodoxies of the "Washington consensus" are viewed with increasing skepticism. Similarly, perhaps the time has come to examine whether the orthodoxies of cultural heritage practice that have held sway over the past decades should be looked at in the light of non-Western cultural contexts. To what extent are concepts of culture and cultural heritage unique to each culture, and therefore require different approaches to preservation?

The etymology of the word "culture" itself hints at how different peoples may regard culture differently. The modern English word "culture" has its roots in a Middle English word of the same spelling that meant "a cultivated piece of land." That Middle English word in turn derived from the Latin word "cultura," meaning cultivation of the soil. In the early 16th century "culture" evolved to include the sense of cultivating the mind, and thereafter gradually assumed the additional meaning of the arts, institutions, and behavior patterns of a people, in which sense it is now given a range of definitions by academics, taking on new shades of meaning as social science thinking evolves. Although the word "culture" as now used encompasses a range of intangible concepts, the origins of the word "culture" are firmly embedded in the soil—what could be more tangible than soil?

Contrast this with the Chinese word 文化 *wenhua*—a two-character word which dictionaries give as the Chinese equivalent of the English word "culture," but whose etymology is entirely different from that of its English equivalent. The original and basic meaning of the first character 文 wen is "the word," while the basic meaning of 化 hua is to change or transform. These two characters both deal with intangible concepts. The word *wenhua* had been used since the ancient Han Dynasty up through the Ming Dynasty in the sense of "using soft power to subdue enemies." It is only in the latter years of the Qing Dynasty in the late 19th century that use of the word *wenhua* is encountered having the meaning of the English word "culture." Since that time, *wenhua* has ceased to have its ancient meaning of subduing with soft power, but has become a very frequently used word for "culture" in its broadest sense.

Do the different etymologies of the English and Chinese words for "culture" suggest different understandings of what culture is, and of how it should be conserved? Whereas in the West "authenticity" and scrupulous respect for the appearance, materials, and physical workmanship of the past is highly valued in conservation practice, in China change is built into the very word for culture.

The word "culture" was introduced to Thailand in the early 20th century. Apparently, no word expressing this concept previously existed in the Thai language. The first attempts to create an equivalent word in the Thai language did not gain popular acceptance. Finally, one Thai scholar devised the word *watthanatham* out of two Sanskrit-Pali roots, *watthana*, meaning "growing" or "increasing," and *tham*, which has a range of meanings relating to ethical teachings, justice, and rationality. This word gained acceptance and was enshrined in the Thai language in the Culture Act of 1942. The modernizing Thai leader, Luang Phibunsongkhram, used the word in the service of promoting nationalism. Subsequent interpretations have given it somewhat broader meanings, but generally still promoting official views of culture.

These examples from three languages demonstrate that "culture" is a word of relatively modern usage, and that the way in which it is rendered in different languages depends on circumstances peculiar to each language. Further study is needed to understand the origins and etymology of the word "culture" in each Asian language, and the extent to which subtle differences in nuance of the word in different languages might indicate different underlying appreciations of culture itself.

This brief discussion of the etymology of the words for "culture" in different languages points to the complexity of cultural heritage issues in Asia. In its work over the past several years in Thailand, the Siamese Heritage Trust of the Siam Society has reflected on the differences encountered in global and local approaches to cultural heritage protection, and on the complex realities of successful heritage protection on the ground in Thailand. These realities are not always well accounted for in established global best practice of cultural heritage protection.

To address these issues on a pan-Asian scale, the Siam Society organized a conference under the title "Heritage Protection: the Asian Experience" in Bangkok on January 25–26, 2019. The conference offered a forum for Asian experts to consider aspects of cultural heritage from their own national or regional perspectives. The fifteen participants, including thirteen who presented papers and two moderators, came from eleven countries: one each from Korea, Japan, Cambodia, Myanmar, India, Malaysia, Indonesia, Singapore, and the Philippines, and two each from Thailand, China, and Laos. All were ethnically and culturally Asian, were either academics or cultural heritage practitioners, and were independent of their governments and international organizations.

The papers addressed four broad issues: the definition of cultural heritage; the involvement of grassroots communities in taking control of their own cultural heritages; the role of law in cultural heritage protection; and enlisting commercial energies to support rather than obstruct cultural heritage protection. The essays are all country-specific; Asia is a vast area, with many different cultures, and no attempt was made by the presenters to reach conclusions that would be valid for the entire region. The styles and topics of the papers are diverse, but taken together they form a pioneering attempt to look at the challenges of cultural heritage protection by Asian practitioners within an Asian context.

The conference and these essays are hopefully only a first step in developing Asian perspectives on heritage protection—perspectives that might in the future influence the policy and methodology of cultural heritage protection carried out by Asian governments, civil society institutions, and local governments. The conference generated great enthusiasm and interest on the part of both the presenters and the attendees. The next step will be to channel that enthusiasm and interest into more tangible form by building Asian networks to promote approaches to cultural heritage protection that are adapted to the cultural, social, and political realities of Asian societies.

Heritage Is the Living Present of the Past

Piriya Krairiksh

Stanley J. Tambiah writes in the conclusion to his study of Thai Buddhism, *World Conqueror and World Renouncer:*

> If we find it difficult or even impossible in many situations today to separate continuities from transformations, it is for the good reason that in Thailand (as in many other post traditional and developing societies) there is a simultaneous reference to "two uses of the past."
>
> The first use of the past is *past as sanction*. This view of the past has two dimensions. It embraces the Malinowskian "charter" theory, which focuses on how people use the past as a legitimator of the present; thus the past is seen as a living present. There is also the further use whereby whatever changes, modifications and innovations are introduced in the present are referred back to a pristine canonical model or event as seen as reflecting it .... The past used in these ways has been a handmaid of authority serving to conserve as well as to adapt. The traditional Thai view of "history" and their use of it is in this tradition of past as sanction ...
>
> But there is also the *past as destiny,* the past seen as influencing the unfolding of the future in a linear pattern. Although there are in Asian intellectual systems intimations and "primitive" versions of this orientation ... yet perhaps it is correct to say that a systematic view of the linking of past and future, event leading to event, as unfolding destiny expressed in ideas such as progress, evolution, development has its origin in Judaeo-Christian traditions of prophecy and infected the East through colonial contact with the West ....
>
> Thai notions of destiny—whether grounded in the past as sanction or in the future as prophecy—are inextricably linked

> with the promises and goals of the Buddhist religion. (Tambiah 1977, 528–30)

Scholars of heritage study followed Tambiah's lead by attributing Thailand's cultural differences from the West to her Buddhist religion. Denis Byrne is a critic of the practitioners of the International Charter for the Conservation and Restoration of Monuments (The Venice Charter), drawn up by the Council on Monuments and Sites (ICOMOS) in 1964, which specifies keeping the original fabric of the monuments (Nikhom 2533/1990: 223–28). Byrne denigrates the "current conservation practice which, privileging 'original' fabric, cuts across Thai local religious practice" (Byrne 1995: 266), and argues that "the continuity which the *stupa,* as a religious monument, represents is primarily spiritual in nature and has little to do with the physical continuity of its fabric or form" (Ibid., 267).

This observation led Anna Karlström to emphasize that:

> In such a discourse, spirituality must be considered and focused upon when developing conservation ethics or heritage management programs. This might lead to a situation where the World (read: Western) Heritage Project becomes gradually overthrown or at least dramatically changed, resulting in greater balance between different discourses, and between materiality and spirituality. (Karlström 2005: 341–42)

Somchart Chungsiriarak also argues for "making a better balance between traditional value and the modern concept." According to him:

> The preservation of a structure's authenticity has never been an aim of such [Buddhist ecclesiastical] activity. Only since Thailand opened the country to the West in the mid-19th century in the reign of King Rama IV [r. 1851–68], a new idea in conservation from Europe has been forming. The substantial change to the modern idea of conservation was evident in the reigns of King Rama VI [r. 1910–25] and Rama VII [r. 1925–35], when relevant laws were passed and organizations established. Yet the traditional concept and practice were still intact and co-existed with the new idea. Their strong influence was seen in the conservation practiced by both government and people which continued to follow the traditional method aiming to "restore

the structure to its former glory." (Somchart 2555/2012: 127, edited)

Byrne reiterates the spiritual nature of monuments by attributing to them a "miraculous efficacy." As an illustration, he uses King Mongkut's restoration of the Phra Pathom Chedi in 1854, when he encased the ruins of the ancient stupa with a new stupa three times its size (Figure 1). "What legitimated Mongkut's enlarged version of Phra Pathom was its continued authenticity as a magical object. The laws of magic constitute their own charter for restoration" (Byrne 2014: 83). Byrne espoused "a 'living heritage' of objects vibrant with efficacy and devotees locked in a consensual embrace with them" (Ibid., 80).

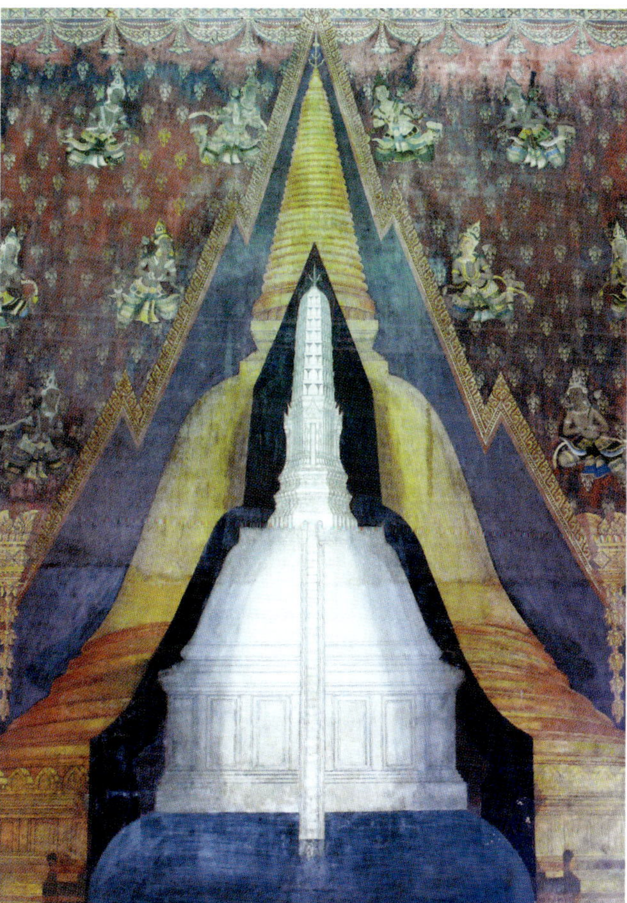

Figure 1. Mural painting by Phraya Anusarn Chittakorn, 1910–25 at Wat Phra Pathom Chedi, Nakhon Pathom, showing the present bell-shaped stupa enclosing the earlier Ayutthaya-period stupa.

Such religious fervor could also wipe out a monument, as for example Khru Ba Śrīvijaya's restoration of the chedi of Wat Suan Dok, Chiang Mai, in 1931 (*Chiang Mai News* 2559/2016), when the only lotus-bud topped stupa in Chiang Mai was demolished (Figure 2a), to be replaced by a modern counterpart (Figure 2b). Khru Ba Śrīvijaya might have thought that the lotus-bud topped stupa, being a symbol of Siam, had no place in Lān Nā.

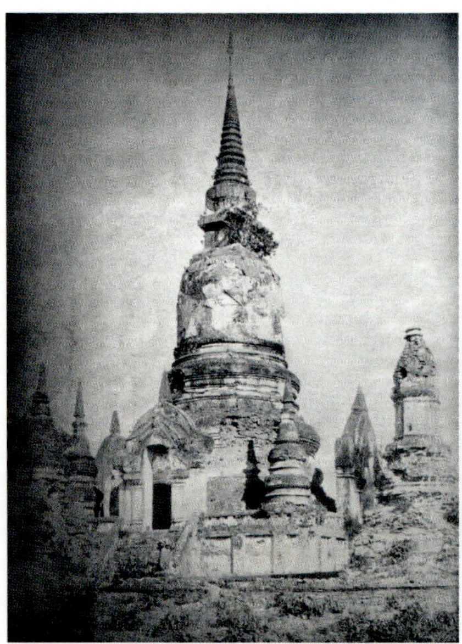

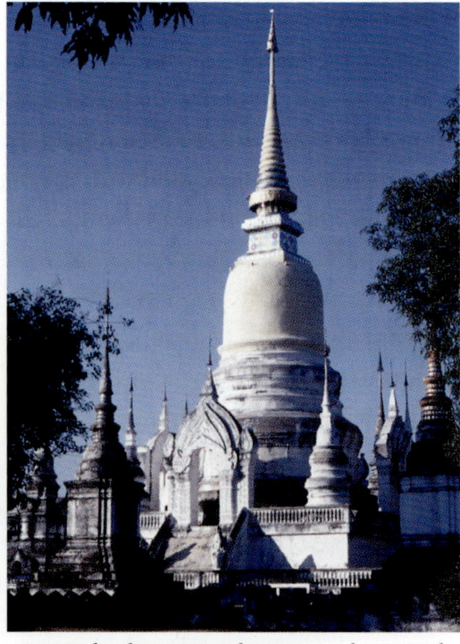

Figure 2. (left) The lotus-bud topped stupa at Wat Suan Dok, Chiang Mai shown in a photograph taken before restoration undertaken by Khru Ba Śrīvijaya in 1931. (Photo: after Ratanapañña Thera 2501/ 1958, Fig.2) (right) After restoration the lotus-bud topped stupa is replaced by a modern stupa.

Maurizio Peleggi also concludes:

> ...that conservation cannot be premised upon seemingly universal—though in fact Western—ideas of aesthetic and historic value, but must reflect in the first place the cultural values and religious beliefs of the community for whom heritage is preserved. (Peleggi 2012: 55)

Peleggi (2017: 25) sees "the traditional approach to restoration as a meritorious act, or meritorious acts seeking to resurrect the *śaksit* [preternatural power] that had dissipated owing to the decay of the cultic object's physical fabric."

Donald Ellsmore succinctly sums up restoration in Thailand:

> In Thailand, the act of building or renovating a sacred Buddhist place is a cherished way of making merit. However, acts of maintenance do not appear to have the same appeal. It is not uncommon, therefore, to witness Buddhist communities in Thailand dedicating very substantial financial and human resources to constructing new temples or related sacred buildings whilst allowing venerable historic structures to deteriorate for want of conservation. Nor is it unusual to witness major changes being made to highly significant places of worship in acts of renewal that show little regard for the original and authentic fabric of the places. In Buddhist belief, these acts of renewal are more highly valued than acts of understated care of building fabric and, as far as it can be determined, there is little official interference in the process. (Ellsmore 2008: 164–65)

Thus, both Thai and foreign scholars agree that conservation in Thailand should be exempted from the rules and regulations of the "Venice Charter" of 1964 and be allowed to pursue its own Buddhist way.

As a Theravāda Buddhist nation, religion was the driving force of Thailand's conservation in the past as well as in the present. Its main objectives were to strengthen faith and prolong the life of the religion.

The goal of traditional conservation, then as well as now, is to preserve and to continue the sanctity of the sacred (śaksit) location. Hence between the 6th and 9th centuries, three reconstructions can be discerned at Chula Pathon Chedi in Nakhon Pathom (Figure 3) (Krairiksh 2012: 55, 88, 270).

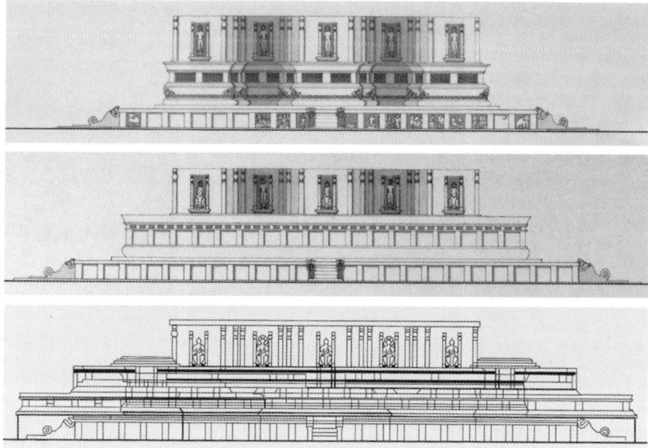

Figure 3. The three stages of the Chula Pathon Chedi, Nakhon Pathom. (After Krairiksh 2012, 55, 88, 270)

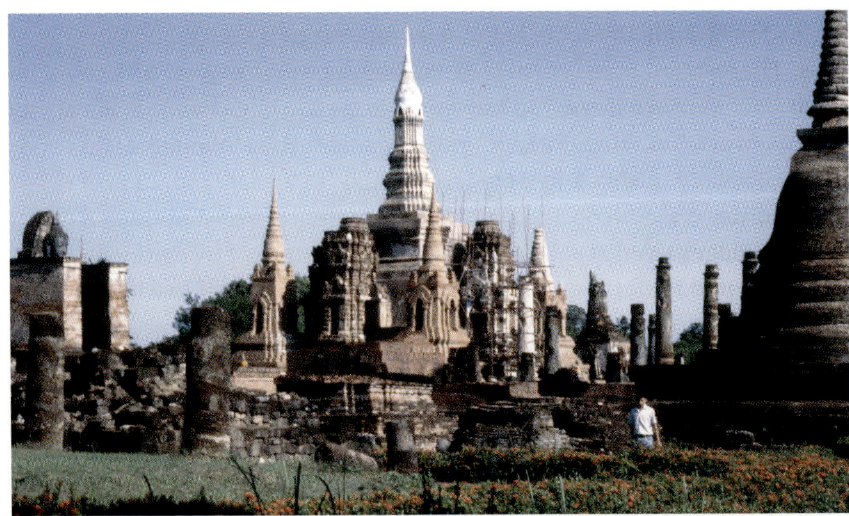

Figure 4. The Great Relic Stupa at Wat Mahāthāt, Sukhothai, reconstructed in the 17th and 18th centuries.

The practice continued into the mid-14th century with the rebuilding of the Mahāthāt (Great Relic Stupa) at Sukhothai over an earlier one (Phra Thāt Luang), which has been overgrown (Prasert and Griswold 1992: 390–92). Many reconstructions of the Great Relic Stupa took place between the mid-17th and mid-18th centuries, when the Mahāthāt assumed its present form (Figure 4) (Krairiksh 2018: 94).

The traditional Buddhist method for conserving an ancient building, therefore, was to construct a new one on top of the old and to continue beautifying it.

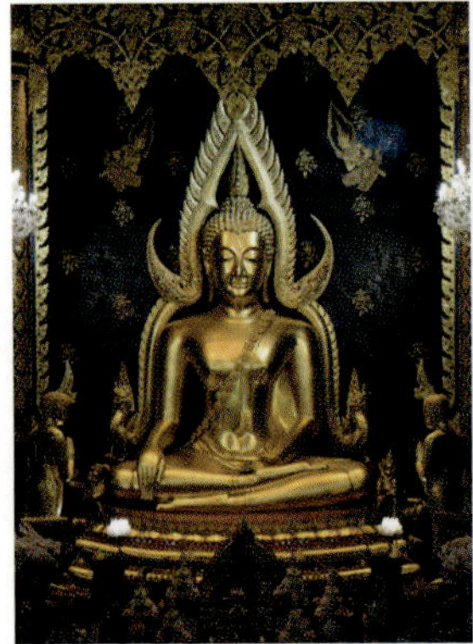

Figure 5a. Phra Buddha Jinarāja, Wat Phra Si Rattana Mahathat, Phitsanulok, 17th century. (Photo © courtesy of Sivakorn Chumprasert)

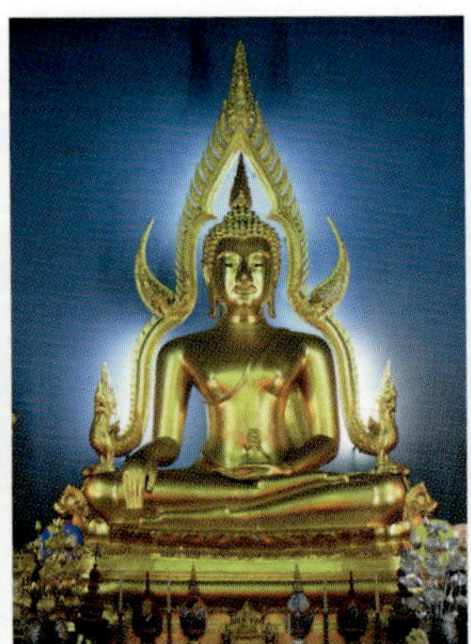

Figure 5b. Phra Buddha Jinarāja, Wat Benchamabophit, Bangkok, cast in 1901.

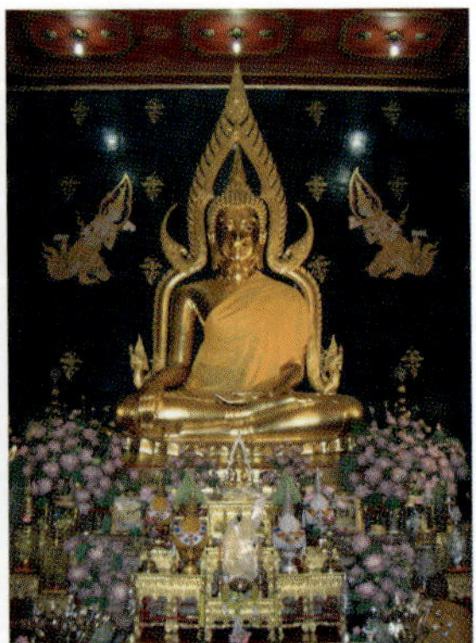

Figure 5c. Phra Buddha Jinarāja, Wat Thai Bodh Gaya, Bihār, India, cast in 1957.

As for Buddha images, the primary aim was to conserve their sacredness. Therefore, copies were made to preserve the sanctity of individual spiritually potent images (Griswold 1966: 37). The best modern day examples are the Phra Buddha Jinarāja image at Phitsanulok (Figure 5a) and its replicas (Figures 5b, 5c).

In order that they would not lose their sanctity as religious icons, broken images were repaired and made whole, as in the case of the stone images, found in pieces at places two or three days travel from Sukhothai, that were brought to Wat Mahāthāt in the mid-14th century "to mend and restore into large, fresh-looking, and . . . exceedingly beautiful statues of the Buddha" (Inscription 2, Prasert and Griswold 1992: 393). An example is the 3.30-meter Buddha found at Wat Mahāthāt and now in the Bangkok National Museum (Figure 6).

When their original homes were ravaged by wars or neglect, images of the Buddha were moved for safekeeping to new locations, as with the celebrated image of Phra Lokanātha from the Temple Royal of Wat

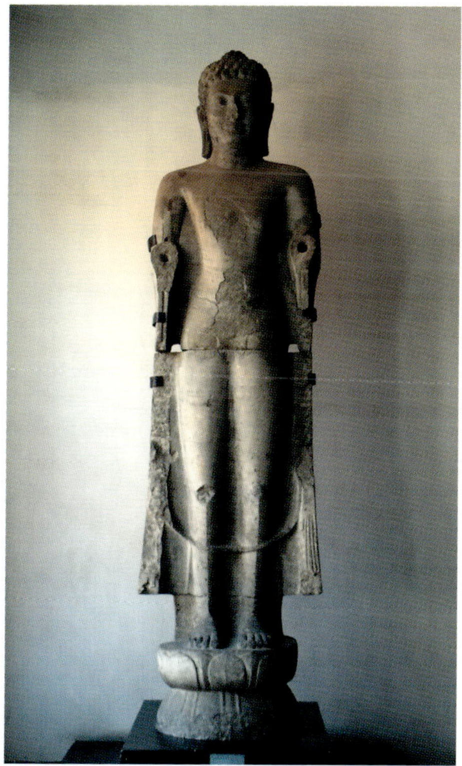

Figure 6. Buddha Amitābha found at Wat Mahathat, Sukhothai. 8th century. Stone: H. 3.30 m, Bangkok National Museum.

Phra Si Sanphet, Ayutthaya, which King Rama I (r. 1782–1809) had brought to Wat Phra Chetuphon, Bangkok, and restored in 1788 (*Prachum charuk,* Vol. 1 2472/1925: 1) (Figure 7). In 1794 the King also brought 1,285 bronze Buddha images from Sukhothai, 383 images from Phichit, and 361 images from Lop Buri to Bangkok to be installed in the same monastery (Figure 8) (Wirawan 2560/2017: 42–55).

To prevent the images losing their sanctity because some physical attributes differed from those considered authentic at the time, many had their head and hands recast to conform to prevailing taste (*Prachum charuk*, Vol. 1 2472/1929: 3). Among them are three famous images from

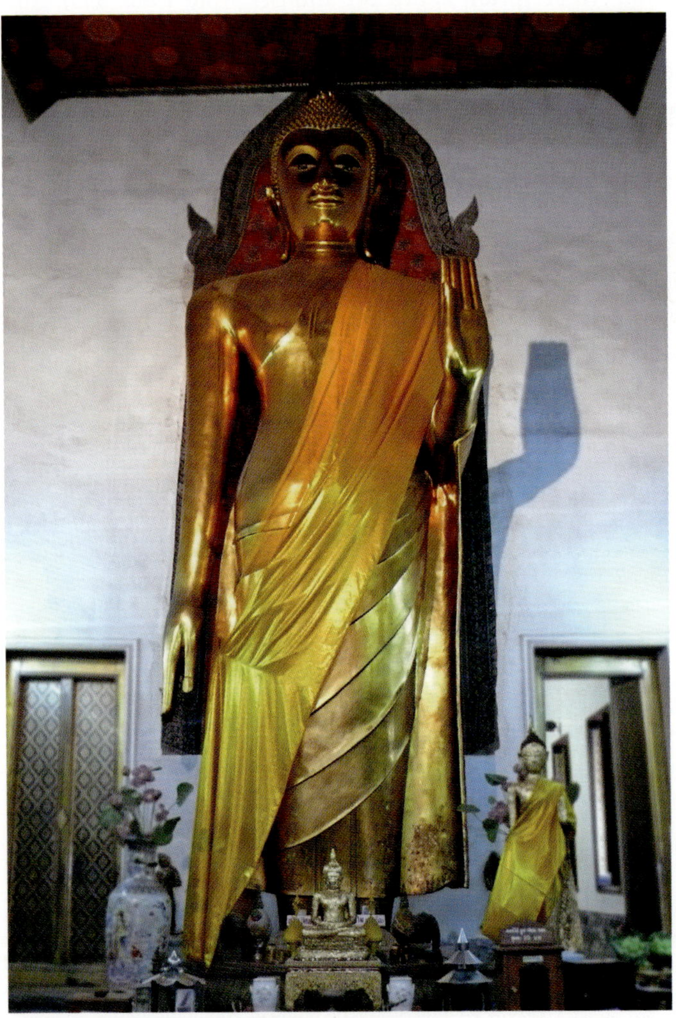

Figure 7. Phra Buddha Lokanātha, brought from Wat Phra Si Sanphet, Ayutthaya. 16th century. Bronze: H. 10 m. Wat Phra Chetupon, Bangkok.

Sukhothai, two of which King Rama I knew by name; they are Phra Buddha Jinarāja (Figure 9a) and Phra Buddha Jinaśrī (Figure 9b). The third, previously known as the Big Buddha, was given the name Phra Śrī Śākyamuni by the King (Figure 9c) (Krairiksh 2018: 64–6).

Peleggi has also pointed out that cultural nationalism is a contributing factor in Thailand's cultural inheritance. Like Tambiah, he sees the institutionalization of the nation's cultural heritage as a reflection of modernization. So, "Siamese monarchs in the late 19th and early 20th centuries manipulated the past to sanction change, via the authority of historical customs, and continuity, via the normative values of newly

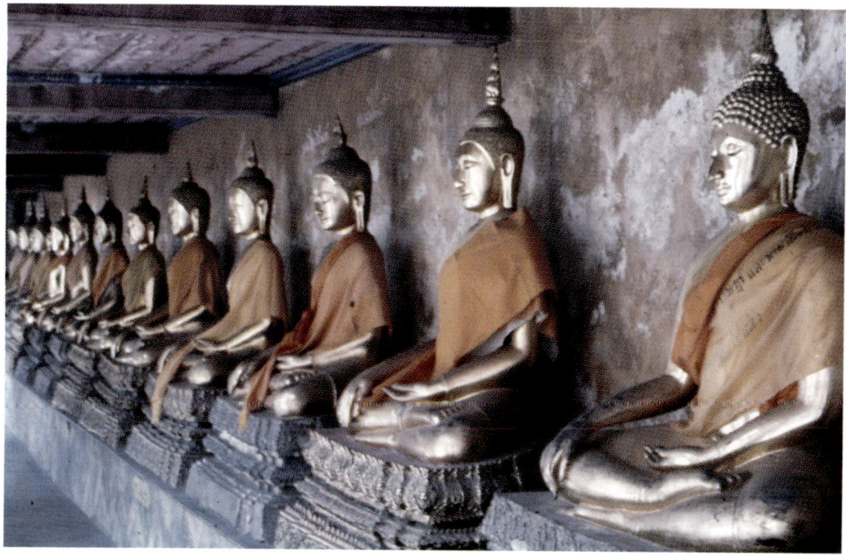

Figure 8. Some of the bronze Buddha images brought from Sukhothai, Phichit and Lop Buri in a covered gallery of Wat Phra Chetuphon, Bangkok.

invented traditions" (Peleggi 2002: 14). He chooses the stone inscription of King Rām Khamhaeng (ca. 1279–98), which King Mongkut claimed to have discovered at Sukhothai, as "a most important symbol of the national identity." (Ibid.)

The modern invention of national historical identity became a source of pride for the Thai nation, in particularly after UNESCO declared Ayutthaya, Sukhothai, Si Satchanalai, and Kamphaeng Phet as World Heritage Sites in 1991. It is:

> ... an acknowledgment of the previous decade of government efforts towards conservation and, indeed, as the ultimate

authentication of the national historical narrative for which the kingdoms of Sukhothai and Ayutthaya were the precursors of the modern Thai nation. (Peleggi 2002, 24)

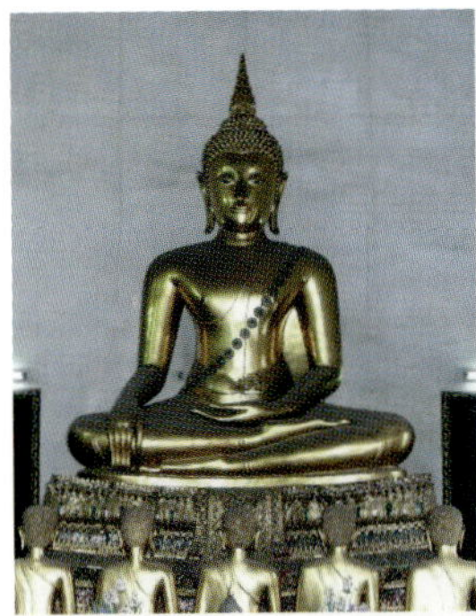
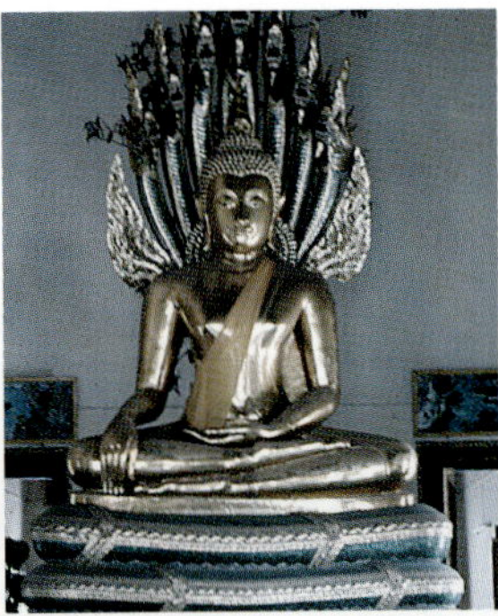
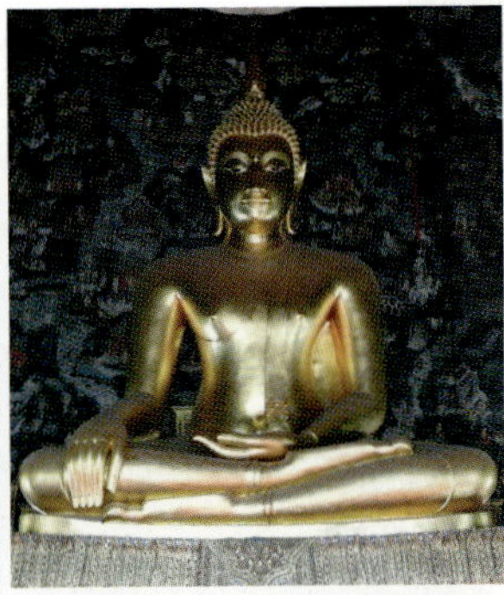

Figure 9a. (left) Phra Buddha Jinarāja, brought from Sukhothai by King Rama I in 1801. Bronze: W. 277 cm. South Vihāra, Wat Phra Chetuphon, Bangkok. Figure 9b. (center) Phra Buddha Jinaśrī, brought from Sukhothai by King Rama I in 1801. Bronze: W. 277 cm. West Vihāra, Wat Phra Chetuphon, Bangkok. Figure 9c. (right) Phra Śrī Śākyamuni, brought from Sukhothai by King Rama I in 1808. Bronze: H. 800 cm. Vihāra Luang, Wat Suthat Thepwararam, Bangkok.

From 1953 to 1987, the Thai Fine Arts Department endeavored to restore the ruins of Sukhothai to its preeminent state in the 14th century, using as its guideline the "Bangkok Charter" (The 1985 Amendments of the Act on Monuments, Antiques, Objects of Art and National Museums of 1961) (Nikhom 2533/1990: 98–100). "Restoration" meant the act of returning a structure to a former state. An example was the Fine Arts Department's restoration of Phra Acana, a brick and stucco Buddha measuring 11.30 meters between the knees, at Wat Śrī Chum. When Prince Narisara Nuwattiwong saw this image in 1901, he noticed that there were about five different levels of molding around the eyes (Narisara Nuwattiwong 2506/1963: 98), suggesting that there might have been at least four restorations before that time (Figure 10a). After restoration by Nai Boonthum Phunsawat, the Fine Arts Department's restorer, any vestige of the image's multiple changes had disappeared and the image has become an example of the idealized 14th century Sukhothai-style Buddha, albeit created in 1953 (*Rai ngan karn sam ruat* 2512/1969: 55) (Figure 10b).

Another example is the Atthārasa image (18 cubits/circa 9 meters high) of the Buddha, one of a pair flanking the Great Relic Stupa at Wat Mahāthāt Sukhothai. As seen in a 1927 photograph, the northern image clearly exhibits Ayutthaya-period physiognomy and the Ayutthaya-era manner of wearing the undergarment (Figure 11a). After being remodeled in 1953, the image conformed to the Fine Arts Department's ideal of 14th

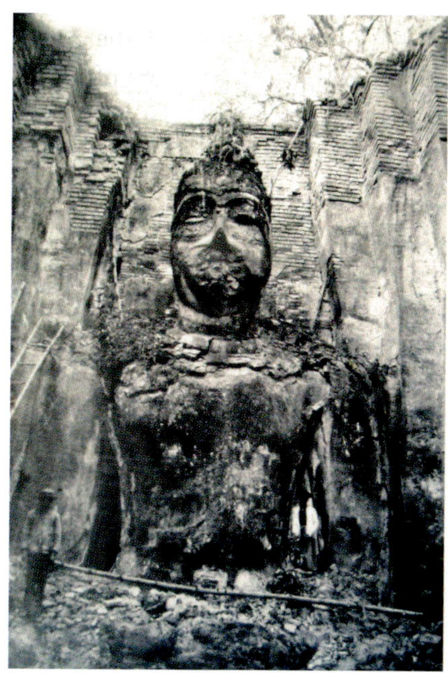

Figure 10a. Phra Acana, Wat Śrī Chum, Sukhothai, photographed by Lucien Fournereau in 1891. (After Fournereau 1908, Vol. II, Pl. IV.)

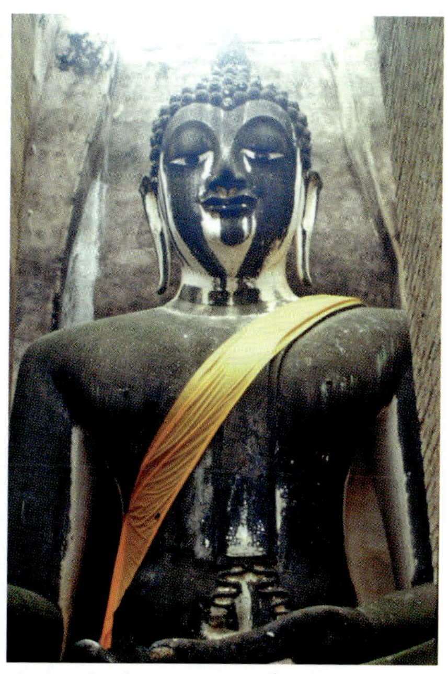

Figure 10b. Phra Acana, Wat Śrī Chum, Sukhothai, modeled by Nai Boontham Phunsawat in 1953.

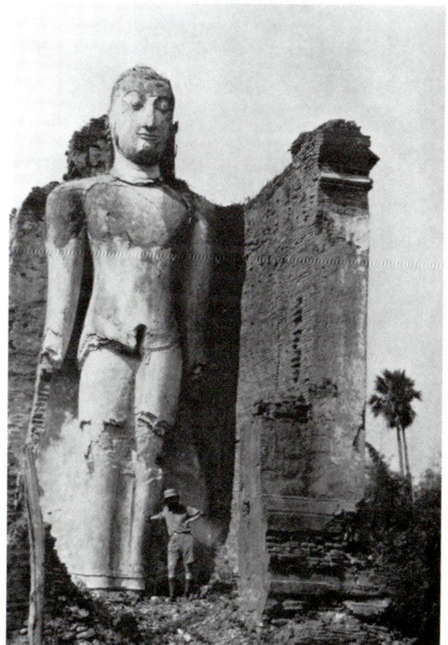

Figure 11a. Phra Atthārasa, late 17th and early 18th century, photographed in 1927. Stucco: H. 9 m. (18 Śok). North Mondop, Wat Mahāthāt, Sukhothai. (Photo after Wales 1973, Pl. 36)

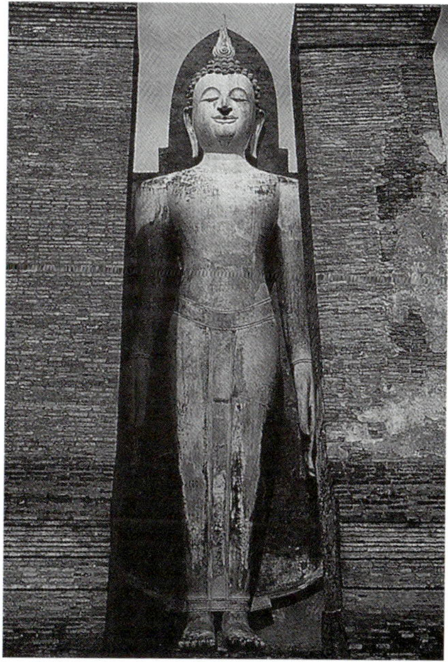

Figure 11b. Phra Atthārasa, restored in 1953. Stucco: H. 9 m. (18 Śok). North Mondop, Wat Mahāthāt, Sukhothai. (Photo after *Kān anurak* 2538/1995, 57)

century Sukhothai-style images (Figure 11b). Nevertheless, the restorer admitted to leaving the Lop Buri-style frontal panel of the robe untouched (*Kān anurak* 2538/1995: 56). Thanks to this omission, the dating of the original image can be confirmed as late 17th to early 18th century.

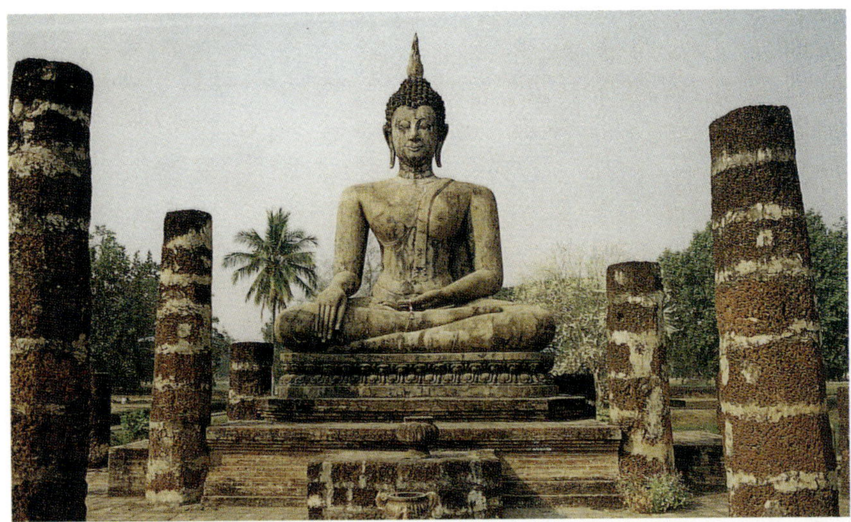

Figure 12. Buddha image in Ubosot erected in 1994. (Photo after *Kān anurak* 2538/1995, 18)

In conjunction with cultural nationalism there is tourism, which demands that heritage sites be worthwhile to visit. In order that tourists would not be disappointed when they arrived at Sukhothai to find only piles of bricks, or nondescript bases of buildings, the Fine Arts Department supplied them with fake Sukhothai-style Buddhas. An example is the stucco Buddha seated on a lotus-petals base in the ordination hall (*phra ubosot*) of Wat Mahāthāt (Figure 12). In 1994, the remains had consisted only of a rectangular base and a few pillars (Ibid., 17).

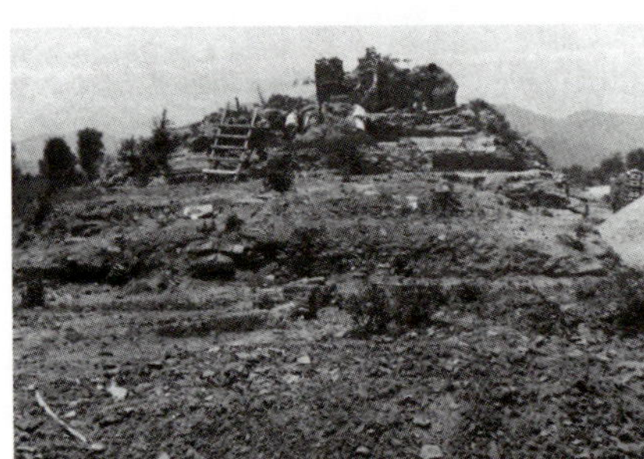

Figure 13a. Wat Mae Chon, Sukhothai, before restoration. (Photo after Krom Silpakorn 2531/1988, 114)

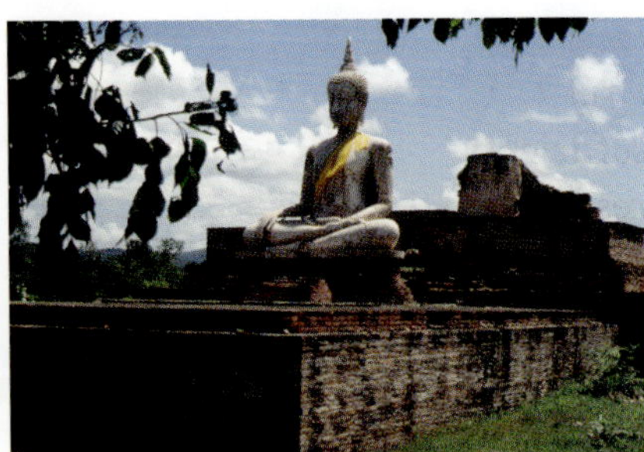

Figure 13b. Wat Mae Chon after restoration.

Similarly, the ruin of Wat Mae Chon, which originally consisted of two brick mounds (Figure 13a), was transformed into the base of a stupa and a congregation hall, on which is placed a seated Buddha image modeled by Nai Boontham Thongsawat (Figure 13b). The Fine Arts Department went so far as to put up images of the Buddha in places where they had never been before, such as at Wat Traphang Ngoen, where a stele of the Buddha Walking in Meditation was erected, representing the Fine Arts Department's equivalent of a garden gnome (Figure 14).

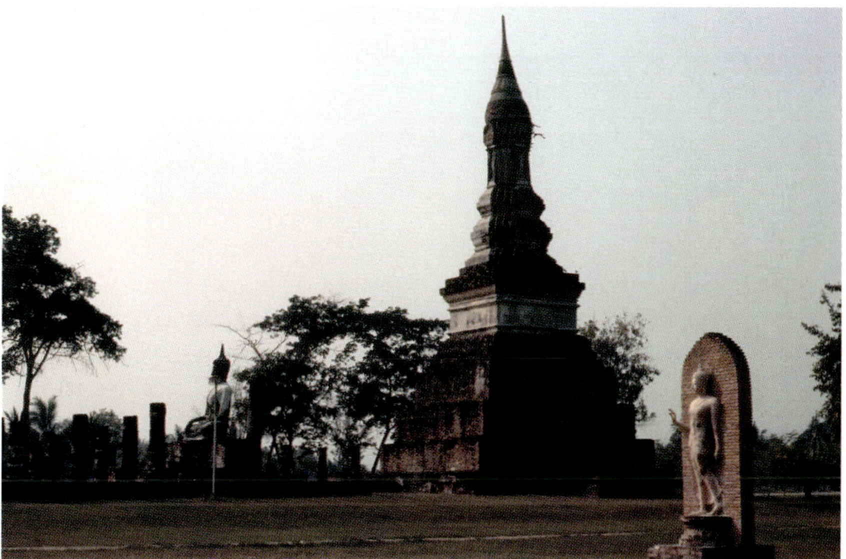

Figure 14. A stele of Buddha Walking in Meditation, brick and stucco. Wat Trapang Ngoen, Sukhothai.

The most spectacular example of the Fine Arts Department's restoration must be the resurrection of the stupa at Wat Sorasak, which in 1965 was a pile of bricks (Figure 15a). In the same year, only a base decorated with fragments of elephant caryatids was constructed (*Rai ngan karn sam ruat* 2512/1969: 12) (Figure 15b). Apparently, this was not sufficiently photogenic for the tourists, so the Fine Arts Department resurrected the whole stupa in 1985 (Figure 15c).

To the north of Wat Sorasak is Wat Son Khāo, where the stupa was restored without the top section in 1965 (Figure 16a). In order to keep company with its neighbor, a new stupa was constructed for Wat Sorasak, with a lotus-bud section reminiscent of the Taj Mahal (see Figure 15c). Unable to withstand onslaughts of criticism, the Fine Arts Department had the offending section removed (Figure 16b).

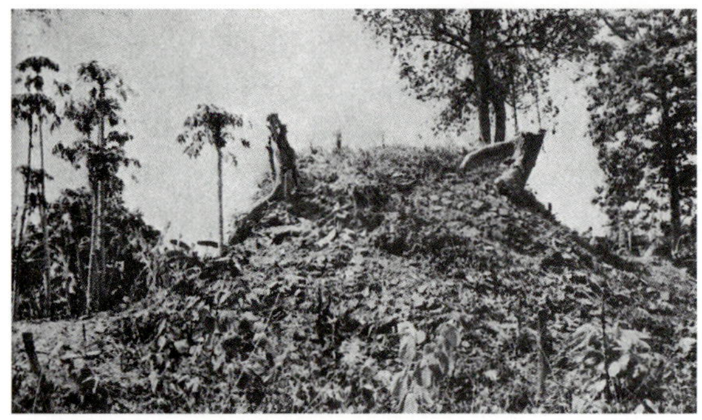

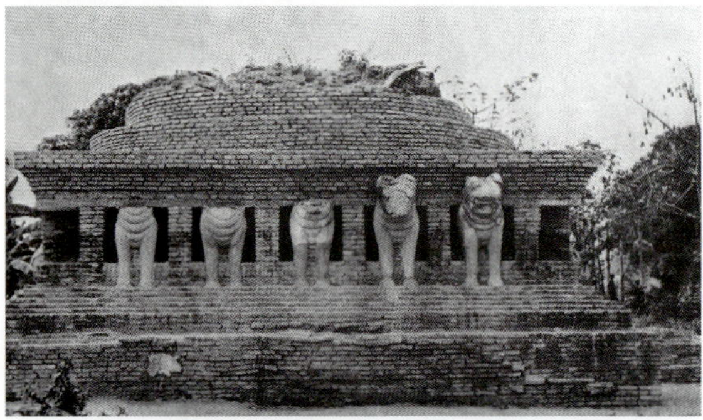

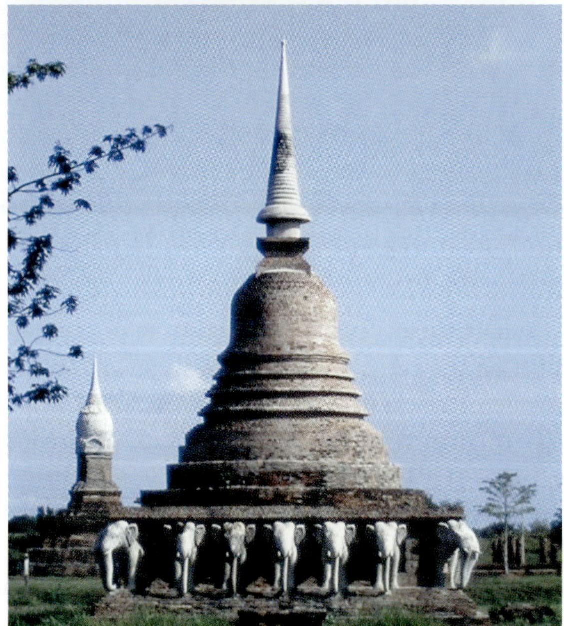

Figure 15a. (top) The stupa at Wat Sorasak, Sukhothai, before restoration in 1965. (Photo after *Rai ngan karn sam ruat* 2512/1969, 41) Figure 15b. (middle) After restoration in 1965. (Photo after *Rai ngan karn sam ruat* 2512/1969, 41) Figure 15c. (below) The stupa at Wat Sorasak and the lotus-bud topped stupa of Wat Son Khāo; both restored in 1982–85.

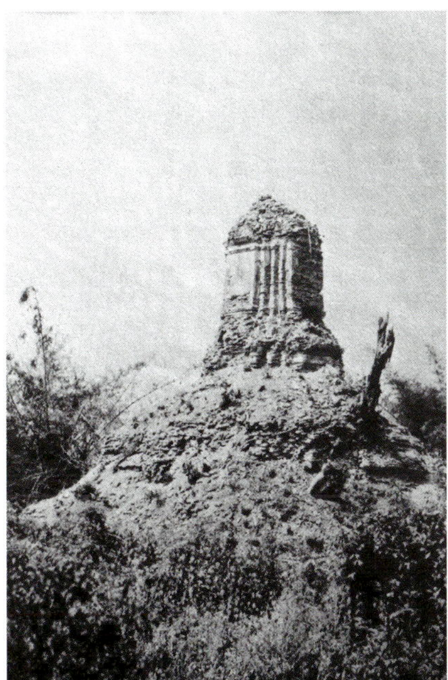
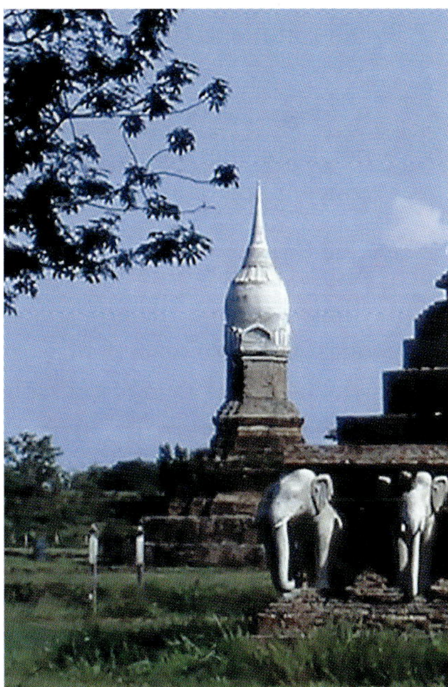
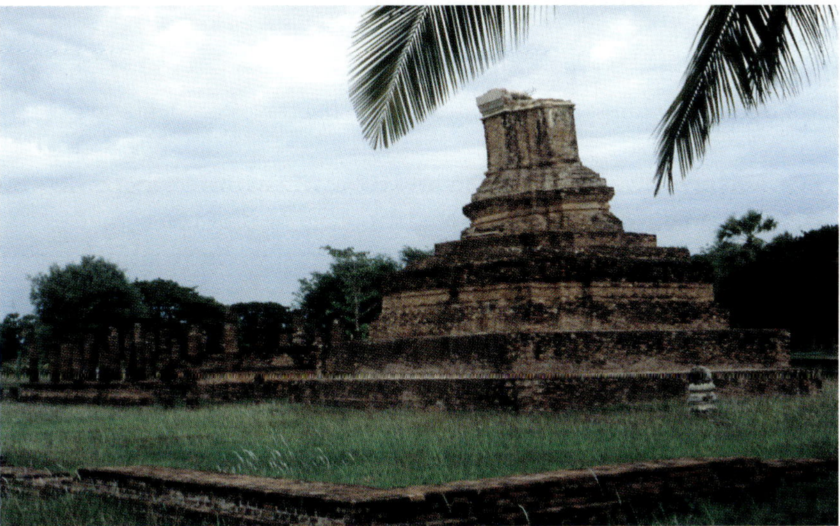

Figure 16a. (top) The stupa at Wat Son Khao, before (top left) and after (top right) restoration in 1965. (Photo after *Rai ngan karn sam ruat* 2512/1969, 39) Figure 16b. (bottom) After the lotus-bud section was removed.

Byrne commented that:

> It seems clear that the over-restoration of Sukhothai resulted not from the state's ignorance of international conservation conventions but from a systematic pursuance of its own agenda.... When the director of the Sukhothai restoration project [Nikhom Musikakhama] justified construction of missing components on the grounds that the statues and structures in question were objects of worship, he signalled the extent to which the heritage discourse in Thailand might differ from its Western counterparts. (Byrne 1995: 278)

Nikhom was following the government's policy of promoting tourism. Such disregard for keeping the original fabric of structures, and the impunity of those responsible for their conservation, cannot be attributed to religious devotion and cultural nationalism alone, but to Theravāda cultural tradition.

Thais are nurtured by Theravāda Buddhism, which means the "Doctrine of the Elders," or the orthodox Buddhist doctrine transmitted through the elders of the Order (Saṅgha). Commenting on the Mahāyāna term for Theravādins, "*sāvaka*" meaning "a hearer," Prof. Ishii says:

> This etymology of sāvaka captures the essential character of the Theravādin monks, men devoted to upholding the Dhamma and Vinaya preached by the Buddha. Their totally passive attitude has virtually precluded any active development of the teachings they hear. (Ishii quoted in Dhammika 2006, 7)

Ishii contined: "They heard and they repeated but they rarely inquire, explored or questioned" (Ibid.). As most Thai men spend part of their life in monkhood, they too take up this attitude.

Although most monks are just "simple uneducated farmers in yellow robe" (Chatsuman Kabilsingh, quoted in Dhammika 2006: 17), they "insist that they should be respected and revered simply because they wear a yellow robe" (Ibid., 46).

Personal experience as a Theravādin monk enabled the Venerable Shravasti Dhammika to catalog some of the characteristics of Theravāda monks, such as hypocrisy, ritualistic bent, negative outlook, being out of touch, selfishness, wastefulness, sectarianism, and ethnocentricity (Ibid.) For example, they "give exaggerated importance to things which appeared to be little more than rituals and formalities (Ibid., x)"; "Theravādins expect you to follow their traditions and not question them" (Ibid., xii); "Theravāda has evolved a whole culture of getting around the rules" (Ibid., 32), such as "by juggling definitions" (Ibid., 34). As monks are role models for Thais, such characteristics are emulated by lay people.

Although socially and theoretically separate from lay society, the Saṅgha has chosen to subjugate itself to secular authority. "Obliged to maintain its unworldliness, the Saṅgha actively sought the patronage of secular authority in the hope that it would thereby prosper. This attitude remains characteristic of today Thai's Saṅgha" (Ishii 1986: 51). However, "The main factor governing monks and monasteries is not Dhamma or even Vinaya but long established tradition and these traditions usually owe more to feudalism and monarchism than they do to anything the Buddha taught" (Ibid., 105).

Inscriptional evidence leaves no doubt that the Saṅgha came under the control of the monarchy ever since King Mahā Thammarāchā I (Li Thai) introduced the Araññavāsī branch of the orthodox Sinhalese Mahāvihāra ordination lineage from Martaban, Lower Myanmar, to Sukhothai in 1361 (Prasert and Griswold 1992: 473). In the same year the king appointed Saṅgkharāchā Mahāswāmi to be in charge of the Araññavāsī monasteries in the province of Śrī Satchanalai (Ibid., 579). In 1406, Mahā Thammarāchā I's grandson, Mahā Thammarāchā III, raised Sangkharāchā Mahāswāmi to the ecclesiastical title of Saṅgkhaparināyaka, or Supreme Patriarch, of the Araññavāsī Ordination Lineage (Ibid., 580).

Complete subjugation of the Saṅgha to state control came in the reign of King Boromatrailokanāt of Ayutthaya (r. 1448–88), who promulgated the Laws of Civil Hierachies (*Phra aiyakān tamnaeng nā phonlaruen*), introducing the *sakdinā* system, under which the status of each man and woman, with the exception of the king, was graded according to the area of riceland (*nā*), theoretically tenable by each person. The heir apparent was entitled to 100,000 *rai* (one *rai* equals 1,600 square meters), whereas a slave was entitled to 5 *rai* (*Rueng kot mai tra sām duang* 2521/1978: 108, 146).

The same law also set up the Department of Ecclesiastical Administration (Krom Thammakān), through which the king conferred clerical ranks (*samaṇaśak*), bestowed titles (*ratchathiṇanām*) and presented monks with insignia of ranks. This Department sent out officers to supervise the behavior of monks in every province. It also set up a law court to try monks for serious offenses (Wales 1934: 93).

The Law of Provincial and Military Hierachies (*Phra aiyakān tamnaeng nā thahān hua muang*), promulgated in 1466, graded monks according to their knowledge of the Pāli scriptures, ranging from 200 *rai* for a novice (*sāmanera*) ignorant of the Dhamma to 2,400 *rai* for a teacher monk (*Phra khrū*) (*Rueng kot mai tra sām duang* 2521/1978: 172). Even a monk entirely ignorant of the Dhamma was entitled to 400 *rai*, which was the equivalent of the lowest official rank (*bandaśak*), and qualified him as a member of the privileged class.

Perhaps the greatest practical effect of Buddhism (at Ayutthaya), wrote Quaritch Wales:

> was the heavy expenditure that was incurred by the government and the onerous demands that were made on the people's personal services, second only to those demanded by war, for the erection of countless shrines and monasteries; while at all times a considerable proportion of the country's manhood was exempted from both military and civil service by the highly developed institution of monasticism. (Wales 1934: 7–8)

Yet neither kings nor commoners would have found erecting shrines and monasteries an onerous task. On the contrary, they would have been delighted to have the opportunity to spend money, or manpower, in order to accumulate merit (*bun*) that would ensure them a better future life. A few months before he died, King Rāma III (r. 1824–51) requested that one fourth of the cash left in the treasury be spent on the completion and maintenance of the monasteries he founded and those under his patronage, totaling seventy-three in number (Thipakornwong 2477/1934: 353, 370).

Commoners also believe that giving alms to the Saṅgha and building monasteries are the most effective way of earning merit. A survey conducted by Tambiah in the Northeast in the 1960s found that constructing a monastery was more meritorious than becoming a monk. Observing the śīn *hā*, the five ethical virtues prescribed for the laity, was at the bottom of the list for acquiring merit (Tambiah quoted in Ishii 1986: 17–8).

Building a new monastery, however, can be disastrous for antiquities found in the same locality, as in the case of two late 12th century Khmer stone radiating Bodhisattva Avalokiteśvara statues in Wat Khuhā Sawan, Lop Buri. In 1928 these two-meter high statues were discovered in a cave at Lop Buri and brought to the Bangkok National Museum to be restored and exhibited there. In 1940 the provincial governor cleared the cave where the statues were found and built a road and a concrete stairway to its mouth. He then asked the museum to return the statues to be put back inside the cave (Figure 17a) (Tri Amatyakun quoted in Huan 2512/1969: 107). Around the same time a wandering monk (*phra thudong*), named Phra Khammī Phutthasāro, took shelter in the cave. A community then grew up in the vicinity, and permission for setting up a monastery was granted in 1962. The monastic boundary was delineated in 1975 and Phra Khammī Phuthasāro was appointed the first abbot of Wat Khuhā Sawan (*Prawat wat* Vol. 5, 2529/1986: 56). After paving the floor of the cave with polished stones and installing an ensuite bedroom at the back of the cave, the abbot must have thought that the two statues could serve him best as door guardians. So he gave each of them a pair of hands holding a sword,

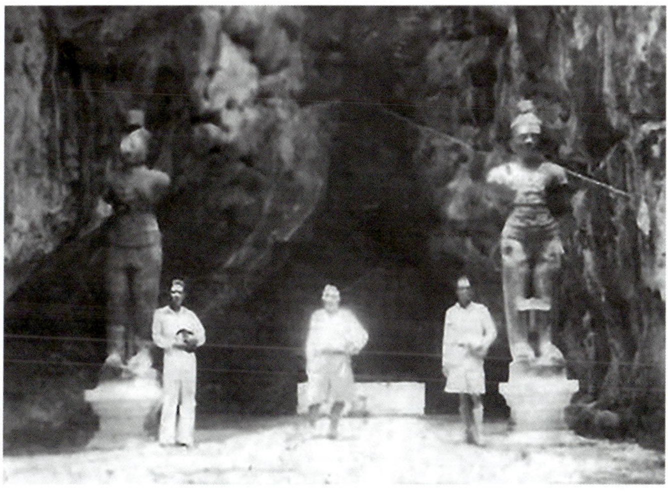

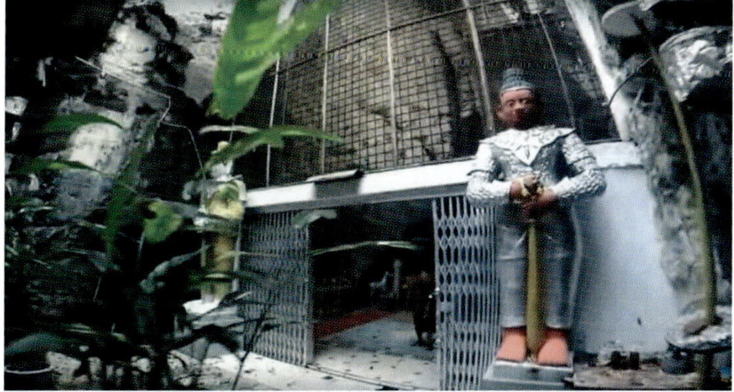

Figure 17a. (top) Radiating Bodhisattva Avalokiteśvara, Wat Khuhā Sawan, Lop Buri, late 12th century, photographed around 1940 after their return from the Bangkok National Museum. (Photo courtesy of Wuttichai Techapichayapakdee) Figure 17b. (bottom) Transformed around 1960s into door guardian named Narong Rit (left) and Prap Narong (right). (Photo after Faiththaistory.com, 2016)

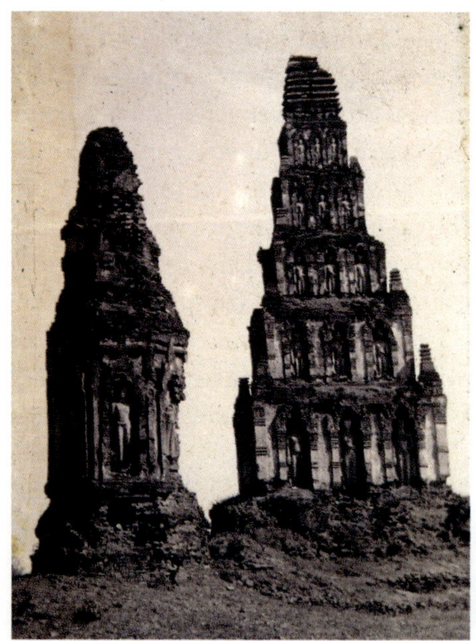

Figure 18a. The ruins of Wat Kukut, Lamphun, Early 13th century, photographed in 1922.

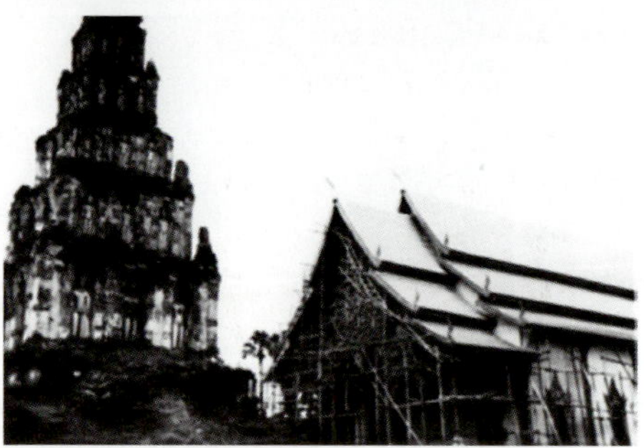

Figure 18b. The Congregation Hall of Wat Chām Thewī, constructed by Khru Ba Śrīvijaya in 1936. Photographed in 1936. (Photo after Oknation, online, 2552/2009)

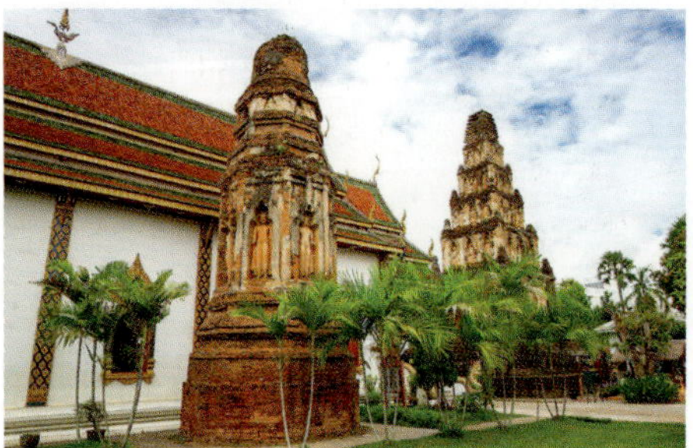

Figure 18c. The Congregational Hall of Wat Chām Thewī. (Photo after Lamphun Cycling, Dekguide, online, 2015)

on which was inscribed their names; one called Prāp Narong, the other Narong Rit (Figure 17b) (Huan 2512/1969: 108).

In the past, building an ordination hall, congregation hall (*wihān*), teaching hall (*kān parian*), or stupa was a means for a layman to make merit, as in the case of Khru Ba Śrīvijaya's founding of Wat Chām Thewī, Lamphūn. In 1936 the celebrated monk was residing at Wat Phra That Haripuñjaya (Salisbury Family 2005: 62). Chao Chakkham Khajornsak, the last heriditary ruler of Lamphūn, together with the government officers and local people, came to ask Khru Ba Śrīvijaya to establish a monastery in the ruins of an abandoned monastery called Wat Kukut. The ruins had been discovered by Prince Damrong Rajanubhab in 1922 (Damrong B.E. 2471/1928: 2), and dated by Coedès to 1218 (Coedès 1926: 192 and Pl.VII) (Figure 18a). The building of the congregation hall began in the same year. It was completed in less than a year and renamed as Wat Chām Thewī (Salisbury Family 2005: 66) (Figure 18b).

Six years earlier Prince Damrong Rajānubhāb had given a lecture on the preservation of antiquities to lieutenant governors (*thesāphiban*) of the then administrative circle (*moṇḍon*) in which Lamphūn was located. He gave three specific instructions:

1. keep to the original appearance; do not change the form and the design according to the restorer's own fancy;
2. do not demolish an ordination or a congregation hall in order to replace it with new one; should a bigger building be needed, construct a new structure instead; and
3. do not construct any new building close to the ruin because it will destroy the dignity of the monument.

He also admonished the lieutenant governors to inform monks under their change of his instructions before they commenced any reconstruction (Damrong 2519/1976: 319–21).

Apparently, his instructions went unheeded. Khru Ba Śrīvijaya defiantly placed his outsized congregation hall next to the base of the square pyramidal stupa and in between the two ancient stupas (Figure 18b). On account of his popularity and prestige, no one has dared to suggest that the offending structure be pulled down so that the two ancient monuments could regain their dignity and have enough space to breathe. Instead, the hall now stands proud as an architectural monument to the memory of Khru Ba Śrīvijaya (Figure 18c).

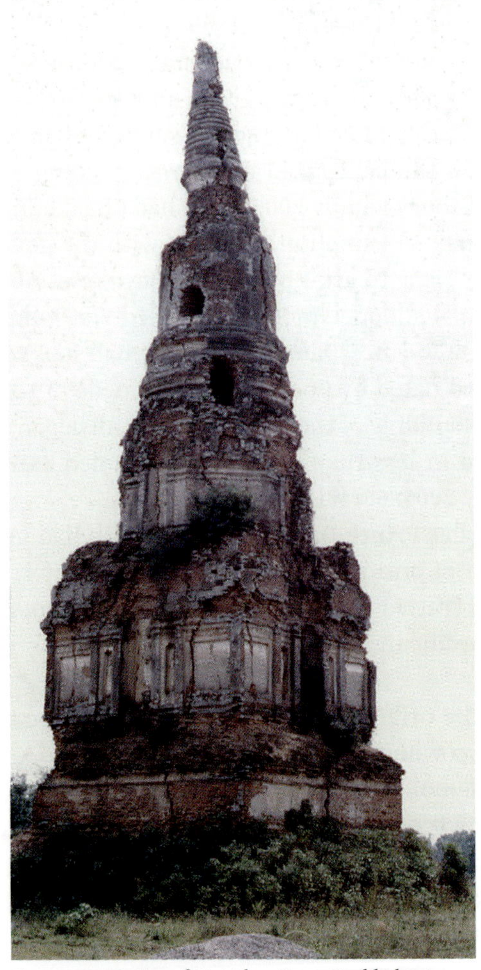

Figure 19a. Cetiya of Wat Phra Kaeo, Sankhaburi, 17th century, photographed in 1977.

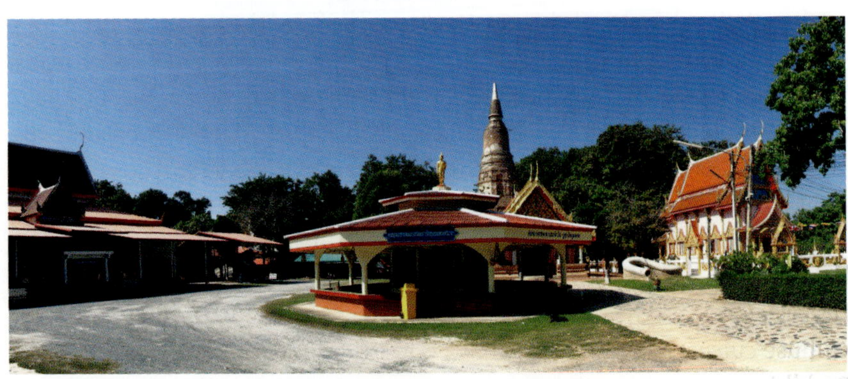

Figure 19b Wat Phra Kaeo, Sankhaburi, in 2019.

Half a century later Prince Damrong's instructions on not building a congregation hall close to an ancient monument again went unheard. As a result, "the most beautiful *cetiya* (stupa) in Thailand" (Figure 19a) according to the National Artist and art historian, Nor Na Paknam (Nor Na Paknam 2516/1973: 23), who compared this *cetiya* to a beautiful woman standing alone in an empty field, lost its glamor among a clutter of nondescript buildings (Figure 19b). Regrettably, religious fervor took hold of the community. Even though the stupa had been registered as a national monument by the Fine Arts Department in 1935, the Department of Religious Affairs condoned the establishment of a monastery at the site in 1976 and an ordination hall was constructed in 1978 (*Prawat wat* Vol.5 2529/1986: 628).

Today the Council of the Elders (Mahāthera Samākhom) has decreed that any abbot who wishes to acquire a higher clerical rank (*samaṇaśak*) must demonstrate that he has a structure or a monument to his credit. To prove it, he must report the cost of its construction—a minimum of one million baht in the Bangkok area. Abbots living in the North, South and East administrative regions have to show a minimum of one hundred and fifty thousand baht. The rationale behind this regulation is that the money raised is a gauge of the candidate's popularity among his congregation (Komchadluek 2556/2013). This requisite put all dilapidated buildings in the Kingdom's monastic compounds in danger of demolition.

The above decree must have contributed to the increase in construction of new monasteries within the years 2004 to 2012. In 2004 there were 40,717 monasteries in the Kingdom, and by 2012 the number had risen to 43,810, an increase of 3,093 monasteries in nine years, or 344 monasteries per year (*Thaipublica* 2013). This statistic supports Tambiah's observation that Buddhism is:

> *expanding* and keeping pace with modernization, urbanization, nationalization, and rising expectations.... In Thailand at least modernization and economic development spell not the demise of religious action labeled 'Buddhism' but probably its intensification. (Tambiah 1977: 267–68)

Since Thailand uses the *past as sanction* and *as destiny*, there is no hope of her conforming to the norms of international conservation and restoration. Rooted in conservatism, traditionalism and nationalism, she will use cultural heritage as she has always done, as a means to promote Buddhism.

References

Byrne, Denis. 1995. "Buddhist stupa and Thai social practice." *World Archaeology* 27, 2: 266–81.

Byrne, Denis. 2014. *Counterheritage: Critical Perspectives on Heritage Conservation in Asia.* New York: Routledge.

Chiang Mai News. 2559/2016. "Burana wat suan dok doi kru ba śrīvichai lae chao luang chiang mai," Retrieved from www.chiangmain-news.co.th/page/archives/539814, accessed September 2018.

Coedès, G. 1926. "Documents sur L'Histoire Politique et Religieuse du Laos Occidental." *Bulletin de l'École Française d'Extreme-Orient*, 25 (1925): 1–201.

Damrong Rajanubhab, Phrachao Borommawongthoe Kromphra. 2471/1928. *Athibāi rayathang long lamnam ping B.E.2465.* Phra Nakhon: Sophon Phiphat Thanakorn.

Damrong Rajanubhab, Phrachao Borommawongthoe Kromphraya. 2519/1976. "Pathakatha rueang sa nguan khong boran." In *Prachum pathakatha* (collected lectures), published in memory of M.C. Ajavadis Diskul on the Occasion of his Cremation, pp. 306–26. Bangkok: Rongphim Phrachan.

Dhammika, Ven. S. 2006. *The Broken Buddha: Critical Reflections on Theravada and a Plea for a New Buddhism.* Singapore: The Nimmala Group.

Ellsmore, Donald. 2008. "Managing Change to Sacred Places: Conservation of the Gothic Revival Church in Asia and the Pacific." In *Karn anurak lae karn chatkarn puchaniyasathan*, proceedings ICOMOS Thailand International Conference 2008 "Conservation and Management of Sacred Places," pp. 158–78. Bangkok: Amarin Printing and Publishing.

Faiththaistory.com. 2016. "Tiaw wat khuha sawan chom tham boran krap sangkhan luang pu khammī lae luang por chun." Retrieved from www.faiththaistory.com/kuhasawan, accessed January 2019.

Fournereau, Lucien. 1908. *Le Siam Ancien*, Vol. II. Paris: Musée Guimet.

Griswold, A. 1966. "Imported image and the nature of copying in the art of Siam." *Essays offered to G. H. Luce*, Vol. II. Edited by Ba Shin et al., pp. 37–73. Ascona: Artibus Asiae.

Huan Phinthuphan. 2512/1969. *Lop buri thī nā ru.* Lop Buri: Hattha koson karn pim.

Ishii, Yoneo. 1986. *Sangha, State, and Society: Thai Buddhism in History.* Translated by Peter Hawkes. Honolulu: University of Hawaii Press.

Kān anurak patimakam wat mahathat changwat sukhothai. 2538/1995. Bangkok: Fai anurak chittakam fapanang lae patimakam tid ti, kong borankhadi, krom silpakorn.

Karlström, Anna. 2005. "Spiritual materiality: Heritage preservation in a Buddhist world?" *Journal of Social Archaeology*, 5, 3: 338–55.

Komchadluek. 2556/2013. "Poet ken tang samanasak phra song thai." Retrieved from www.komchadluek.net/news/lifestyle/152251, accessed September 2018.

Krairiksh, Piriya. 2012. *The Roots of Thai Art.* Translated by Narisa Chakrabongse. Bangkok: River Books.

Krairiksh, Piriya. 2018. "Phra Mahathat, Sukhothai, Revisited." In *The Renaissance Princess Lectures in Honour of Her Royal Highness Princess Maha Chakri Sirindhorn on Her Fifth Cycle Anniversary*, pp. 48–96. Bangkok: The Siam Society.

Krom Silpakorn. 2531/1988. *Thamniap boransatan uthayan prawattisat Sukhothai*. Bangkok: Rongphim Hatthasil.

Lamphun Cycling, Dekguide. 2015. "Wat chām thewī." Retrieved from www.lamphuncycling.com/main/3373-2/, accessed January 2015.

Narisara Nuwattiwong, Somdet Chaofa Krompraya. 2506/1963. *Chot mai ra ya thang pi phitsanulok*. Phra Nakhon: Rongpim Phra Chan.

Nikhom Musikakhama, ed. 2533/1990. *Tidsadi lae naew patibat kān anurak anusorn sathan lae laeng boran sathan*. Ekasan kong boran khadi mai lek 1/2532 B.E. Bangkok: Krom Silpakorn.

Nor Na Paknam. 2516/1973. *Tiaw muang silpa u-thong*. Bangkok: Rongphim Fueang Nakhon.

Oknation Blog. 2552/2009. "Wat chām thewī wat sud tai tī khru ba śrīvijaya burana." Retrieved from oknation.nationtv.tv/blog/ze- bolamphun/2009/12/02/entry-1, accessed January 2019.

Peleggi, Maurizio. 2002. *The Politics of Ruins and the Business of Nostalgia*. Bangkok: White Lotus.

Peleggi, Maurizio. 2012. "The unbearable impermanence of things: Reflections on Buddhism, cultural memory and heritage conservation." In *Routledge Handbook of Heritage in Asia*, edited by Patrick Daly and Tim Winter, pp. 55–68. New York: Routledge.

Peleggi, Maurizio. 2017. *Monastery, Monument, Museum: Sites and Artifacts of Thai Cultural Memory*. Honolulu: University of Hawai'i Press.

Prachum charuk wat phra chetuphon, Vol. 1. 2472/1929. Phra Nakhon: Sophon phiphatthanakorn.

Prasert Ṇa Nagara and Griswold, A. B. 1992. *Epigraphic and Historical Studies*. Bangkok: The Historical Society.

Prawat wat thua rācha anachak, Vol. 5. 2529/1986. Bangkok: Kong phuttha sāsana sathan, Krom karn sāsana, Krasuang sueksa thi ka.

Rai ngan karn sam ruat lae khut thang burana boran watthu sathan muang kao sukhothai por. sor. 2508–12 (B.E.). 2512/1969. Phra Nakhon: Khana kammakarn prap prung burana boran sathan changwat Sukhothai lae changwat Kampaengphet.

Rueang kot mai tra sām duang. 2521/1978. Bangkok: Krom Silpakorn.

Ratanapañña Thera. 2501/1958. *Jinakālamālīpakon*, translated by Saeng Monwithun. Phra Nakhon: Krom Silpakorn.

Salisbury Family and Friends. 2548/2005. *A History of Kruba Sriwichai (The Buddhist Saint of Northern Thailand) A Story of making way up to Doi Suthep and a Historical Chronicle of Wat Phra That Doi Suthep*. Chiang Mai: Sutin Press.

Somchart Chungsiriarak. 2555/2012. "Thai's Attitude and Concept in Conservation of Historic Structures from Past to Present." *NAJUA*, Vol.8 (September 2554/2001–2555/2012): 106–27.

Tambiah, S. J. 1977 [1976]. *World Conqueror and World Renouncer: A Study of Buddhism and Polity in Thailand against a Historical Background*. Cambridge: Cambridge University Press.

Thaipublica. 2013. "Sathiti chī cham nuan wat poem kuen pī la 300 wat! yuk rung rueang khong śāsana laew jing rue?" Retrieved from thaipublica.org/2013/12/monastery-institution-2/, accessed September 2018.

Thiphakornwong, Chao Phraya. 2477/1934. *Phra rat cha pong sawadarn krung rattanakosin ratchakarn ti 3*. Phra Nakhon: Rong pim śrī hong.

Wales, H. G. Quaritch. 1934. *Ancient Siamese Government and Administration*. London: Bernard Quaritch.

Wales, H. G. Quaritch. 1973. *Early Burma—Old Siam: A Comparative Commentary*. London: Bernard Quaritch.

Wirawan Naruepiti. 2560/2017. *Karn muang rueang phra phut tha rup*. Bangkok: Matichon.

Integrating Local and International Perspectives into Legal Frameworks: Problems and Challenges

Sujeong Lee

INTRODUCTION

The legal frameworks for heritage conservation in any society reflect certain theories, principles, and contemporary attitudes. They codify the social and cultural norms and practices of that society. In Asia heritage law tends to reflect Western perspectives rather than local ones, yet the applicability of Western ways of understanding heritage and practicing conservation have been questioned. There have been attempts to revise laws and regulations by integrating more local perspective. In order for legal frameworks to be practical tools for protecting intrinsic and extrinsic heritage values for transmission to the next generation, it is necessary to study how indigenous perspectives may be consolidated into existing frameworks.

This chapter aims to provide both a theoretical and practical platform for re-examining key elements of legal frameworks. It examines how a value-based approach, rational decision-making, and understanding of heritage as a resource should form the foundations of legal frameworks. It argues that legal frameworks based on international perspectives can only be effective in practice when they are supplemented by local perspectives for identifying and sustaining values. Taking Korea as a case, it addresses problems on the absence of local perspectives and provides a set of recommendations, including proposals to increase public involvement.

The first Cultural Heritage Protection Act, drafted after Korea's independence in 1945, was much influenced by Western or non-local perspectives. It was enacted in 1962, following a Japanese act on such matters as the definition and classification of heritage, legal structures, and role of state in protection. There have been many claims that local perspectives should be integrated into the legislation, but without success. As a result the material-based perspective has played an important role in assessing heritage values while spiritual or contextual considerations have been neglected although they play an important role in interpreting the intrinsic values of heritage in Korean culture.

The first section explains three international principles and perspectives which should be the foundation of the legal frameworks: value-based approach, rational decision-making, defining heritage as a resource. Presenting several cases, the second section explains the role of local perspective in assessing values, and the third addresses the problems of current Korean legal frameworks. There is a need to re-examine the prevailing material-based approach, enhance a value-based process by providing a set of detailed guidelines for practice, and improve the quality of impact assessment by inviting public participation. The last section provides a set of recommendations for the revision of legal frameworks.

THREE PILLARS OF INTERNATIONAL PRINCIPLES AND PERSPECTIVES IN LEGAL FRAMEWORKS

A legal framework for heritage sets out what to preserve and how to preserve it. Based on the contemporary understanding of heritage, the framework provides procedures and guidelines to implement principles in management. Many legal frameworks, including in Korea, have been influenced by international debate and experience. Although the local perspective and cultural context can play an important role in improving its effectiveness in practice, they have been less respected and reflected. This paper lays out the three basic requirements for a legal framework from the international perspective, and then examines how local perspectives can be integrated into each requirement.

The first requirement is a value-based approach. UNESCO's World Heritage system understands value is the essence of heritage passed down through generations (UNESCO 1972, Article 1). Korean law defines heritage as a container of different values (Cultural Heritage Protection Act, Article 2). Value is the object that we target to manage, and is the most important criterion in decision-making. Therefore, UNESCO's Operational Guidelines and Korea's legal provisions set out the processes for managing value and the criteria for decision-making based on a value-based approach. This approach can be divided into three steps: value identification, value preservation, and value dissemination, as displayed in Table 1.

Table 1. Three steps of value-related activities

Value Identification	Value Preservation	Value Dissemination
research	physical intervention	reinterpretation
scientific examination	conservation, repair, restoration,	education
documentation	reconstruction,	site visit and experience
interpretation	preventive conservation	commercial use
designation	risk management	etc
etc	etc	

The above is not a one-time process but is cyclical and repetitive because the ways of identifying, sustaining, and disseminating values change over time. For a site that is identified as heritage and preserved through generations, these steps may be repeated by different generations and different communities.

Value identification includes all types of research and scientific examination needed to identify all of a site's different values. Such activities provide the information for identifying each value and weighing the significance of the heritage. At this step, it is important to identify all attributed values and clarify where those values are imprinted as tangible and intangible elements of the heritage. If the value is misunderstood or misinterpreted due to limited information, conservators or decision-makers cannot determine the scope of physical intervention or choose the techniques and materials at the next step. Therefore, the legal framework should encourage multi-disciplinary research, such as scientific analysis and archival research to collect all related information.

Value preservation includes all types of intervention to sustain values, such as conservation, restoration, reconstruction, and risk management, which sustains value by guarding against loss from external threats. Any decision made before and during those activities depends on the values identified in the previous step. Although the aim of this step is to conserve all of the different values as much as possible, not all can be preserved in practice. In order to recover artistic integrity of a degraded painting, for example, the oldness or age value of the work can be compromised. Repainting the wooden components of Buddhist buildings for aesthetic reasons as well as for protection from biological damage effaces the historical layers of traditional pigments. The legal framework must provide a set of criteria for weighing the significance of different types of value in order to guide decision-making.

Value dissemination shares the values with the society. Heritage is owned by community or the general public, hence the legal framework should provide a platform for them to enjoy its benefit. Understanding the value is a precondition for value dissemination. If the values are not clearly identified, it is difficult to decide what should be shared. Legal statements need to specify how the identified value can be presented to the public in an efficient way.

The second requirement of a legal framework is to set out a logical process and criteria of rational decision-making. A value-based approach is achievable only when legal provisions provide a well-designed procedure for impact assessment. Because the essence of heritage lies in its values and significance, any impact on those values needs to be thoroughly examined before taking decisions on any intervention to heritage. Rational decision-making aims to prevent any loss of value. If the approval of a planning application will inevitably affect the value of the heritage, legal provisions should specify ways to mitigate the negative impact. A process is needed to analyze potential changes in values as well as a set of criteria for making a rational decision. The legal framework should ensure a way of reaching an objective decision by specifying who can be a decision-maker and what can be done if a decision should be re-examined.

The third requirement of a legal framework is its ability to reflect contemporary perspectives on understanding and managing heritage. The early concept of heritage focused on material aspects of heritage as remains of history. The aim of conservation was to freeze and retain a certain form or style of a specific period. This thinking evolved in the mid-20th century towards an understanding of heritage as an inheritance from one generation to the next to connect the past, present, and future. Not only physical remains but also various types of intangible apects of a society, such as spirit, belief, tradition, and cultural activities, have been recognized as objects to protect. The aim has shifted from conserving material aspects into sustaining values. Led by Western countries, such as the UK, the perspective on heritage is now evolving again. The official agency, Historic England, defines historic environment as "a shared recourse" to improve the quality of life of a society (English Heritage 2008: 19), meaning that value preservation is not the final goal but a means and precondition of benefitting the public by utilizing heritage to improve the quality of our lives. Legal statements need to secure community involvement so that people can clearly understand and manage the values of their heritage, and find a way of benefitting themselves.

INTEGRATING A LOCAL PERSPECTIVE INTO THE LEGAL FRAMEWORK

Heritage value is socially constructed by a community which creates, recognizes, and interprets heritage over time (Tomaszewski 2008: 34). Different cultures make judgements about the authenticity of heritage in different ways, by assessing such elements as form and design, materials and substance, use and function, traditions and techniques, location and setting, and spirit and feeling (UNESCO 2004: xxiii). Form and design, for example, play an important role in assessing artistic or religious values in Western culture. In Korea, tradition and techniques are important aspects because making Buddhist objects is part of religious practice for accumulating good karma. Artistic values are much influenced by the aesthetic taste of a specific time and culture, and can vary greatly across cultures on such dimensions as the material or spiritual aspect, the focus on a single building or the harmonious arrangementof many buildings, and so forth.

The ways of understanding and identifying the values of heritage are deeply connected to the questions of what and how to preserve. UNESCO's World Heritage Convention recognizes the Outstanding Universal Value for all humankind, examining the meanings of heritage in the context of world history. Once the Outstanding Universal Value of a site is identified and inscribed on the World Heritage List, then the impact of the listing on the site's value, as a result of development or intervention, is closely examined.

Article 2 of Korea's Cultural Heritage Protection Act understands heritage as outcomes of human activities on items that have historical, artistic, academic, and scenic values. The values used to assess these outcomes are universal to humankind but distinctive to local history and tradition. The scenic value, for example, should reflect a Korean perspective on understanding heritage in relation to nature. It does not mean only natural beauty which has been created by natural processes, but also qualities constructed by spiritual beliefs or the meaningful arrangement of buildings in a natural setting. *Poongsu* (*feng shui* in Chinese), for example, is an important traditional theory for understanding the natural environment and the harmony with man-made structures and objects, such as houses, pavilions, and tombs. A pavilion with a mountain at the back and small stream in front based on *Poongsu* principle creates scenic value in a designed garden. The style, form, and age of the pavilion can be supplementary elements in assessing the heritage value of a scenic site.

In order to reflect local perspectives in assessing and conserving heritage values, it is important to set out criteria and guidelines in legal frameworks, and make them available in official documents so that objective judgements can be made in decision-making. Local perspectives play an important role in such guidelines. Historic England's guide for listed buildings, scheduled monuments, and registered parks and gardens is a useful example. Employing a value-based approach, *Principles of selection for listed buildings* (Historic England, 2008) provides overarching criteria of assessing values. The "architectural and historic interest" is a statutory criterion for listing. These guides interpret the values, authenticity, and integrity of heritage for an English context, and provide applicable criteria to assess the architectural and historic interest of different types of their heritage. The guide for selecting maritime and naval buildings, for example, considers the geographical fact that England has the longest coastline in relation to its land mass in Europe, and highlights the significant factors for defining items of heritage in naval and maritime history.

In Korea, legal frameworks reflect the local context in setting out decision-making criteria rather than value assessment criteria. Recognizing that there is likely to be continuing development around heritage sites, the Cultural Heritage Administration of Korea provides objective criteria for decision-making on planning applications to meet the public interest. In 2018, for example, regulations about installing solar panels within 500 meters of the boundary of heritage were added to the criteria for planning permission. These regulations came in response to a new government policy to encourage installation of solar panels on ecological grounds. The 2018 White Paper on Renewable Energy encourages solar panel installation on building roofs, redundant agricultural fields, and even lake surfaces (Ministry of Industry, Trade and Energy 2018: 82–3). As such installations may affect the visual experience of a heritage site, new criteria were provided to allow each planning application to be independently examined and resolved by experts on the possible impact on the heritage. However, legal frameworks still need to provide criteria for value assessment to improve the applicability of decision-making criteria in the impact assessment process.

HISTORICAL AND SOCIAL CONTEXT OF TANGIBLE HERITAGE PROTECTION IN KOREA

Before the modern concepts of "monument" and "conservation" were adopted in Korea in the early 20th century, buildings were repaired when age or damage had severely limited their use. It was the Japanese colonial government which recognized the importance of traditional buildings as material evidence of history that should be protected. The colonial authority surveyed and dismantled many Korean wooden buildings, studied them, and then reconstructed or refurbished them in a Japanese style for political purposes as well as for their relevance to the study of Japanese buildings. Japanese learning on the concept of heritage and conservation, which came from the west during the Meiji Period in the late 19th century, was applied in the 20th century to repair deteriorated heritage sites in the colonized land of Korea. Japanese influence was imprinted on Korea's early conservation practice and legal frameworks.

Korea's first Cultural Heritage Protection Act, enacted in 1962, copied a Japanese act of 1954 which in turn was influenced by Western concepts and principles for understanding heritage as historical remains and national identity. Subsequent revisions were limited to additions and amendments of clauses without any major changes in structure, definition, and principles of management for the last half century. The concept of heritage has evolved over the last fifty years but this has not been reflected in Korea's legal framework. There has been no attempt to integrate local perspectives for assessing heritage values along with international principles.

Over the last sixty years since gaining independence from Japanese rule, government has played a leading role in conservation: outlining a heritage policy, endorsing acts and regulations, implementing them in practice, and managing conservation projects for nationally and locally valued heritage sites, contributing public funds, and providing technical and scientific knowledge. The government has served as the leading actor in heritage research and management because of the role expected by Korean society in connection with national history. After the Japanese Colonial Period (1910–45) and the Korean War (1950–53), public interest focused on economic development, leaving to the government the responsibility of restoring the tangible heritage that displayed the long-lost dignity and identity of the nation. The government's priority was to recover national identity by using heritage as a material witness. Repairing damaged heritage sites, reconstructing destroyed buildings and devising legal frameworks to designate and conserve them was the government's priority, as tangible heritage is the visible manifestation of the richness of a culture and the proof of its long history.

For Korean cultural heritage, which had experienced a dark age of colonization and war for almost fifty years, the government focused on two things: prioritization of the older, and development of scientific knowledge. Government gave priority to the excavation, survey, identification and designation of ancient capital cities rather than anything newer. Government also accelerated scientific research on traditional materials and techniques for their conservation but ignored the importance of establishing philosophical and theoretical grounds to explain why, how and what to preserve. Ancient capital cities and old buildings are the monuments that visibly represent the long history and dignity of the ancient kingdoms of Korea. In addition, the repair techniques and scientific knowledge were key to repairing the damaged material remains.

Korea's economic development in the 1970s and 1980s, as well as its political stability in the early 1990s, laid the foundations for building public interest in cultural heritage and citizen involvement in decision-making. People started to enjoy more leisure hours and to seek educational family activities, which led to an increasing number of day-long visitors to heritage sites. Growing interest in cultural heritage was accompanied by interest in its conservation. What to conserve became not only governmental interest but also the public interest. The demolition of the rear part of Seoul city hall, almost a century old, evoked public criticism of the Seoul municipal government for the destruction, and of the Cultural Heritage Administration for its neglect of a historic building.

Decisions on cultural heritage conservation no longer belonged only to the government. The public began to participate. In 2000 the National Trust of Korea was established, and an Act on the National Trust of Cultural and Natural Heritage was passed in 2007. More non-governmental organizations took interest in heritage learning and protection. The government realized there was a need to lay down principles for discussing, sharing, and implementing a suitable approach to decision-making on heritage, recognizing that conservation is not a top-down practice with the government as the sole decision-maker but a social process in which the public should share responsibility.

In addition, heritage sites were recognized as a resource for tourism which could deliver economic benefit to the local community. Value dissemination is now an important objective for both the government and the public in Korea. Heritage has to be re-defined as a resource to improve the quality of life.

Government-led heritage management has made it possible to develop systematic frameworks in various areas of need; setting out legal frameworks and implementing procedures, creating the list of heritage sites to be valued and protected, and establishing academic foundations for training younger generations and for studying conservation techniques. In the 1990s Korea began to debate whether the Cultural Heritage Protection Act should be subdivided for different types of heritage and activity. The historic city, in particular the ancient capitals which played an important political, social, and cultural role in Korean history, was the first type of heritage to have an independent law in 2007. In 2010, legislation on repair and conservation practice, on the certification of conservators for nationally designated heritage, and on related work was separated from the Cultural Heritage Protection Act. Separate acts were devoted to the excavation and protection of buried objects in 2011, and to intangible heritage in 2015. At present the government is preparing legislation on education, promotion, and natural heritage. The five pieces of legislation now in place are as follows:

Cultural Heritage Protection Act (1962)
Special Act on Preservation and Promotion of Ancient Capitals (2007)
Act on Cultural Property Maintenance, etc. (2010)
Act on Protection and Inspection of Buried Cultural Property (2011)
Act on the Safeguarding and Promotion of Intangible Cultural Property (2015)

Korean legal framework has three levels with a well-established hierarchial structure. At the first level is an act which states the overarching principles and procedures, enacted by parliament; at the second level are presidential decrees which provide detailed procedures; and at the third are ministerial regulations with more specific administrative information and specific guidelines. In addition, there are sub-level guidelines issued by the Cultural Heritage Administrator or the Ministry of Culture, Sports, and Tourism.

However, the Korean government has not focused on the principles of conservation, which provide the philosophical and theoretical perspective for reasoning why and deciding what to conserve and how to conserve it. These principles are typically copied from international documents, such as charters, without modifying them for local practice. As a result, the decision-making on cultural heritage and its conservation has often been inappropriate, illogical, inconsistent, non-transparent, and baffling for the public. The Korean government has followed international principles such as "minimum intervention," "reversibility," and "restoration or reconstruction based on accurate information" without adapting these principles to the Korean context and to the nature of local practice. The lack of appropriate principles for value identification and value conservation has made it difficult for government to communicate and work with the public in the process of value dissemination.

LACK OF SPECIFIC GUIDELINES FOR VALUE-BASED APPROACH

Munwhajae in Korean is a legal term for all types of heritage, both tangible and intangible, cultural and national. Its literal meaning is "cultural property." *Munwha*, meaning culture, was a new term translated from Japan during the Meiji Period. *Jae* means "property, something valuable, or asset." *Munwhayusan*, literally meaning cultural heritage, appeared first in the press in 1935 (Anon 1935), and *munwhajae* appeared a little later in 1946 (Anon 1946). Both *munwhayusan* and *munwhajae* were used for the same meaning of something valuable or something inherited from the past. *Munwhajae* became favoured as the legal term through the first Cultural Protection Act in 1962 which copied the 1954 Japanese law. It is not known why *munwhajae* was favoured as the legal term. There was no discussion or research on the meanings of these words. It probably came about through copying the Japanese law. Over the last five years, experts have debated changing to *munwhayusan*, without any resolution.

In 2017, expert opinion divided three ways on the terminology to be used in a new law. Some favoured continued usage of *munwhajae* or "cultural property," while others favored "cultural heritage" or "national heritage," arguing that the term heritage is widely used both internationally and locally, including UNESCO's World Heritage List. This argument, between concepts from Japan or international practice, shows the failure to develop a local perspective even after more than a century. Before the terminology is chosen, the meaning and substance of the term should be studied and discussed.

Heritage is a modern concept. Developed from the interest in human history and material evidence, its meaning has evolved over time. Many subdivisions of heritage have appeared to cover both tangible and intangible types as well as both man-made and natural objects. The concept has spread from the west into the east. Countries have taken on the duty of listing their important heritage sites and protecting them. Civic societies and the general public are empowered to play an important role in decision-making in the developed countries. However, latecomer countries like Korea are still struggling to understand the concept, redefine it for their cultural context, and render it in legal language. These are challenging tasks.

The definition of *munwhajae* in the 1962 act states:

> Article 2 (Definitions) (1) In this Act, the term "cultural property" means the following:
>
> 1. Buildings, classical books, calligrapher works, ancient documents, paintings, sculptures, crafts, etc and other tangible cultural products which are of the highly historical or artistic value and other archeological data corresponding thereto (called as tangible objects);
> 2. Drama, music, dance, craft technique, etc. and other intangible cultural products which are of the highly historical, artistic, academic, and scenic value (called as intangible objects);
> 3. Folklore material: public morals and customs relating to clothing, food, housing, occupation, religion or an annual event, etc. and clothes, tools or houses used therefor that are essential to the understanding of changes and progress in the national life (called as folklore material).

The legislation avoids clearly defining cultural property, and instead defines three sub-types, tangible objects, intangible objects, and folklore materials. In 1999, a brief definition was added before listing the types:

> Article 2 (Definitions) (1) The term "cultural properties" used in this Act means the artificially and naturally shaped national and global properties which possess the highly historical, artistic, academic and scenic values and fall under each of the following subparagraphs.

This addition highlights the concept of "values," following the Western perspective that perceives heritage as something valuable. However "values" may include subjective implications and myriad meanings which require further explanation and guidelines in practice. In addition, it is necessary to understand how heritage has been perceived and how the perception has evolved.

The present legal framework does not provide a clear methodology or guidelines for understanding how heritage value is exhibited in material remains. Identifying the tangible and intangible elements which form the value is an important step in deciding whether a certain site or artefact should be designated as heritage and placed under state protection. However, the present legal framework fails to provide objective criteria for making such identification in practice. It only states that:

> Article 23 (Designation of Treasures and National Treasures)
>
> The Administrator of the Cultural Heritage Administration may designate important cultural heritage as treasures, following deliberation by the Cultural Heritage Committee.
>
> The Administrator of the Cultural Heritage Administration may designate cultural heritage of great importance for humanity and without parallel in human history, among the treasures under paragraph (1), as national treasures, following deliberation by the Cultural Heritage Committee.

In addition, the Cultural Heritage Protection Decree, which lays down the standards and procedures for the designation of treasures and national treasures under Paragraph (1) and (2) of Article 23 of the Cultural Heritage Protection Act, provides lists of qualifying types of heritage in Appendix 1 without any specification of the criteria for decision-making. It also uses ambiguous phrases such as "those with much historical, academic, aesthetic, and technical values," "those with significant meanings," and "those which are a rare example."

Such criteria cannot form the basis for rational decision-making based on accurate information and an appropriate analysis of the significance of the heritage. As a result, the Cultural Heritage Administration has not been able to elaborate a full spectrum of values for heritage which can serve as a useful reference in deciding what can and cannot be allowed in conservation work. Heritage professionals do not recognize the importance of values in their daily practice and decision-making.

HERITAGE AS HISTORICAL REMAINS NOT AS RESOURCE

Wonhyeong, with a literal meaning of "original form," is a core entity and overarching local principle in the Korean legal framework. However, its meaning is ambiguous, hence a lack of guidelines for applying the concept has generated a gap between principle and practice. The concept was created as part of understanding heritage as material remains, but is no longer a viable principle. The concept highlights material aspects, based on the concept of heritage as historical remains, and ignores heritage as an inheritance or resource.

In 1999 a principle for protecting heritage was added to the Cultural Heritage Protection Act. It states:

> Article 2–2 (Basic Principle of Protection of Cultural Properties)
> The basic principle of preserving, managing, and utilizing cultural properties is to maintain their original forms.

There are two key points in this definition: 1. historic, artistic, academic, or scenic values are the key attributes for an object to be included as "cultural property," and the ultimate goal of conserving heritage is to protect and deliver such values for both present and future generations; 2. "original form" is the key criterion to guide decision-making for the conservation and management of heritage values.

The way that "values" and "*wonhyeong*" are linked in Korea's legal framework is also found in the 1972 World Heritage Convention. Korea's four values and UNESCO's Outstanding Universal Value are core elements in defining cultural property or World Heritage. Korea's *wonhyeong* and UNESCO's authenticity and integrity determine the values and the attributes to sustain values. However, the concept of *wonhyeong* has not been scrutinized and discussed in the same way that the concept of authenticity has been discussed in the international community. *Wonhyeong* has a fixed meaning of "original form," which excludes the intangible aspects of tangible objects.

Two questions may be raised here. How should we assess the various types of value of heritage in practice? What is "original form" and how does it relate to values? These two questions introduce a tightly interwoven issue in actual practice, in particular for value-based processes, because original form plays an important role in assessing the value of heritage. For example, the value of a monument may partly lie in the multiple historical layers from different periods that are still present in its surviving fabric. Were this monument to be returned to its original form by removing the material, technological, and aesthetic traces of changes made since its creation, its historical value would be compromised and misunderstood by future generations.

Defining original form as the earliest form has led to slippage between principle and practice, as exemplified in the case of Sungnyemun (National Treasure No. 1, southern gate of the old capital of Seoul). During the Japanese colonial period, the city walls were lost to road construction.

During the Korean War, part of the roof was destroyed by a bomb (Figure 1). In 1961, the Korean government planned to restore the gate to its earliest form from the 14th century, but this form proved impossible to identify due to later changes and additions (Lee 2002: 228). The principle of restoring to the original form (which was the earliest form) could not be carried out in practice.

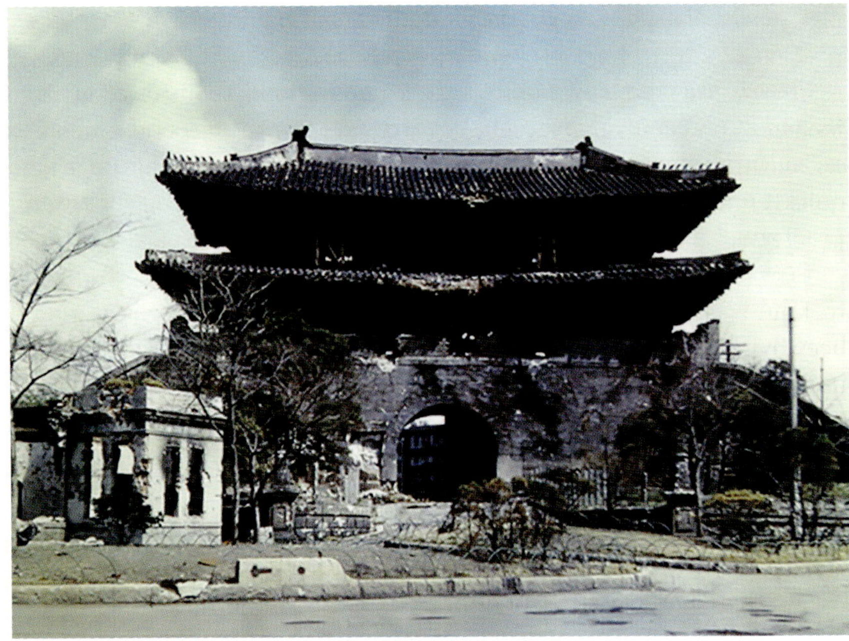

Figure 1. Sungnyemun gate after bombing during the Korean War. (Photo © National Archive of Korea)

From the 1970s to the present, restoring *wonhyeong* has been a major aim in the government's projects on heritage (Lee 2018: 60–1). In the 1970s, conservation of Geungnakjeon, Hall of Western Paradise in the Bongjeongsa temple replaced the form from the Joseon Period (1392–1910) with the form imagine from the Goryeon Period (935–1392). The wooden floor, which is suitable for the present Buddhist practice where worshippers sit on the floor, was replaced by a tile floor more suited to the earlier period when visitors entered wearing shoes and stood for worship. As a result, the building became a dead monument that is no longer compatible with contemporary rituals despite the fact that the building is still in daily use as part of a living monastery. The temple had to install a Joseon-style wooden floor on the top of the tiled floor for convenience in daily use. Also in the 1970s, in the conservation of Bulguksa temple, the concept of *wonhyeong* was applied not only to a single building but to the entire site. The original form of the individual buildings was considered less important than the original layout. As a result, many buildings in the complex were reconstructed based on assumptions, which goes against international recommendations such as the Venice Charter. Despite the reconstruction of buildings based on assumptions, the site was listed as a World Heritage Site in the 1990s.

The phrase "original form" first appeared during the Japanese colonial period, and became a prominent concept in the process of reformulating national identity after the Korean War. However, the concept was quickly established as meaning "the earliest form." and there was no scrutiny of its usage in a social or cultural context. Why did Korean society establish its meaning as "earliest form" and why was this accepted so easily and quickly? The answers to these questions will show how to tackle the problems.

The modern concept of preserving material remains was introduced to Korea in the early 20th century. Before then, material objects had been regarded as manifestations of sublime spirits, useful knowledge, useful teachings, respected principles, and human values. Therefore, the material aspect could be changed and replaced as long as it reflected the intangible substance. It is not clear exactly when the concept of heritage in regards to cultural value was created or introduced in Korea. However, it is clear that certain political and social changes, such as the Japanese annexation and rapid influx of Western culture, drew attention away from the traditional spirit, which had been Koreans' reason for valuing the physical remains. Koreans began to recognize material remains that helped to preserve national identity because these remains visually and tangibly displayed the long history and rich cultures of the people, which had faded under the Japanese regime.

This perspective on material remains was probably strengthened after the Korean War, when many historic sites and monuments were destroyed. In turn, this focus on material remains has changed the perspective on the relationship between material and intangible substance. Valuing heritage as material evidence of the past and recognizing that conservation of heritage is a social duty has indoctrinated many with a belief that the intangible elements of heritage are subordinate to the material substance. As a result, material remains become the center of interest, and the significance of intangible elements is undermined. Furthermore, a belief has emerged that the earliest form of a building or monuments can physically manifest the long-lost national identity damaged by the Japanese invasion and the Korean War.

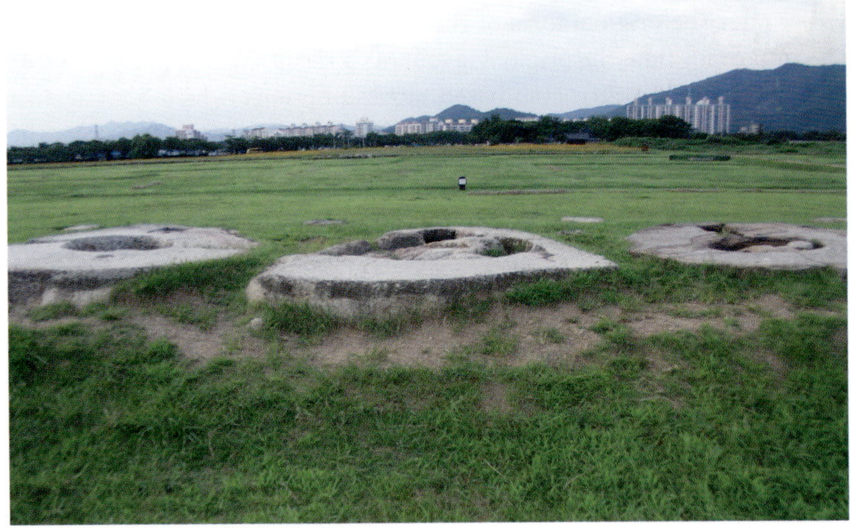

Figure 2. Hwangryongsa temple. (© author)

However, such a static approach toward "original form" has created two problems in actual practice. First, this approach has neglected the importance of physical historical layers in heritage, therefore creating a dilemma in deciding which layer is to be preserved and which others can be sacrificed. Second, this approach has ignored other elements which contribute to the values of heritage, such as original materials, techniques, settings, and spirits of heritage. As a result, certain (mostly important) aspects of heritage values have been lost in the process of physical intervention for conservation.

In order to tackle these problems, the Cultural Heritage Administration has recognized the need to re-examine the principles, revise the concept of "original form," and provide a new framework for using the principle in actual practice.

First, the definition of original form should be revised. Although the literal meaning of original form implies the physical and tangible aspect of heritage, its meaning should be explicitly re-defined to include not only the visible form but also various elements which shape the form such as material, techniques, settings, and spirits of heritage, as noted in the 1994 Nara Document on Authenticity. Second, the principle should not be a goal in itself but a methodology to achieve the goal in practice. It should be the criteria for making decisions. Considering that the ultimate goal of heritage conservation, management and utilization is to maintain the value of heritage, the principle of "preserving original form" should be a tool for decision-making to achieve this goal.

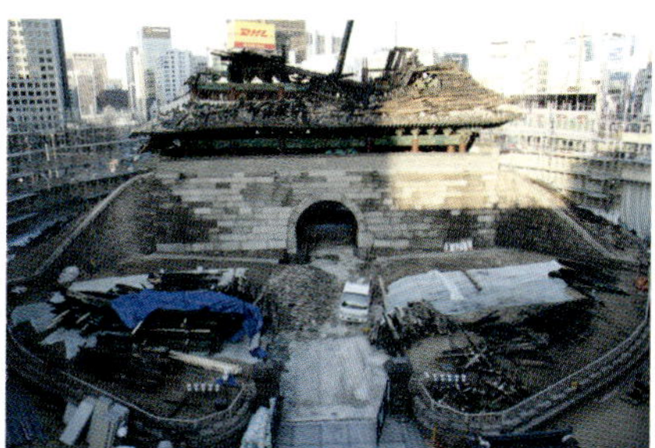

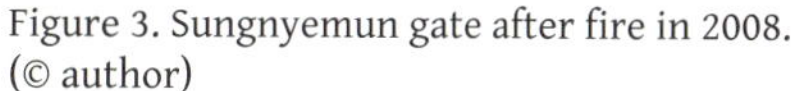

Figure 3. Sungnyemun gate after fire in 2008. (© author)

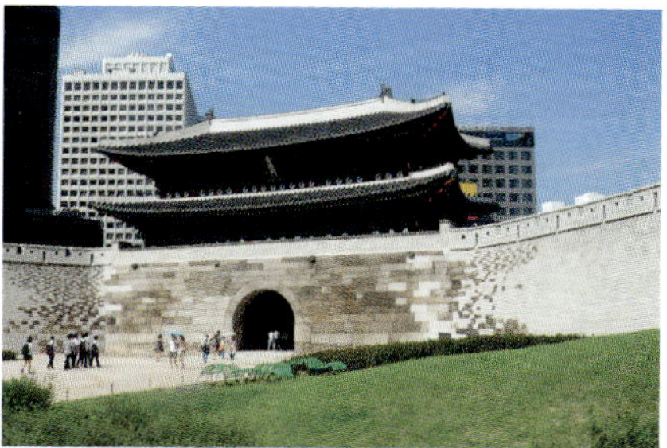

Figure 4. Sungnyemun gate after restoration. (© author)

Internally within the Cultural Heritage Administration, some think that the principle of "preserving original form" should be removed from the legal framework because "original form" can be interpreted in so many different ways, resulting in paradoxical and controversial decision-making in cases of restoring ruined or totally destroyed heritage sites. The Hwangryongsa temple site in Gyeongju (Figure 2) and Sungnyemun gate in Seoul, which was destroyed by fire and reconstructed (Figures 3 and 4), are prime examples. However, the removal of the principle would generate new problems, such as no principles of conservation in law and no practical criteria on what to conserve in practice. Therefore, it is necessary for the Cultural Heritage Administration to re-examine the meaing of *wonhyeong* and re-define the meaning of the word so that it can be practiced as a useful principle in practice.

NO LOCAL PERSPECTIVE, NO CLEAR GUIDELINES IN DECISION-MAKING

Wall paintings of the thousand Buddhas in the main hall of Mihwangsa temple were dismantled in 2017 for conservation (Figures 5 and 6). Due to deterioration and damage over many years, conservators and scientists advised that the paintings should be removed from their old locations and mounted on backing paper. The surfaces were then cleaned and missing parts were repaired and repainted. The Cultural Heritage Administration claims they have not decided whether the paintings will be returned to their original place. As they have been separated from the walls, they are no longer an intrinsic part of the building but are individual religious and artistic objects, with implications for the value of the walls and also of the building. This procedure was pursued in order to protect the historical remains and the material aspect of the heritage, however the decision took no consideration of the religious association between the paintings and the building, which is based on the Korean tradition of presenting religious teaching in material form.

The paintings were made during the later Joseon Dynasty (1392–1910) when the hall was built. The thousand Buddhas were enshrined on the walls between pillars, on brackets, and on the surface of beams inside the hall. Most historical wall paintings are made with natural pigments on a clay base, hence these wall paintings are unique and rare heritage, which have been preserved in situ for more than 250 years. They depict

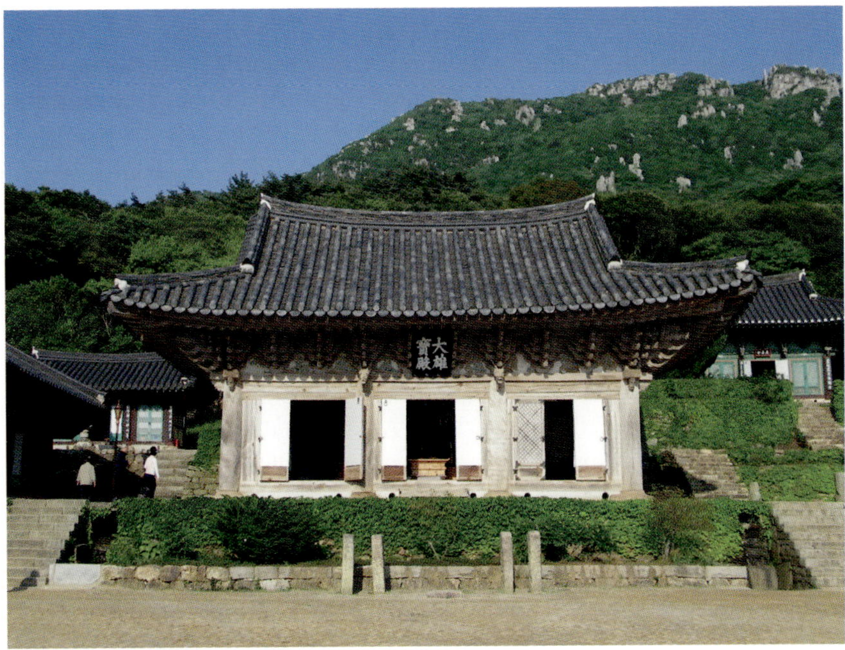

Figure 5. Main hall of Mihwangsa temple. (© author)

the different faces of the thousand Buddhas, expressing a core theology of Mahayana Buddhism that every human being has a Buddha nature to be enlightened through practice. The paintings are an integral part of the hall. The decision to separate the paintings from the building should have considered the impact on the building's value, not only the preservation of the paintings' historic and artistic values. The Cultural Heritage Administration, the authority behind the decision, has claimed that it was following legal procedure (Noh 2017; Cultural Heritage Administration of Korea 2017).

The religious value can be sustained when the paintings remain attached to the walls, sanctifying the main hall. However the building was designated as national heritage without taking into consideration the significance of the paintings in relation to the building. Scholars have acclaimed the rarity and significance of the now paper-mounted paintings without thinking of their religious value as an integral part of the building.

Such problems have been caused by the lack of local perspective in the step of value assessment, in particular, the failure to recognize the intangible aspect of heritage. Buddhist scroll paintings called *gwaebul,* which are used in outdoor rituals, manifest important artistic and

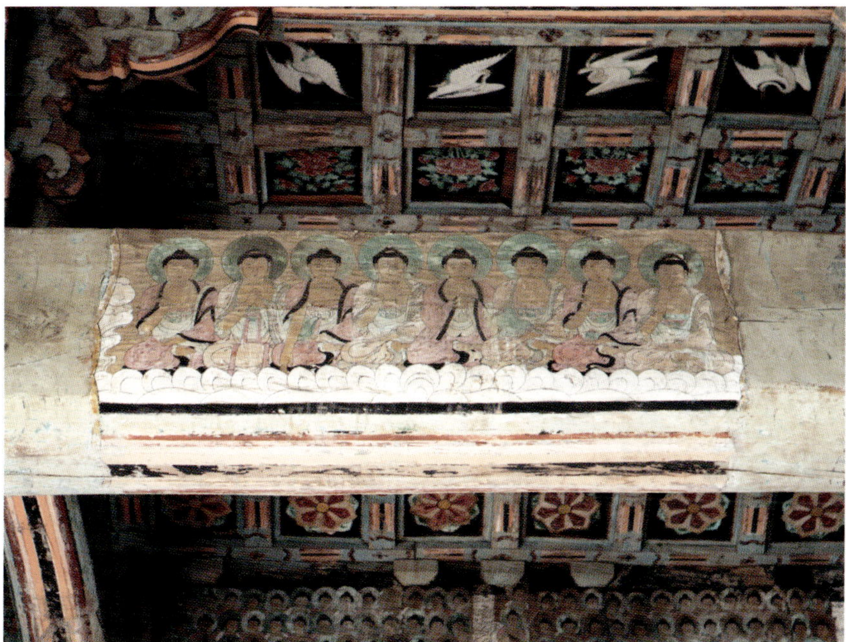

Figure 6. Painting of Thousand Buddhas. (© author)

historic values in themselves but also play an important and integral part in Buddhist ritual (Figure 7). Because they depict a Buddha or a scene of preaching from a Buddhist text, they are placed at the center of the courtyard, yet they are only one element in the outdoor event. Their religious value exists within the context of the Youngsanjae ritual, which is designated as both Korean Intangible Heritage (No. 50) and UNESCO Intangible Cultural Heritage. On the day of the ritual, the courtyard is sanctified with paintings of guardians, flags, carriers for dead spirits and many other material elements. At the end of the ceremony, all the material objects except for the scroll paintings are traditionally burnt to symbolize the Buddhist philosophy of emptiness and impermanence.

However, although the scroll paintings and the Youngsanjae ritual were both inscribed in both the national and international list, there was no information on the relationship between tangible painting and intangible ritual as one entity. Therefore, many scroll paintings have been preserved for sustaining their artistic and historical values while their religious values have been lost. Buddhist rituals have been performed in a place decorated by photocopied paintings and cheaply manufactured offerings. Even though many scroll paintings have been repaired, they do not have the opportunity to come out to the courtyard to host a ritual. If the legal framework provided a set of guidelines for recognizing the local distinctiveness of paintings, rituals, and other related objects as

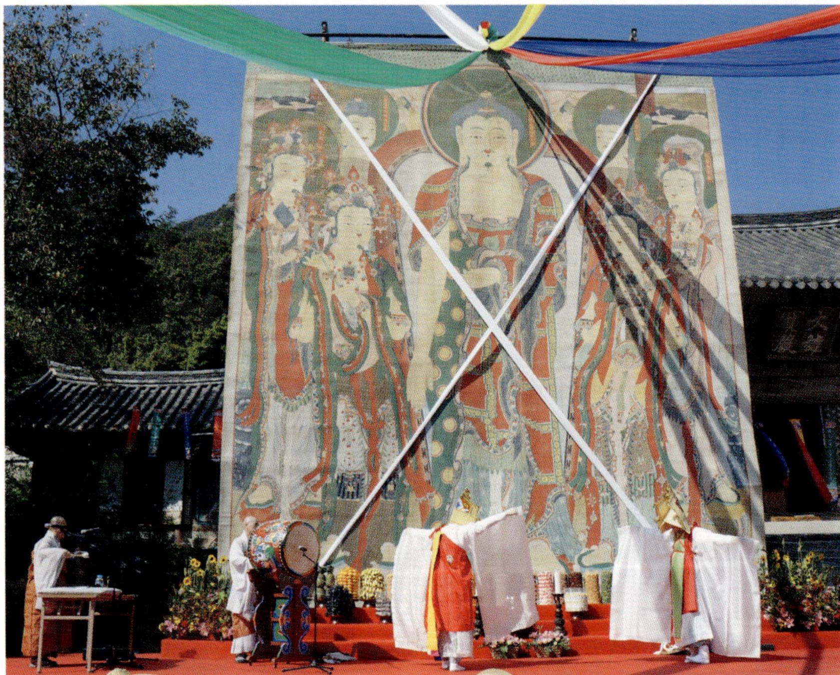

Figure 7. Big scroll painting and rituals in Naesosa temple. (© author)

one entity, then the ways of sustaining and disseminating value could be differently decided.

Both the Korean legal framework and UNESCO's World Heritage policy have provisions for assessing the impact of decision-making on heritage. However, detailed procedures and criteria, which take into consideration both local and international perspectives, have not been established. As mentioned earlier, a World Heritage Site recognizes values for mankind whereas a nationally designated site recognizes the significance in national history. The legal framework should provide a set of systematic procedures and criteria for decision-making to sustain values from both perspectives.

The plan to construct a new bridge on the Geumgang River in Gongju, which will have impact on heritage that is both internationally and nationally designated, demonstrates the importance of the legal framework for impact assessment. Until the early 20th century, there were only bridges for pedestrians. Transport between the north and south of the old capital city of the Baekjae Kingdom (18–660 BCE) was by boat. The Gongsanseong Fortress was built on the south of the Geumgang River so that the river would serve as a natural moat protecting the capital. In 1932 during the Japanese Colonial Period, a railway bridge was built and later converted into a road. Recognizing the historical value of the introduction of new material, the bridge is listed in the Cultural Heritage Administration's National Registry List. However, only one lane is now used because of structural problems.

After many requests for a new bridge, a member of parliament secured a budget of 4.4 billion dollars from the Ministry of Land and Transportation in 2016. In 2017, the Gongju Municipal Government submitted to the Cultural Heritage Administration a planning application for a four-lane bridge adjacent to the old bridge and fifty meters away from the border of the fortress, which is a site both internationally and nationally designated, hence its value has been assessed from two different perspectives based on two different legal frameworks. The impact assessment should therefore be conducted from two different perspectives for a value-based rational decision-making.

Under Korean law, a planning permission within 500 meters of the border of a Historic Site should be examined by the National Committee of Cultural Heritage and decided by the Cultural Heritage Administration of Korea. This impact assessment is based on the site's listing as national heritage and hence on the relevant values. Any assessment based on the international perspective of a World Heritage Site should be separate. In addition, Gonsanseong Fortress falls under the Special Act on Ancient Capitals Conservation and Promotion.

In the conservation and management plan found in the *Nomination of Baekje Historic Areas for Inscription on the World Heritage List*, there is an explicit statement that the landscape of the Geumgang River and surrounding hills is important for the fortress (Republic of Korea 2015, 109). *Comprehensive plan for conservation and promotion of ancient capital*

Gongju states that all traffic between the residential area to the north and the old capital area to the south should be diverted outside the historical area (Gongju Municipal Government 2014: 197).

The Outstanding Universal Value of the fortress within a historic city should be an important consideration in any rational decision. Even though the impact on the value of the Historic Site can be mitigated, the conservation plan should ensure that the fortress is sustained as World Heritage of Outstanding Universal Value. The impact on traffic, tourism, commercial activities, and local communities in a historic but living city need to be taken into account. However, the impact of this planned bridge needs to be assessed from the perspective of both its World Heritage status and the Ancient Capitals listing. Although there is no legal requirement, the Cultural Heritage Administration has strongly recommended that Gongju City conduct an impact assessment from the World Heritage perspective. A new plan for the location and size of the bridge will be submitted after the World Heritage impact assessment is completed.

A WAY FORWARD FOR A VIABLE LEGAL FRAMEWORK

Since the early 20th century, heritage and its conservation has developed in concept and practice. The legal framework has been revised in parallel with change in international perspectives, yet there remains a challenge to integrate local perspective for improving the legal framework's viability in practice. This chapter argues that a value-based approach, rational decision-making, and understanding heritage as a resource to improve the quality of life can be possible only once the gap between international principles and local practice is closed by integrating local perspectives. Three changes are needed.

First, guidelines for value identification should be drafted and published. These guidelines should recognize the four values (historic, artistic, academic, scenic) manifested in different types of heritage, and should reflect local perspectives on creating and understanding heritage. The meaning of each value should be clarified to help identify both tangible and intangible elements of values. It is also necessary to have a guide for writing up a statement of significance. A full explication of the concept of *wonhyeong,* its relationship to values, and the principles for conservation should be provided so that decisions can be made in a consistent, rational, and transparent manner.

Second, the procedures and criteria for impact assessment should be re-examined and revised. The present provisions limit the scope of impact assessment, omitting some important factors affecting heritage values. The criteria for impact assessment should include World Heritage perspectives as well as considerations relating to ancient capitals.

Third, the legal framework should make space for public participation. At present, there is no official procedure to hear public opinions on development affecting heritage values or on alterations to historic sites or buildings. All decisions on heritage affect the historic environment of a society, hence the decision-making authority should hear the opinions of different stakeholders, experts, and civic societies. In England there are five National Amenity Societies who must be notified by local government on any decision for partial or total demolition of listed buildings or scheduled monuments (Historic England 2019). There are also civic preservation societies, which can be consulted on planning applications in a region. In addition, each local government posts all planning applications submitted so that neighbors can provide their opinions during a public consultation period before a decision is made. York Civic Trust, for example, monitors all planning applications within the Conservation Area and may offer its opinion. In order for a civic society or the general public to contribute to rational decision-making, they must have access to the requisite knowledge and the opportunity for ethical participation.

References

Anon. 1935. "*Munwhayusan* in Joseon, distinctiveness and the way of transmission." *Donga Daily Newspaper*, February 11, 1935.

Anon. 1946. "Let's care about old *munwhajae,* celebrating the week of caring treasures and ancient remains." *Donga Daily Newspaper*, April 21, 1946.

Cultural Heritage Administration of Korea. 2017. "Official explanation on the dismantling the wallpaintings of a thousand buddhas." Cultural Heritage Administration, October 11, 2017.

Cultural Heritage Protection Act (First enacted in 1963, last revised in 2018).

DCMS (Department for Digital, Culture, Media and Sports). 2010. *Historic England Principles of selection for listed buildings* (revised in 2018). assets.publishing.service.gov.uk/government/uploads/system/uploads/attachment_data/file/757054/Revised_Principles_of_Selection_2018.pdfassets.publishing.service.gov.uk/government/uploads/system/uploads/attachment_data/file/757054/Revised_Principles_of_Selection_2018.pdf

English Heritage (later Historic England). 2008. *Conservation principles, policies and guidance for the sustainable management of the historic environment.* https://content.historicengland.org.uk/images-books/publications/conservation-principles-sustainable-management-historic-environment/conservationprinciples policiesguidanceapr08web.pdf/content.historicengland.org.uk/images-books/

publications/conservation-principles-sustainable-management-historic-environment/conservationprinciplespoliciesguidanceapr08web.pdf/

Gongju Municipal Government. 2014. *Comprehensive plan for conservation and promotion of ancient capital Gongju*. Gongju Municipal Government.

Historic England. 2019. Amenity societies and other voluntary bodies. historicengland.org.uk/advice/hpg/publicandheritagebodies/amenitysocieties/historicengland.org.uk/advice/hpg/publicandheritagebodies/amenitysocieties, accessed April 2019.

Historic England. *Listing selection guides.* historicengland.org.uk/listing/selection-criteria/listing-selection/historicengland.org.uk/listing/selection-criteria/listing-selection/

Lee, Gangkeun. 2002. "Sungnyemunyeonggu" (A study of Sungnyemun: about restoration and history of maintenance.) *Misulsa* 19, 207–35.

Lee, Sujeong. 2018. "Redefining authenticity in Korean context, focusing on authenticity of form." In, G. Wijesuriya and J. Sweet, ed., *Revisiting Aauthenticity in the Asian Context*, ICCROM-CHA, pp. 55–63. www.iccrom.org/sites/default/files/publications/2019–03/revisiting_authenticity_cha-2_web.pdf

Ministry of Industry, Trade, and Energy, *2018 White Paper on New Regeneration Energy.* knrec.or.kr/file/2018%EC%8B%A0%EC%9E%AC%EC%83%9D%EC%97%90%EB%84%88%EC%A7%80%EB%B0%B1%EC%84%9C.pdf

Noh, Hyeongseok. 2017. "Why dismantled wall-paintings of a thousand buddhas?" *Hangyerae Daily Newspaper*, October 10, 2017.

Republic of Korea. 2015. *Nomination of Baekje Historic Areas for inscription on the World Heritage List, Appendix 1 Conservaton and management plan of Baekje Historic Area.* Republic of Korea.

Tomaszewski, A. 2008. "Introduction on the topic of the conference." In A. Tomaszewski, ed., *Values and criteria in heritage conservation: Proceedings of the international conference of ICOMOS, ICCROM and Foundazione Romualdo Del Bianco, 2–4 March 2007 Florence*, pp. 33–4.

UNESCO. 1972. *World Heritage Convention*. UNESCO.

UNESCO. 2004. "Nara Document on Authenticity." In K. Larsen, ed., *Nara conference on authenticity: Proceedings*, pp. xxi–xxv. UNESCO.

Thailand's Conservation Laws and Evolving Heritage Values

Yongtanit Pimonsathean

Law is one of the most effective tools to ensure good protection and management of cultural heritage sites. Based on international practice influenced by European philosophy and experiences, the universal concepts and principles of heritage conservation evolve over time and thus require an updated and responsive regulatory framework to cope with contemporary social, economic, and political demands. Moreover, the Eurocentric values-based conservation has been recently challenged by the growing support for alternative approaches such as the living heritage, the inclusion of the intangible dimension, and historic urban landscape. This has made the legislative issue in heritage conservation more complicated. In Thailand there is a question: after ratifying several international charters and conventions, is the values-based conservation well-established? If not, how can Thailand reach beyond the values-based approach? This paper simply deals with the values-based versus the existing Thai conservation legislative framework.

To help identify the need for a more comprehensive and responsive regulatory framework, this chapter explores the Thai conservation laws in this paper in five sections. The first reviews regional challenges in heritage conservation to the values-based approach. The second reviews existing heritage conservation laws in Thailand and identifies some issues in the context of the values-based approach. The third part presents the current situation of heritage sites through several cases to prove that there are real problems in heritage conservation in the country. The fourth part reviews conservation laws from countries that have already followed the values-based approach in order to set a benchmark for a legislation framework. The final part presents recommendations for Thai conservation legislation.

INTRODUCTION: REGIONAL CHALLENGES AND VALUES-BASED CONSERVATION APPROACH

For more than two decades, countries in Asia have shared common challenges in heritage protection and management. Such challenges are massive degradation, misuse, and loss of cultural heritage sites, mostly linked to rapid urbanization, rural to urban migration, overemphasis on fulfilling tourism demand, focus on single monuments, and isolation of conservation from the contemporary urban development process (UNESCO 2016: 91; UNESCO Bangkok 2009; Stubbs 2009: 325–29; and Stovel 2004: 108–9). One among several factors causing threats to heritage is the lack of regulatory controls (UNESCO Bangkok 2009: 3). Thailand is perhaps one of the best cases of this challenge in the region.

Despite its claim to a rich cultural heritage, Thailand is losing heritage sites very rapidly under the contemporary socio-economic atmosphere. The term "heritage" here includes all signs of human achievements that help people to realize their cultural identity, and to mentally and spiritually use them to balance their quality of life (Feilden and Jokilehto 1998: 11). Therefore, all those ancient monuments or archaeological sites protected by the current law are only a part of what is called cultural heritage today. Anything outside the category of ancient monuments and archaeological sites is not really protected by any law. Hence, existing law is inadequate for protecting (and enhancing) what is seen and understood as cultural heritage by the people. The non-registered heritage such as urban shophouses, private houses, and traditional villages, are the main focus in this paper.

The significance of non-registered heritage is often recognized by people in the non-governmental sector. The existing law does not provide opportunity to receive assistance or support to safeguard this heritage. The way a heritage site is evaluated can be explained by a review of different conservation approaches. According to Poulios (2014: 19–29), in modern times there are three main approaches to heritage conservation: material-based approach, values-based approach, and living heritage approach.

The material-based approach is the practice of conservation which emerged between the 19th and mid-20th centuries with a focus on the work of experts in the preservation of the materials or fabric of heritage places. The sites considered as heritage under the material-based approach tend to be great architectural works and archaeological sites.

The values-based approach, which developed since the 1980s, is currently practiced in most countries in Europe, North America and Australia, and is advocated by the World Heritage Operational Guidelines. This approach still emphasizes the work of experts but allows for a participatory process involving multiple stakeholder groups that utilize the heritage. In the values-based approach, the meaning of heritage has been expanded from great works to include ordinary, everyday life pieces of human creation.

The living heritage approach, which is now emerging in the postmodern era, is more radical in increasing the role of local communities in decision-making processes over both protection and utilization of heritage.

Although there are signs of the living heritage approach in some programs such as a SEAMEO-SPAFA project in Phrae (Tanprawat 2009; Poulios 2014), the practical application of today's mainstream values-based approach is still limited in Thailand. The focus on a single monument, and lack of protection and management tools for non-registered heritage, show that Thailand has not yet comprehended the merit of the values-based approach in heritage conservation practice.

The values-based approach is documented in international reference materials such as Australia ICOMOS' Burra Charter, the Getty Conservation Institute's conservation process, and the World Heritage Operational Guidelines. The process starts with evaluating the cultural significance of a site by certain criteria, followed by applying methods of treatment or intervention appropriate to the site's significance, and lastly designing a management scheme to sustain the value and promote the proper utilization of the site. Each step in the process requires active participation from all stakeholders. These requirements of the values-based conservation process will be used here to analyze the heritage laws in Thailand and other countries.

REVIEW OF EXISTING HERITAGE CONSERVATION LAW IN THAILAND

Thailand has only one law that directly deals with the protection and conservation of tangible cultural heritage, which is the Monuments, Antiques, Objects of Art and National Museums Act B.E. 2504 (1961) as amended up to 1992. However, due to the broader meaning of cultural heritage, other relevant laws are also reviewed here. These are: the City Planning Act B.E. 2518 (1975) as amended up to 2015; the Building Control Act B.E. 2522 (1979) as amended up to 2015; and the Enhancement and

Conservation of National Environmental Quality Act B.E. 2535 (1992). The review follows an analytical method by examining three components of the fundamental legal principles which are: a) authorization, the manner in which the regulations are enabled; b) discretion, the manner in which the regulations are written; and c) delegation, the manner in which the regulations are administered (Sitkowski and Russel 2007: 5).

The Monuments, Antiques, Objects of Art and National Museums Act 1961

The Monuments, Antiques, Objects of Art and National Museums Act ("Monument Act" in short) has its roots in the establishment of the first national museum in 1868, followed by a law to preserve ancient objects in 1923, and a law on the export of ancient objects and art objects in 1926. After the political revolution of 1932, The Monuments, Ancient Objects, Art Objects and National Museums Act was promulgated in 1934 before being superseded by the current law in 1961.

On authorization, power to register, annul, protect and maintain a monument under this Act is granted to the director general of the Fine Arts Department (FAD), Ministry of Culture. Any property worthy of conservation can be registered a monument regardless of ownership. There is no enabling law to confer such power on any other government authority. So heritage conservation in Thailand is a centralized and top-down procedure.

On discretion, the status of a monument is evaluated by statutory criteria on age, method of construction, and its importance for history, archaeology and art (Section 4). Once registered, a monument cannot be demolished (Section 10), any intervention needs approval from the director general (Section 7 bis.), and violations will be punished (Section 32). In 1985, the FAD issued the one and only supplementary document, The Departmental Regulations on the Methods of Conservation of the Monuments, which broadly follows the Venice Charter of 1964. The Venice Charter is considered one of the main documents of the material-based conservation approach (Poulios 2014: 19). Heritage conservation in Thailand is still effectively based on a material-based conservation approach.

On delegation, all the power of decision-making in the whole conservation process rests with the director general. The FAD has regional offices across the country but in practice all the management resources (budget, manpower, and equipment) are under central administration. Since the management is strongly centralized, there is little chance for participation by stakeholders, particularly local people, in the utilization of heritage.

The City Planning Act 1975

The second law is the City Planning Act 1975. The law replaced the previous British-influenced Town and Country Planning Act enacted in 1952. The current law is influenced by the modern concept of city planning from the United States through the intervention of the USAID program and a team of American planning consultants who prepared an urban plan for Bangkok in the early 1960s (Sternstein 1982: 109). According to the Act's definition (Section 4), the conservation and restoration of sites or objects of artistic, architectural, historical, and archaeological importance is one of the objectives of city planning. A heritage conservation area can be demarcated under this law, by one of two tracks. The first track is by having the area zoned for conservation in the comprehensive plan of land use drawn up when land use and building regulations are stipulated (Section 17). The second track is through a project-based proposal under the specific area plan process (Section 28). This paper does not examine this second track as there is no example of its implementation.

Under this city planning law, authorization again rests at the central level. The land use plan and zoning regulations for any city are adopted as ministerial regulation. A specific area plan needs an act with cabinet approval. City planning in Thailand has little participation from local authorities and residents as the decision-making is at the central level.

Under the planning law, there is discretion in both control and guidance measures. On the control side, the law regulates building use, height, size, type, bulk, set-back distance, and other aspects to ensure a good townscape and environment (Section 17). On the guidance measures, tools to promote heritage conservation can be established. Recently in Bangkok, a study has been made on the transfer of development rights (TDR) or air right transfer. This is expected to help the conservation of heritage buildings owned by the private sector. There is no provision for the protection of individual buildings in the law. The role of the city planning law is to protect the townscape rather than heritage buildings.

Under the planning law, there is delegation of power to local officers for preparing, monitoring, and implementing a comprehensive plan, but the decision on delegation is made by the national planning board at the central level.

The Building Control Act 1979

The Building Control Act 1979 replaced several building construction laws enacted between 1936 and 1972. These old laws, which predated the planning law of 1975, had played a role in land use zoning and regulation.

The first regulation for a Bangkok conservation area was initiated in 1984 under the building control act, prior to adoption of the first comprehensive land use plan in 1992. According to the 1979 Act, a conservation area can be demarcated for the benefit of environmental protection, city planning, and architecture (Section 8).

Under the current Building Control Act, the authorization to demarcate a conservation area can be done at the central level in the form of a ministerial regulation (Section 8) or by local ordinance (Sections 9 and 10), depending on the context. This law is the only channel which allows a municipality and local residents to protect their heritage area. There are examples of local ordinances for the benefit of conservation areas in the cities of Bangkok, Chiang Mai, Chiang Khan, Chiang Rai, and Songkhla.

There is discretion in the regulations on building use, height, set-back distance, bulk, type, and other aspects of a building's character. Similar to the planning law, the Building Control Act does not cover the protection of individual heritage buildings.

On delegation, local officers are granted power to inspect, monitor, and permit or deny development proposals in the conservation area.

The Enhancement and Conservation of National Environmental Quality Act 1992

This law ("Environment Law" in short) was introduced during the national promotion of localization and civic participation in the 1990s, replacing the environment law of 1975. The term "environment" is defined in the law as "physical and biological substances created by both nature and humans" (Section 4). Similar to the planning and building control laws, a conservation area for environmental protection can be designated under this law (Section 43). The environmental protection area has many categories, including one labelled *sing waedlom silpakam* in Thai, literally meaning "artistic environment," but "cultural environment" is a less ambiguous translation. The designation of a cultural environmental protection area requires consent from local stakeholders. In general, a cultural environmental protection area is designated as a last resort when there is no proper protection measure in place and there is an urgent need for protection. The only place where this provision has been implemented is the old quarter of the city of Phuket.

Authorization under this law rests at the central level under the Ministry of Natural Resources and Environment. The designation of a cultural environment protection area is done by a Ministerial Regulation

(Section 43) or Ministerial Announcement (Section 45), depending on the local context. The power to adopt, amend, or annul rests with the minister.

Discretion is similar to that provided by the planning and building control laws but there are better provisions on several aspects, including management to effectively protect the environment.

Delegation is also similar to the planning law where local officers have a duty to monitor, grant, or deny development projects and proposals from private developers.

Table 1: Summary of regulating aspects of conservation laws in Thailand

Regulating Aspects	Laws Related to Conservation			
	Monument Act 1961	City Planning Act 1975	Building Control Act 1979	Environment Act 1992
Protection of individual building (no demolition)	/	-	-	-
Conservation area	-	/	/	/
Land use restriction	-	/	-	/
Building use restriction	-	/	/	/
Density control	-	/	/	/
Building type and size	-	/	/	/
Building character	-	/	/	/
Management methods	-	-	-	/
Incentives	-	/	-	-
Non-registered buildings	-	-	-	-

Among these four conservation laws, the monument law has the distinctive provision for registering, protecting, and maintaining heritage properties, while the other three laws (planning law, building control law, and environment law) have similar functions to protect the landscape by imposing restrictions on new development, rather than on existing heritage buildings (see Table 1). This similarity results in possible overlaps and conflicts. As the monument law covers only ancient monuments and archaeological sites, there is still no proper legal document to protect non-registered heritage in Thailand.

On May 29, 2019, the new City Planning Act was announced in the Royal Gazette. This law superseded the City Planning Act of 1975. There are two changes that may provide opportunity for the people to protect their heritage. The first change is that a conservation area can be declared at national, regional and provincial levels as one of the policies for guiding the city's future growth. The second change is the power to prepare and adopt the city plan is given to local administrations. The plan prepared by local administration can be adopted in the form of local ordinance, not ministerial regulations.

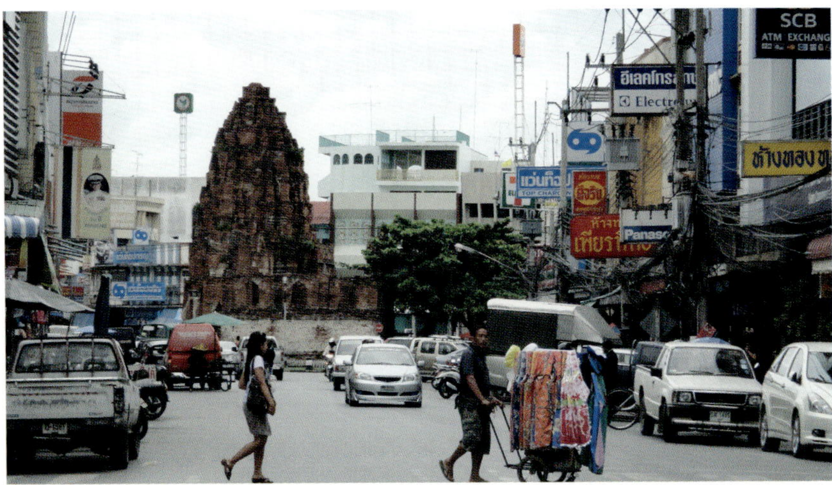

Figure 1. Prang Khaek in Lopburi's modern urban setting.

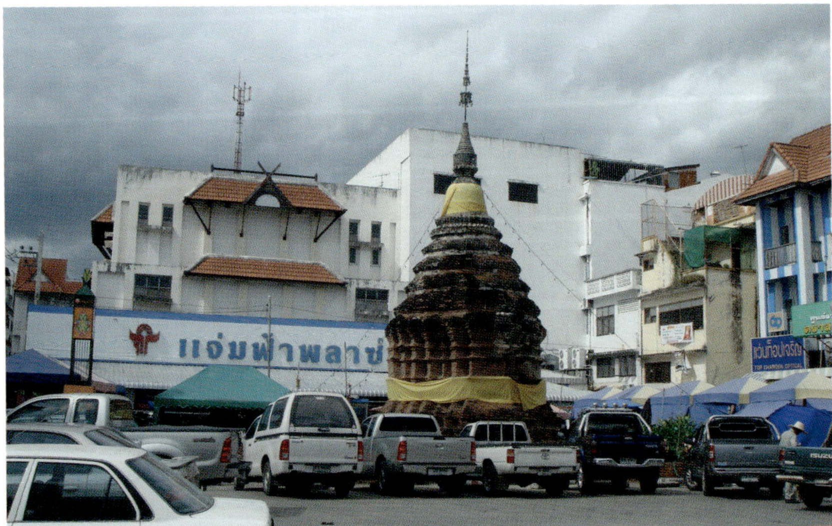

Figure 2. An isolated pagoda in Lamphun.

SITUATION OF CULTURAL HERITAGE SITES IN THAILAND

To demonstrate the inadequacy of Thai heritage laws using the values-based approach, some examples of the situation of heritage sites, both registered and non-registered, are presented here.

The first case shows how FAD's registration of heritage focuses on single monuments rather than their whole setting and context. In Thailand there are several registered monuments situated in a chaotic urban environment. Examples are Prang Khaek in Lop Buri (Figure 1) and a pagoda in Jaemfa Plaza in Lamphun (Figure 2), while there are several similar examples in Phimai (in the province of Nakhon Ratchasima), Chiang Mai, Ayutthaya, and so on. The focus on single monuments goes along with the failure to integrate any consideration of heritage sites into the urban development process. As a result, heritage sites cannot fulfill their function as past achievements of human kind that help people realize their cultural identity. They are just human-made structures that are now old and dead.

Another case shows how the focus on a single monument results in a change in traditional use once a building is registered as a monument. An example is a *sim* or traditional northeastern-style ordination hall at Wat Phrathat Kham Khaen in Khon Kaen province (Figure 3). The temple was registered as national heritage in 1987 and the *sim* and wall

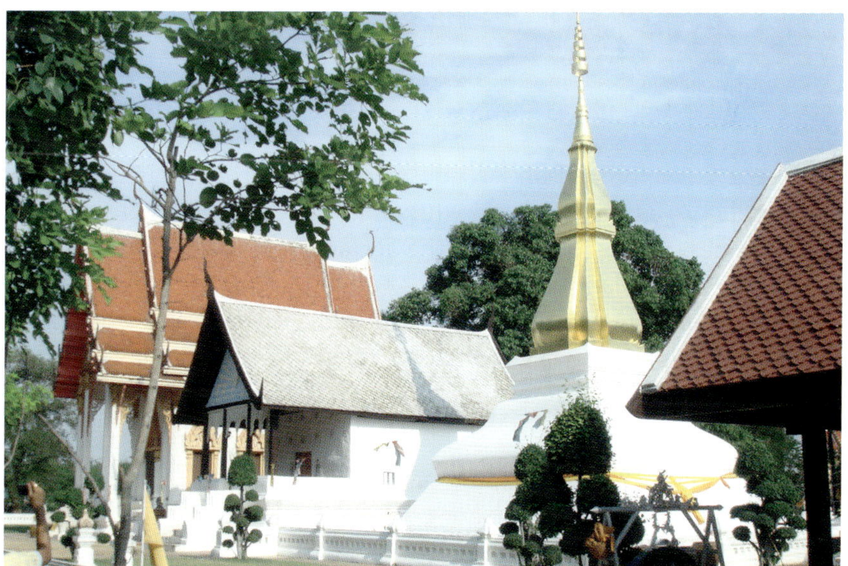

Figure 3. New ordination hall (far left with red tiled roof) was built next to the old sim (middle) at Wat Phrathat Khamkaen, Khon Kaen.

were designated as monuments. Close to the old *sim*, another ordination hall was built in contemporary style and took over the function of the former *sim* that was left vacant as showcase of northeastern tradition. The functional and religious value of the old *sim* was lost. This gives rise to a question of who has the authority to value the heritage as well as issues of authenticity in the usage, continuity, and spirit of the place.

For non-registered heritage which is the main focus of this paper, the first example is from the city of Phuket, where the old quarter has been under central government protection through the environment law since the mid-1990s. Despite a strong conservation movement among local citizens, there has been no enforcement at the local level. The central government has taken charge of protecting the old quarter that contains shophouses, mansions, and other buildings in the old Straits Settlement style. Unfortunately, such protection has limited control over the height, size, use, and style of new infill and replacement buildings.

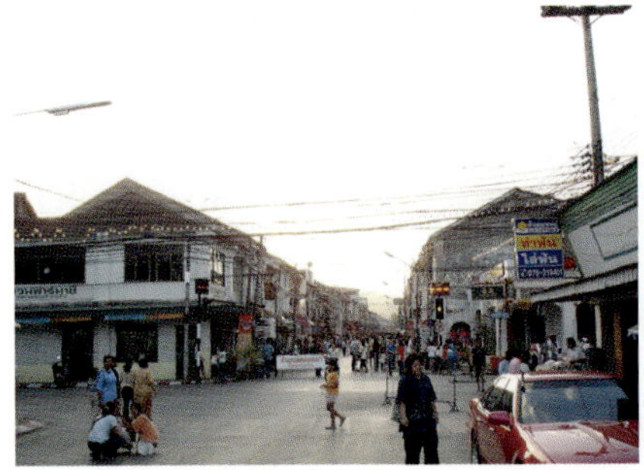

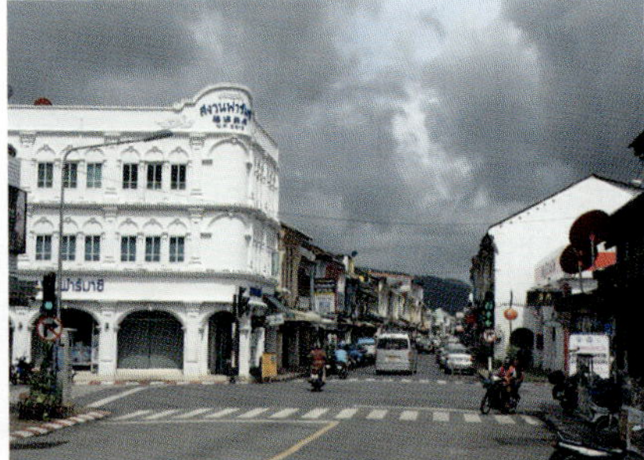

Figure 4. Replacement of a non-registered heritage building (left) with a building in retro old Phuket style (right) at the corner of Talang road in the old quarter of Phuket town.

There is no protection of non-registered heritage buildings and this has led to many incidents where old buildings are replaced with modern ones. An obvious case is the replacement of an old shophouse at the corner of Talang road (Figure 4). In 2011, the two-storey pre-war shophouse with earthen tiled roof was demolished and replaced by a re-invented old Phuket style shophouse of three-storeys at the maximum allowable height of 12 meters. According to the municipality which had responsibility for approving the building, the new structure followed the central government's regulations for Phuket old town conservation. Besides the loss of a heritage building, the replacement disrupts the historic townscape of the old city. Under the existing law, such incidents can occur in a conservation area through the discretion of the local authority. There is therefore a tendency to lose more and more heritage buildings in Phuket due to the existence but inadequacy of the conservation law.

In Bangkok's Chinatown, the importance of heritage buildings has been realized for many years by residents, communities, researchers, and even some non-conservation government authorities. Threats to demolish shophouse communities in Luen Rit, Weong Nakhon Kasem, and Charoenchai have been in the public attention for more than a decade (Figure 5). In 2014, the Luen Rit case was resolved by a long-lease agreement between the landlord and residents which included a commitment to conserve the 200 plus shophouses under a newly established community-based corporation. In the case of Woeng Nakhon Kasem and Charoenchai, the solution is still uncertain.

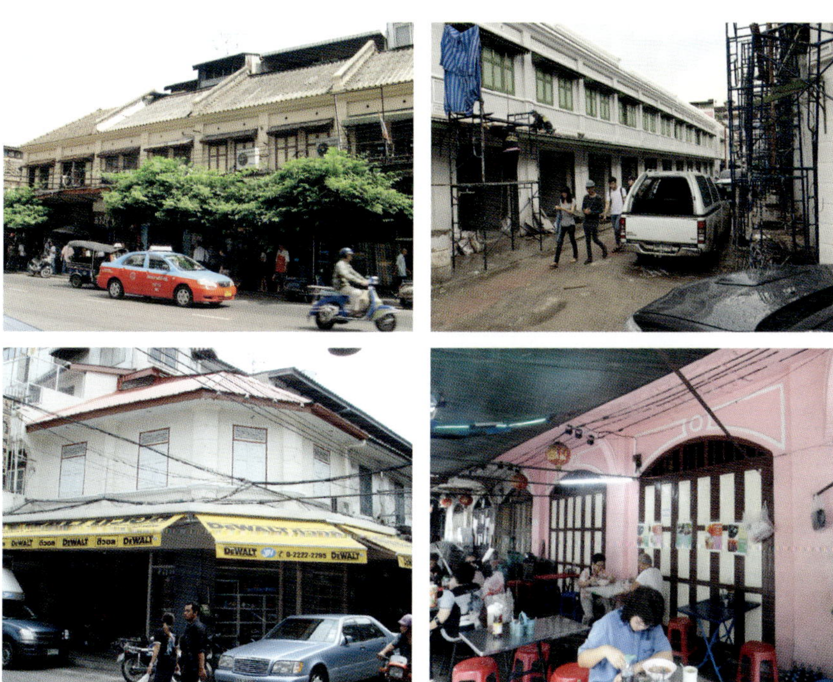

Figure 5. Old and historic shophouse of Luen Rit in 2007 (above left); under restoration in 2018 (above right); Woeng Nakhon Kasem (below left); and Charoenchai (below right).

From 2013 to 2015, after work had begun on building a subway line through Chinatown, residents of old shophouse communities in Chinatown submitted petitions to the National Human Rights Commission (NHRC) requesting for help in conserving the community. The existing local ordinance on conservation, promulgated in 1999, was found to control only the height of new constructions around important religious places but gave no protection to heritage buildings. Around the same time, the planning department of the Bangkok Metropolitan Administration (BMA) conducted a survey of potential heritage buildings in Chinatown, finding thousands of buildings that have architectural or historical significance, none of which was registered as heritage by any law. The NHRC then called for more comprehensive measures to protect Chinatown and the area adjacent to the north as they had evolved since the establishment of Bangkok as the national capital in the late 18th century. The BMA and the National Conservation Committee for Bangkok (Rattanakosin Committee, in short) responded to the NHRC's plea by setting in process a plan for a conservation area with proper measures.

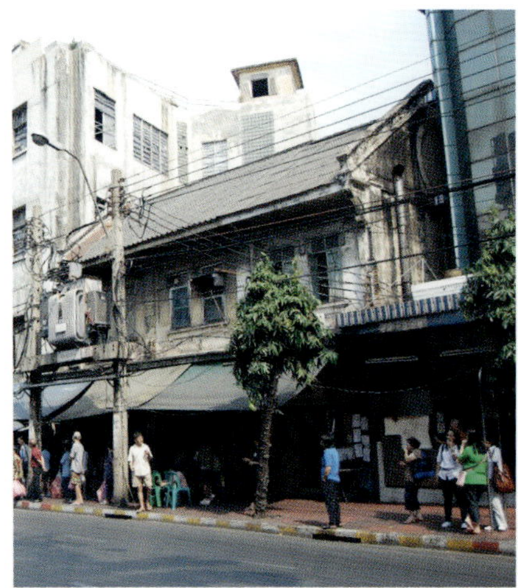

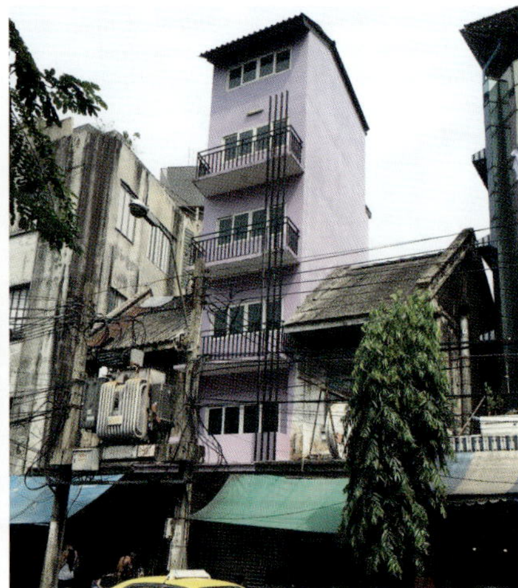

Figure 6. Non-registered heritage shophouses on Charoenkrung Road before and after development permitted in 2015.

This process threw up an interesting case. District officials were invited to participate in the survey and inventory of heritage buildings and the hearing of the results and the preliminary inventory. Even so, these officials have low awareness of the importance of heritage buildings. The district authorities approved a proposal to develop a site occupied by a row of three two-storey heritage shophouses on the oldest business thoroughfare called Charoenkrung road, replacing the middle unit with a seven-storey modern structure, creating visual chaos in a historic part of Chinatown (Figure 6).

These cases demonstrate that central and local authorities are remiss in the conservation of non-registered heritage. In 2015, a journalist interviewed a deputy director of the Fine Arts Department (FAD) as the central-level conservation authority and the director of the Planning Department of the BMA as local authority about the cultural significance of the Charoenchai shophouses and the prospects for their protection. The FAD executive stated that the department protected only places with distinctive cultural value and long history, and suggested some other government office might be helpful (despite the fact that the FAD is the only authority that can register heritage by law!). The director of the BMA Planning Department pointed out that Thailand has no law to protect these buildings and called for the community to prove that the community is significantly older than others (Yongcharoenchai 2015). These responses from central and local authorities demonstrate very well that there is no proper conservation law to meet the needs of the Thai people in contemporary society.

The values-based conservation approach has clearly not yet arrived in Thailand.

LEARNING FROM OTHER COUNTRIES

In order to understand the practical relationship between conservation law and the values-based approach, cases of countries that have already put in place laws shaped by the values-based approach are presented. The countries are England, the United States, and Japan. The review includes a brief explanation of the evolution of conservation laws and then a summary of current laws that follow the values-based approach.

England: timeline

This review of English conservation law is mostly based on the works of Pickard (1996), Ross (1996), Delafons (1997), Hobson (2004), and information from the official website of the Department for Culture, Media and Sport (DCMS).

The English conservation movement can be traced back to John Aubrey's archaeological and historical studies in the 1670s, followed by John Ruskin's critique on conservation philosophy in the 1840s, and a private voluntary effort by the establishment of a Society for the Protection of Ancient Buildings by William Morris in 1877. The first legislation, the Ancient Monument Protection Act, was enacted in 1882 (updated to the Ancient Monuments and Archaeological Areas Act 1979), focusing on ancient monuments and archaeological sites which are called "scheduled monuments" in the law. Between 1944 and 1947, the Town and Country Planning Act introduced another type of heritage, known as "listed buildings," meaning those having architectural value, mostly in urban settings and still inhabited. Local government was authorized to prepare and implement local plans. In 1967, local governments were allowed to designate conservation areas under the Civic Amenities Act (superseded by amendment of the Town and Country Planning Act in 1990). The first conservation area was designated in Lincoln town in the same year. In 1983, the National Heritage Act decentralized the responsibility to manage different types of heritage to local authorities. In 1989, a change in the Finance Act exempted listed buildings of paying value added tax (VAT). In 1990, civic consultation was required in the designation and amendment of conservation areas under the Town and Country Planning Act, and local governments were granted discretionary power to give grants or loans for the repair of buildings of architectural or historic interest.

United States: timeline

This review of the United States' heritage conservation law is based on Fowler (2003), Fitch (1990), Murtagh (1990), Tyler (2000), and information from the website of the National Parks Service (NPS).

The early movement of heritage conservation (known as historic preservation in the US) began with a movement to save the Independence Hall in Pennsylvania from demolition in 1816 and a campaign by Ann Pamela Cunningham to preserve George Washington's Mount Vernon in Virginia in 1853. The first conservation legislation, influenced by the national parks concept, was the Antiquities Act of 1906 which protected mainly the archaeological sites and ancient objects. In 1922, the Standard State Zoning Enabling Act provided legal support for urban heritage buildings by granting power to local governments to regulate zoning. The first local zoning ordinance for historic preservation appeared in Charleston, North Carolina in 1931. In 1966, the landmark National Historic Preservation Act was passed and has been the core conservation legislation until today. In 1976, the federal government's tax reform provided tax incentives for historic preservation. In the 1980s, the amended Historic Preservation Act enabled federal, state, and local governments working in partnership to identify, evaluate, and protect historic places through the certified local government program.

Japan: timeline

This review of Japan's heritage law is based on Asano (1999), Ho (2003), Sorensen (2004), Radzuan et al. (2014), Kakiuchi (2014), and information from the official website of the Agency for Cultural Affairs (Bunkacho) and Professor Nobuko Inaba from Tsukuba University.

The origin of heritage law (called cultural property law in Japan) arose from concern over the loss of art objects and religious places after Western intervention and vandalism in the 1860s. The first legislation, the Historic Objects Preservation Proclamation, was issued in 1871 and the Historic Shinto Shrines and Buddhist Temples Preservation Law was enacted in 1897. In 1919, two conservation-related laws were enacted: the Preservation of Historic Sites, Places of Scenic Beauty and Natural Monuments Law, and the City Planning Law. In 1929, the religious buildings protection law of 1897 was repealed and replaced by a new law to cover government historic properties, the National Treasures Preservation Law. In 1933, the short-life Important Art Objects Preservation Law was enacted to prevent old timber houses from being dismantled and sent abroad. In 1947, the decentralization law, the Local Autonomy Law was passed and in 1950, a new heritage consolidation law, the Law for the Protection of Cultural Property was enacted and remains in effect until today. In 1954, the 1950 law was amended to grant power to local governments to protect and register cultural property via local regulations. In 1968, there were three important advances: the power to formulate and adopt city plans was granted to local governments; the Agency for Cultural Affairs was established to deal with various categories of cultural property under national code of conduct; and the first local historic ordinances under the amended city planning law were issued in Kurashiki and Kanazawa cities. In 1975, the Protection of Cultural Property Law was amended to introduce the Preservation District for Groups of Traditional Buildings (roughly comparable to England's Conservation Area and the United States' Historic District) as a category of cultural property. In 1996, the "listed buildings" system was introduced in the cultural property law, and property tax incentives were introduced later. In 2004, the law was extended to another type of cultural property, the cultural landscape.

Synthesis

The evolution of heritage conservation laws in the three countries reviewed above follows a similar pattern, with five key aspects:

1. **Diversification of cultural heritage beyond ancient monuments.** In all three countries, there was a similar shift from ancient monuments to a broader definition of heritage. In England, heritage falls into two main types, namely scheduled monuments managed under ancient monument law and listed buildings managed under town and country planning law.

In the United States, five different types of historic places—prehistoric or historic district, site, building, structure, and object—are identified in the National Historic Preservation Act 1966 (Section 300308). In Japan, the definition of cultural property has been gradually broadened and diversified by adding new types to the cultural property protection law. At present, there are six types of cultural property—tangible cultural property, intangible cultural property, folk cultural property, monuments, cultural landscape, and groups of traditional buildings—and two specific types of conservation techniques for cultural property and buried cultural property (Articles 71–152). With the diversification of heritage types, there has also been a diversification of evaluation criteria and conservation methods which allow both government and citizen to cooperate in the practice of heritage conservation.

2. **Elaboration of criteria for evaluation.** The conservation laws of the three countries share another similarity in their evaluation criteria which can be divided into two levels: general, and type-specific. The general criteria are stated either in the primary law or statutory criteria (in England and Japan) or in a supplementary document (in the United States). The type-specific criteria are often stated in supplementary documents. For instance, the four criteria for registering all types of American national historic places are found in a supplementary document of the National Parks Service, while the type-specific criteria for listed buildings in England are found in a supplementary document of the Department of Culture, Media and Sport. These criteria are announced publicly on websites and may be used as guidance by anyone to participate in the process of identifying and registering heritage. Stating the criteria in supplementary documents (also available on websites) allows flexibility and responsiveness to changing heritage values, and transparent reference when discretionary power is used.

3. **Devolution of power.** In all three countries, there has been devolution of the power to protect, register, manage, and maintain heritage places from central to local governments in the form of partnership. This evolution has evolved in both heritage law and city planning law. In England, where the national-level body called English Heritage certifies all heritage properties, the preparation and evaluation of proposals is conducted at the local level using relevant criteria. In the United States, the zoning act has granted power to local governments since the 1920s. In 1980 legislation under the historic preservation law made it possible for federal, state, and local governments to work in partnerships. In Japan, power to register and manage sites was devolved by the 1954 law and the

city planning law of 1968. The central-local partnership is framed by a set of standards or principles and an evaluation process mandated by the central government. The readiness of local government to participate is measured in the United States and recently in Japan.

4. **Complementary city planning law.** City planning law contributes a great deal to heritage conservation, particularly for properties which are not ancient monuments. Since it deals with citizens' needs and aspiration for their own locality, a conservation area or historic district is initiated under the city planning process rather than the ancient monument process. This has been the case in England under the listed buildings and conservation areas in town and country planning law in 1947 and 1968 respectively; in the United States, under the zoning ordinance since 1931; and in Japan, under the zoning ordinance since 1968. Zoning of conservation areas was made possible by the devolution of power over city planning. Zoning ordinances must comply with heritage law in identifying and protecting important buildings.

5. **Conservation incentives.** The diversification of heritage, especially the introduction of listed buildings and conservation areas or historic districts, allows a far larger number of privately-owned properties to be entered on the inventory of national and local heritage. In England, the number of scheduled monuments is counted in thousands while the number of listed buildings (mostly privately owned) is more than half a million. All three countries provide both direct and indirect incentives to private property owners. In England there are grants, heritage lottery funds, and inheritance and value added tax incentives. In the United States, there are several tax programs such as rehabilitation tax credit, property tax abatement, and conservation easements. In Japan, repair grants and property tax program are also in place. All these have been established by amendments of relevant laws on heritage and finance.

FINDINGS AND CONCLUSION

From this review of Thailand's laws, the current situation of heritage sites, and the conservation legislation based on the values-based approach in England, the United States, and Japan, what are the gaps in Thailand's conservation legislation which should be filled in order to bring about better conservation practice?

Table 2 shows that Thailand already has heritage protection laws and city planning laws which might form a basis for values-based conservation but the provisions in both types of law do not take account of the evolving conception of heritage. Comparison with the legislation in the three countries reviewed above highlights the following gaps in Thailand's conservation legislation.

1. Lack of diversification of heritage types. Old shophouses, traditional timber houses, vernacular buildings, modern movement buildings, early industrial buildings, and other structures cannot be registered as heritage. In other countries, systems to evaluate, protect and manage such buildings have been introduced either by amendment of heritage law or provisions in the planning laws. This should be the first step to move Thailand forward in conservation legislation.

2. Multi-level registration of heritage. Thailand has only one, national-level register of heritage which does not give opportunity for protecting various types of heritage. In the three countries reviewed, there are several registers to accommodate different types of heritage. Multi-level registers of heritage also provide different types of protection and management responsibilities.

3. Transparent criteria for evaluation. Thailand has never publicly announced the criteria for heritage evaluation and selection. The statutory criteria in the monuments law are broad and vague, and often create disagreement among professionals. Apart from FAD regulations announced in 1985 following the Venice Charter, no other documents have been released to help conservation practice.

4. Devolution of power in heritage law. The values-based approach requires participation of stakeholders in all steps of the conservation process. Stakeholders are more easily involved when power is decentralized from central to local bodies. It is unfortunate that in Thailand there is no such devolution in heritage law. In the three countries reviewed, central government works in partnership with local authorities in the identification, evaluation, protection, and maintenance of heritage through partnership programs which can solve problems such as lack of budget and human resource in managing heritage sites.

5. Devolution of power in city planning law. The merit of civic involvement in city planning receives little attention from the government. The three case studies show that decentralization of planning facilitates residents' support for conservation areas.

6. Conservation incentives. Only one type of heritage is protected by law with funds from the government budget. The government has not provided any financial incentives for conservation of other types of heritage.

Table 2: Comparison of Thai conservation laws under values-based approach

Legislative Provisions	Laws Under Values-Based Approach			
	England	United States	Japan	Thailand
Existence of heritage protection law	Since 1882	Since 1906	Since 1897	Since 1923
Existence of planning law (or zoning)	Since 1909	Since 1922	Since 1919	Since 1952
Conservation area designated by law	Since 1967 (Lincolnshire)	Since 1931 (Charleston)	Since 1968 (Kurashiki & Kanazawa)	Since 1984 (Bangkok)
Diversification of heritage types	1947 (Planning law)	1966 (Historic preservation law)	1950 (Cultural property law)	Nil
Multi-levelled heritage register	Yes	Yes	Yes	Nil
Elaborate criteria for selection and evaluation	Yes	Yes	Yes	Nil
Devolution of power in heritage law	1983	1980	1954	Nil
Devolution of power in planning law	1967	1922 (Zoning)	1968	Nil
Conservation incentives	Since 1953 (Inheritance Tax)	Since 1976	Since late 1990s	Nil

Three measures are needed to move conservation legislation in Thailand towards a values-based approach.

First, a comprehensive survey of different types of heritage should be conducted in order to create an inventory recognized by central government. This project does not start from a zero base. There have been a number of studies by academic institutions and the Thailand Research Fund office of non-registered heritage including old shophouses, vernacular architecture, traditional villages and neighborhoods, modern movement, and industrial heritage. With such research, evaluation criteria can be established as a basis for heritage diversification.

Second, the existing training-based program for heritage practitioners should be transformed into a competency-based program. The values-based approach requires substantial skills, knowledge, and capabilities as well as the right attitude for coping with new challenges in heritage conservation planning and management. Existing training courses focus mostly on conservation techniques (the material-based approach) and conservation principles which are taken from foreign literature and often not compatible with the Thai context. A competency-based program will help practitioners to achieve the required skills through practical hands-on activities related to the values-based approach such as the preparation of proposals for evaluation, knowledge management practices, interpretation of historical context, heritage impact assessment, civic participatory techniques, and conflict resolution.

Lastly, a real and effective civic participation process should be promoted. After devolution of power in both heritage law and city planning law in the three countries reviewed, local citizens have become real supporters of heritage conservation. In Thailand, despite a government commitment to decentralization (meaning devolution, not de-concentration of central power) in the 1990s, little progress has been made. In the current political context, the focus should be on civic involvement which can promote the values-based approach to a certain degree.

References

Asano, Satoshi. 1999. "The Conservation of Historic Environments in Japan." *Built Environment* 25, 3. 236–43.

Delafons, J. 1997. *Politics and Preservation: A Policy History of the Built Heritage 1882–1996.* London: E and FN Spon.

Feilden, B. M. and Jokilehto, J. 199). *Management Guidelines for World Cultural Heritage Sites.* Second edition, Rome: ICCROM.

Fitch, James Marston. 2001. *Historic Preservation: Curatorial Management of the Built World.* Fifth printing. Charlottesville: University Press of Virginia.

Fowler, J.M. 2003. "The Federal Preservation Program." Chapter 2 in Stipe, R.E. (ed.), *A Richer Heritage: Historic Preservation in the Twenty-First Century*, pp. 35–89. Chapel Hill and London: University of North Carolina Press.

Ho, Chin Siong. 2003. *An Introduction to Japanese City Planning.* Johor Bahru: Universiti Teknologi Malaysia.

Hobson, E. 2004. *Conservation and Planning: Changing Values in Policy and Practice.* London: Spon Press.

Kakiuchi, E. 2014. *Cultural Heritage Protection System in Japan: Current issues and prospects for the future.* Discussion paper 14–10, Tokyo: National Graduate Institute for Policy Studies (GRIPS). Retrieved from www.grips.ac.jp/r-center/wp-content/uploads/14-10.pdf, accessed December 15, 2018.

Murtagh, W.J. 1990. *Keeping Time: The History and Theory of Preservation in America*. New York: Sterling.

Pickard, R.D. 1996. *Conservation in the Built Environment*. Singapore: Longman.

Poulios, I. 2010. "Moving Beyond a Values-Based Approach to Heritage Conservation." *Conservation and Management of Archaeological Sites* 12, 2: 170–85, doi: 10.1179/1753 55210X12792909186539.

Poulios, I. 2014. *The Past in the Present: A Living Heritage Approach—Meteora, Greece*. London: Ubiquity Press. doi: http:dx.doi.org/10.5334/bak.

Radzuan, I.S.M., Fukami, N., and Ahmad, Y. 2014. "Cultural heritage, incentives system and the sustainable community: Lessons from Ogimachi Village, Japan." *GEOGRAFIA Online Malaysian Journal of Society and Space,* 10, 1: 130–46. Retrieved from umexpert.um.edu.my/file/publication/00003334_106858.pdf, accessed January 2, 2019.

Ross, M. 1996. *Planning and the Heritage: Policy and Procedure*. 2nd edition, London: E & FN Spon.

Sitkowski, R. J. and Russel, J. 2007. "Form and substance: What New York land use lawyers need to know about form-based land development regulations." *New York Zoning Law and Practice Report*. 8, 3: 1–12.

Sorensen, Andre. 2004. *The Making of Urban Japan: Cities and Planning from Edo to the Twenty-First Century*. London: Routledge.

Sternstein, L. 1982. *Portrait of Bangkok*. Bangkok: Bangkok Metropolitan Administration.

Stovel, Herbert. 2004. "Approaches to Managing Urban Transformation for Historic Cities." In Lung, D. (ed.), *The Conservation of Urban Heritage: Macao Vision*. Cultural Institute of the Macao S.A.R. Government, pp. 103–20.

Stubbs, John H. 2009. *Time Honored: A Global View of Architectural Conservation*. New Jersey: John Wiley & Sons.

Tunprawat, Patcharawee. 2009. *Managing Living Heritage Sites in Mainland Southeast Asia*. Unpublished doctoral dissertation, Silpakorn University, Bangkok, Thailand.

Tyler, N. 2000. *Historic Preservation: An Introduction to Its History, Principles and Practices*. New York: W.W. Norton & Company.

UNESCO. 2016. *Culture, Urban, Future: Global Report on Culture for Sustainable Urban Development*. Paris.

UNESCO Bangkok. 2009. *Hoi An Protocols for Best Conservation Practice in Asia: Professional Guidelines for Assuring and Preserving the Authenticity of Heritage Sites in the Context of the Culture of Asia*. Bangkok: UNESCO Bangkok.

Yongcharoenchai, Chaiyot. 2015. "Changes close in on hidden Chinatown." Bangkok Post, Spectrum Section, 19 July 2015, retrieved from www.bangkokpost.com/news/special-reports/626920/change-closes-in-on-hidden-chinatown, accessed December 5, 2018.

Taking Ownership and Taking a Stand: Heritage Activism in George Town

Khoo Salma Nasution

Those of us involved in heritage advocacy and practice may have started with a focus on the conservation of physical-historical fabric, but we have gradually expanded our scope to include the continuity of social-traditional intangible heritage. Through our engagement with the cultural communities, voices have emerged in the public sphere to articulate the social, economic, and political dimensions of these issues.

George Town in Penang, Malaysia, faces two broad challenges. Firstly, economic forces that push the city to embrace higher property values and, in so doing, transform the historic-physical fabric and patterns of use. Secondly, the planning imperative of modern transport infrastructure which attempts to adapt the city to the car. Due to the collusion between politicians and business, these forces are constantly brought to bear on the cultural and natural heritage.

Since George Town was listed as UNESCO World Heritage in 2008, the buildings and townscape of one square mile are nominally protected by legislation. However, the physical-historical fabric is still being chipped away instead of being maintained and carefully renewed. Inappropriate infill and over-renovation for repurposing and "adaptive reuse" are the rule rather than the exception.

Local communities are vulnerable to loss of livelihood, insecure tenancy, displacement, and other disruptions to the neighborhood. Street art proves more attractive to visitors than the historic walls they are painted on, but this means that the historic city serves only as a backdrop or theater set. As some local stakeholders, going with the flow, venture into commercial activities, the character of streets and neighborhoods is gradually transformed by tourism and gentrification.

The UNESCO branding serves the political agenda, with arguably more resources spent on the management of appearances than on heritage itself. Articles about George Town range from hyped-up success stories to those evoking the hyperbolic "UNESCO-cide." For heritage advocates having to battle ill-informed decisions, the few small victories feel hollow compared to the endless series of losses, compromises, and missed opportunities. In this situation, heritage advocates in George Town have expanded into matters of the public realm, joining forces with urbanists and environmentalists.

We are among the communities across the world having to take ownership of heritage. Heritage seems like a low priority compared to the larger issues. Yet, it is the protection of the historic-physical fabric that contains the wisdom of conserving energy and resources, and the protection of social-traditional local communities that creates resilience and democratic space for alternative development discourses. The championing of the public realm, including the ideas of walkability, social inclusion, open space, and urban forestry, now extends to the hinterland of the heritage area, motivating an energized local response to the greatest challenges of our times—environmental degradation and climate change.

THE BEGINNINGS OF THE HERITAGE MOVEMENT IN PENANG

Citizens in a developing economy may have aspirations to preserve their historic buildings as a sign that the city or nation has "arrived." Historic preservation is made possible through a combination of legal protection, private or public funding for conservation, and popular interest in heritage, which supports the political will to make heritage a part and parcel of urban development. It is then necessary to build capacity to safeguard and conserve, to ensure that knowledge and skills are retained and enhanced, and to constantly enlarge the scope and reach in response to new information and changing notions of heritage.

Many years ago, as a young heritage advocate, the picture looked simple to me. Our mission was to create public awareness so that society would realize how important heritage is. The historic city would provide a conducive and inspirational setting for people to realize their creative potential based on their rich past. We needed to educate owners to conserve their buildings and politicians to put into place the necessary laws to protect heritage, and these groups, together with individual and corporate philanthropists, would have to provide funding for conservation. In order to convince politicians and community leaders, we could tell them that our heritage is a resource for educating the younger generation as well as for generating income through beneficial use and tourism.

George Town properties had been under the Control of Rent Act since just after the World War II. Tenants paid cheap rent while minimally maintaining their homes, and sometimes chief tenants made money from subtenants. The property value was low as it would be difficult to "get rid" of tenants to fetch better rentals. Rent control was phased out from 1997 to 2000. Had the then raging building boom not been curtailed by the Asian Financial Crisis of 1997, many heritage properties would have been redeveloped as soon as the owners could recover them from the tenants. About half the residents moved out over a few years. Several hundred shophouses were left derelict and several hundred more were compromised by the activity of swift breeding, which was only banned in 2013.

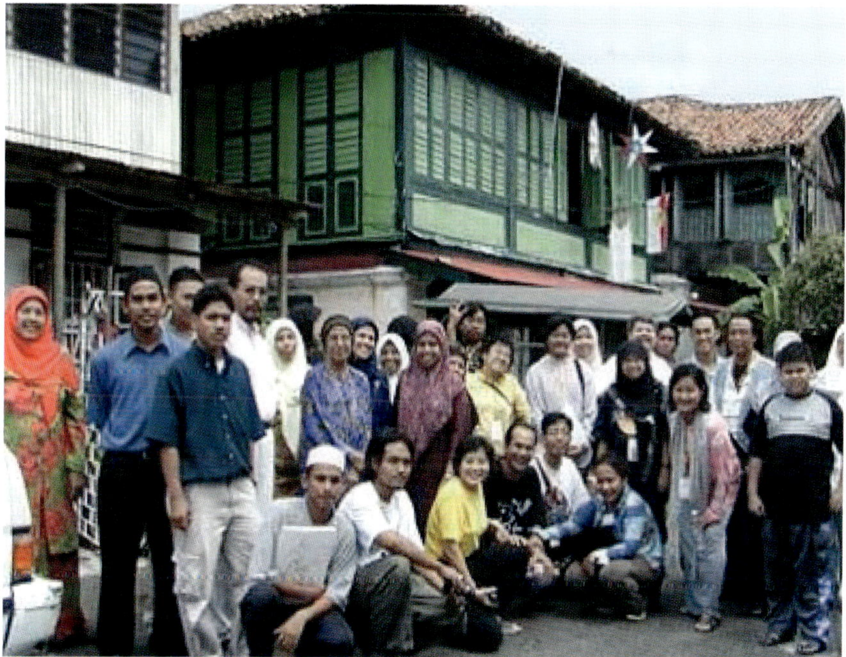

Figure 1. Local residents of Lebuh Acheh and Penang Heritage Trust leaders defending the Acheen Street Mosque compound houses against a proposed redevelopment, 2003/2004. (Photo © SN Khoo)

In 2008, Melaka and George Town, the Historic Cities of the Straits of Malacca, were listed as UNESCO World Heritage. This coincided with several other events—a spike in budget air travel, a new trend in boutique hotels and hipster cafes, the opening of a new cruise terminal, and the reopening of the airport after renovations. Over the next several years the increase in tourism was also encouraged by the flourishing of local arts festivals such as the annual George Town Festival and Jazz Festival, the rising popularity of Penang food and the street mural phenomenon, the explosion of social media and selfie tourism, the expansion of tourist arrivals from China, and so forth. Penang's beach tourism had been losing out to the beach resorts of southern Thailand, but now city tourism picked up the slack.

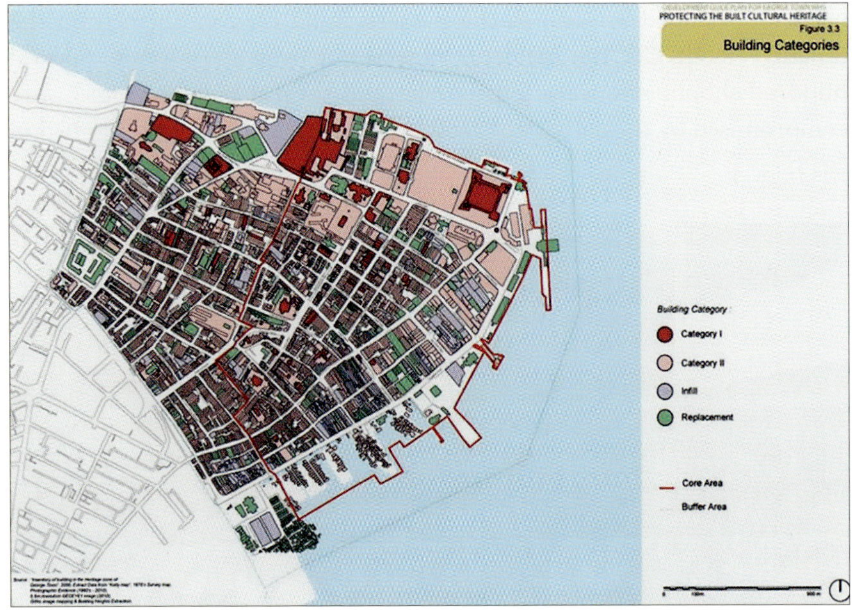

Figure 2. Map of UNESCO World Heritage Site in George Town. (George Town Special Area Plan)

Penang Heritage Trust (see www.pht.org.my) had been promoting heritage conservation since 1986 and cultural tourism since the 1990s. Through its Penang Story program, started in 2001, we promoted community histories so that local communities could start to "take ownership" of their heritage. Complementing the PHT, the Nanyang Folk Culture reached out to the Chinese-educated sector from the 1990s, whereas Arts Ed started to use the city for arts and cultural education of young people from the early 2000s.

In 1998, the Penang Heritage Trust prodded the Penang state government to invite UNESCO and the nomination process was initiated in collaboration with the federal museum authorities, precursor of the National Heritage Department. At the same time, a coalition of NGOs called Penang Forum was formed in 2009 to stop an urban megaproject, articulate environmental issues in light of increasing urban pressures to reclaim land and cut the hill slopes for building housing properties, and promote the imperative of a shift to public transport over private vehicle expansion.

The Penang Heritage Trust, Nanyang Folk Culture and Arts Ed formed CHAT (Cultural Heritage Action Team) and helped the Penang government to set up the World Heritage Office. This was incorporated as the George Town World Heritage Incorporated, which had a mission to monitor and manage the World Heritage Site in 2010. It also undertook much useful work in terms of conservation education and documentation. A Special Area Plan, to be implemented by the local council, was undertaken by a planning consultancy and also tapped the knowledge of the CHAT network. The Penang Island Municipal Council, later the Penang Island City Council from 2014, being the statutory body for approvals and permissions, also set up a Technical Review Panel, to review applications affecting existing heritage buildings, infill, or replacement buildings in the World Heritage Site.

Although heritage guidelines were articulated in the UNESCO nomination, much wrangling went on about how strict development control should be applied. The dos and don'ts became clearer after the Special Area Plan was gazetted in 2016. Ironically, that was the year when George Town World Heritage Incorporated began to depart from its original direction and eventually seemed to give up any pretense of "monitoring" and "managing" the site. Instead, it appeared to prioritize extending its international heritage relations and staging of events, apart from continuing with some educational functions.

The first public restoration project of the Syed Alatas Mansion, way back in 1993, may have started some people on the track to learning about heritage conservation, but had limited impact as most heritage properties were still under rent-control and tenanted at the time. The UNESCO Asia-Pacific Heritage Awards for the restoration of Cheong Fatt Tze Mansion (2000), Penang Han Jiang (Teochew) Temple (2006) and Suffolk House (2008), helped to expose more people to the virtues of conservation. From 2010, the George Town Grants Program was disbursed by Think City, a subsidiary of Khazanah, the federal investment arm. Think City has since augmented its role in spearheading urban regeneration, pulling in international bodies such as the Aga Khan and Getty Foundation.

Meanwhile, UNESCO intervention in George Town heritage issues took the form of monitoring missions or advisory/warning letters. This happened three times: the first time in 2009 to check on four approved high-rise hotels at heights above the agreed guidelines; the second time in 2011 to check on swift-breeding activity damaging the heritage buildings; and the third time in 2016 to check on a proposed elevated transport infrastructure converging at a massive transport hub at the edge of the George Town World Heritage Site.

HERITAGE AS A STATE AGENDA

While heritage usually starts out as a matter of community concern, the success of this effort is expected to lead to mainstreaming in the state or national policy. From the days of Ruskin and the birth of the National Trust more than a hundred years ago, this was the trajectory of heritage protection in the UK. This is what happened in the west. In France, I believe, a different trajectory was followed, and *patrimonie* was always seen as more of a government responsibility. As heritage becomes a matter of state or national profiling, several things should happen: the expansion of knowledge, jobs, institutions, legislation and the bureaucratization of heritage protection. Once government is in charge, the community role in advocacy is supposed to "wither away."

In Penang, after having successfully pushed for UNESCO heritage recognition, heritage advocates and activists envisioned an early retirement. For the first few years, we worked with George Town World Heritage Incorporated to build capacity, anxious to pass on our knowledge and contacts to the civil service, ideally creating jobs for young architects and planners, or new graduates in heritage management, museum studies, and the like.

Within the living, working city, intangible cultural heritage was something that was sustained by the community, but when the repeal of rent control and subsequent rental hikes triggered a collapse of the community eco-system and the loss of livelihoods, it became urgent to document and recommend strategies for safeguarding heritage.

UNESCO status resolved some problems because it meant that state and business have agreed that George Town would be conserved, and that the ways it would be conserved would be guided by international expectations. Unfortunately, it also brought in new problems, related to tourism and money. Most tourists have a superficial understanding of heritage, for example, indiscriminately supporting boutique hotels that are badly restored. Tourism is a cycle and if we are not careful, we will be killing the thing that we love (cultural heritage), or the goose that lays the golden egg (heritage as a resource for tourism).

As the hype about George Town heritage buildings, food and street murals grew, tourism—or rather the prospects of tourism—pushed the heritage city into a frenzy of property speculation, evictions, and illegal conversions of properties into "heritage hotels." Tourism revolved around street mural selfie trails, café and food hunts, and theme-park like attractions billed as "museums."

After 2008, funds and institutional support was finally available for heritage. The original promoters of heritage, particularly the Penang Heritage Trust, were deemed too outspoken, and were hardly given a steerage role to guide the flourishing heritage industry. In the light of other emerging organizations and agencies which are funded and supported by the state, the Penang Heritage Trust decided to stay relevant by focusing on its advocacy role. However, we continued to support and assist George Town World Heritage Incorporated in a practical and low-key manner. Meanwhile, another group called George Town Heritage Action also started to issue heritage alerts about evictions and illegal or inappropriate works.

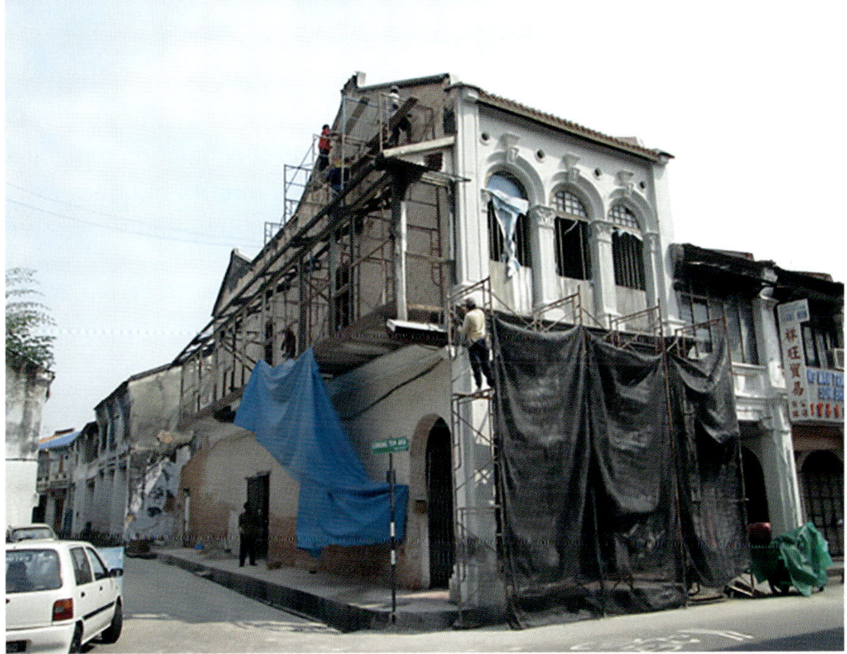

Figure 3. Without adequate monitoring, repairs are often done badly or with inappropriate materials; cement instead of lime plaster is used in repairing this shophouse. (Photo © Mark Lay).

While we might see historic preservation, environmental conservation, cultural education, and urban regeneration as a public interest, it seems that the state authorities tend to view tourism as a public interest because of its supposed role in driving economic growth. For us, tourism could be just one of several means to sustain heritage, but for the state, heritage might be seen as just a means to sustain tourism, and the concern is more with the quantity rather than the quality of tourism.

Although political patronage has always been a factor in moving heritage forward, from around 2013 onwards, political patronage acquired a distinct flavor. Politicians moved into the social space of local community to coopt the arts and traditional organizations where possible, and to aggressively confront those organizations which resist cooptation.

CONTESTATIONS

The following examples illustrate how the heritage agenda was seized by the state, or rather the controlling political party, and how projects or programs that were heavily backed by politicians resulted in contestations over cultural traditions.

The clan jetties

The first example is about the clan jetties on the eastern waterfront of the George Town World Heritage Site. As the inner city was emptying following the repeal of rent control, some pockets of population remained in the clan jetties. Although they are more than a century old, they exist at the tolerance of the state because these structures, built over the water, are on temporary occupation licenses. If not for their inclusion in the UNESCO World Heritage listing, these jetties might have already been demolished. Recently, a 2018 poll identified the clan jetties as the leading tourist attraction in Penang among tourists from China.

Politicians have attempted to exploit the popularity of the jetties for their own purposes. In 2016, the state government decided to stage a state cultural festival on the eighth day of Chinese New Year, on the same night as the traditional celebration of the annual Jade Emperor's birthday in the close vicinity. The government insisted that the jetty community had no right to protest against the state festival, as it was not on their land. In response, T-shirts targeted the chief minister with the slogan, "not your dad's land."

During a separate state attempt to extend the jetty for the purpose of staging events, a resident lamented that the jetty was now divided into several factions, partly for political reasons, but also because some jetty-dwellers took advantage of commercial opportunities while others shunned commercialism and complained about the invasion of privacy. The worst of the contestation seems to be over, as seen in a proposal by the present state assemblyman (late 2017) to introduce measures to curb over-tourism.

Thaipusam chariot processions

The second example concerns the Thaipusam chariot processions which start from George Town World Heritage Site. The trustees of the Penang Nagarathar Thandayuthapani Temple (also called the Nattukottai Chettiar Temple) have been managing a silver chariot procession since around 1890. On the first day of a three-day event, the chariot is drawn by bullocks from the Chettiar temple in town along a 4-kilometer journey to their temple near the waterfall; on the second day, devotees carrying "yokes" (*kavadi*) walk from the Mahamariamman Temple to the Waterfall Hilltop Temple; and on the third day, the chariot makes its way back to the Chettiar temple in town. The second-day procession is managed by the state-controlled Penang Hindu Endowments Board.

After completing the rebuilding of the Waterfall Hilltop Temple in 2012, the deputy chief minister as chairman of the Penang Hindu Endowments Board questioned the Chettiars' monopoly over the Thaipusam chariot procession, and proposed that a second chariot should be introduced, starting from the Mahamariamman Temple and making its journey to the foot of the Waterfall Hilltop Temple. This meant two chariots would proceed on the first day with different but contiguous starting points and destinations, with more than 90 percent of the journey along the same route lined with devotees' stalls (*pandal*). In 2017, the Penang Hindu Endowments Board started the first golden chariot procession, with the new chariot starting the journey 90 minutes or so ahead of the silver chariot.

The contestation arose out of age-old class antagonism within the Indian community. However, added to this was the allegation that the Chettiar trustees are Indian nationals and that the donations collected by the Chettiars were being repatriated to India. The donations collected during the golden chariot procession would be instead channeled to local scholarships. In 2019, the Penang Hindu Endowments Board launched a bigger and grander golden chariot for the procession, pulled by devotees. On allegations of animal cruelty, the deputy chief minister warned the Chettiars against the use of bullocks to pull their chariot.

Siaboey park

The third example focuses on the contestation for the Siaboey area which is adjacent to but outside the World Heritage Site. Siaboey, which means the "edge of town," is a 5.5 acre site which started to be cleared in the 1970s as Phase V of the KOMTAR urban renewal project. In 2004, the market was moved out leaving the Victoria-era cast iron market building vacant. By that time, the KOMTAR project had long lost momentum, and the area was proposed for a park. Most of the shophouses had been progressively destroyed, leaving twenty-four houses to be restored as part of the rehabilitation area.

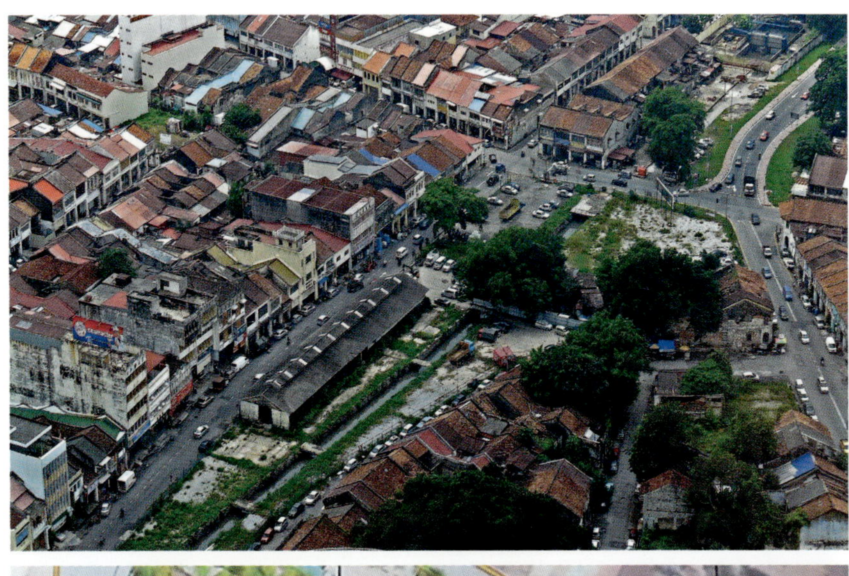

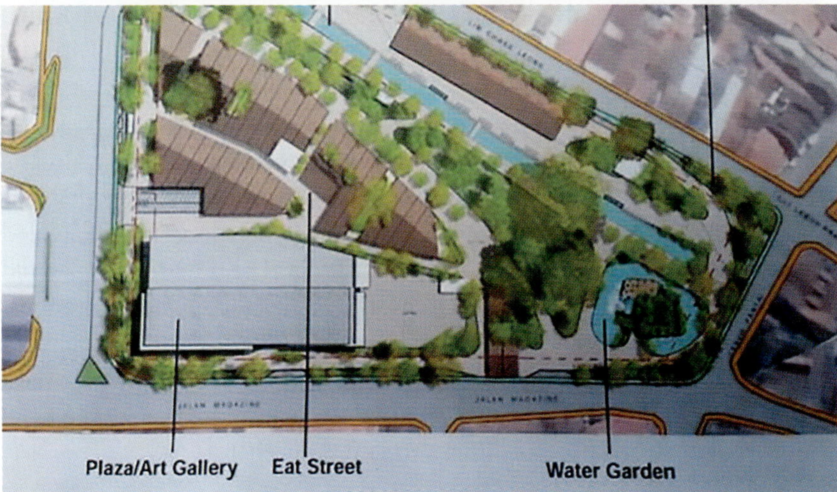

Figure 4. (top) The old Prangin Market and Prangin Canal at the Siaboey site (Photo © SN Khoo); (bottom) The original park proposal shown at "Siaboey Reborn" exhibition, September 2015.

Siaboey had been the city's wholesale market for more than a century, with goods brought in by canal. A historian pointed out that the Prangin creek had been turned into a canal in 1804 by the British East India Company as part of the town's fortifications during the Napoleonic wars.

The boundary of the World Heritage Site should logically have included the other side of the canal, and such a modification of the nomination area was proposed even before the UNESCO listing, but was never followed up.

A proposal was now drawn up to divert drain water to a new culvert, and to use the historic granite-lined canal as a water feature. The market, canal, and twenty-four shophouses were to become the historic attractions of the proposed Penang Heritage Arts District, amidst park-like surroundings.

All was well when the chief minister launched "Siaboey: Reborn" in September 2015. Then he had a change of mind and, six months later, announced that the site would be converted into a transport hub, linking an elevated light-rail line, two monorail lines, a tram line, and most likely incorporating a multilevel car park. The Penang Heritage Trust immediately organized a public talk to report what it knew about the latest plans.

When it became clear that the Penang Transport Council would not reconsider the transport hub proposal, the city councilor representing Penang Forum wrote a letter to UNESCO, with extensive attachments, to alert UNESCO about a project that might impact negatively on the setting of the UNESCO World Heritage Site. Instead of reviewing the project, members of the Penang authorities, including the general manager of George Town World Heritage Incorporated, promptly berated the city councilor for stepping out of line, accusing him of "back-stabbing," and even "treason."

Further delays took place after an archaeological dig uncovered the canal locks, providing irrefutable evidence of Prangin Canal's historical importance. After agreeing to shift the transport hub by a few meters south, a new plan was unveiled in 2018. Compared to the 2015 plan, this plan appeared fragmented and immature, for example, proposing climatically-inappropriate glass roofs on the twenty-four shophouses.

The Siaboey park is necessary for ecological balance and for maintaining the quality of openness at the edge of the World Heritage Site. The aim of imposing development control within the sight lines of the World Heritage Site and creating a visually sympathetic "broader setting" and functionally supportive "tertiary zone" can only be realized through the Local Plan. Further contestation is expected over the new Structure Plan and Local Plan.

The transport hub at Siaboey was part of the US$10 billion Penang Transport Master Plan which also envisioned a 19.5 kilometer highway that would traverse existing neighborhoods, parks, and ecologically fragile hills near a famous Buddhist temple. The schools along the alignment had sent in objections in 2016 but to no avail. We produced visuals to show how ugly the elevated light-rail and monorail lines would be and how they would disrupt the vista of the World Heritage Site. Matters quietened down until the Environmental Impact Assessment containing detailed information and visuals were released in July 2018.

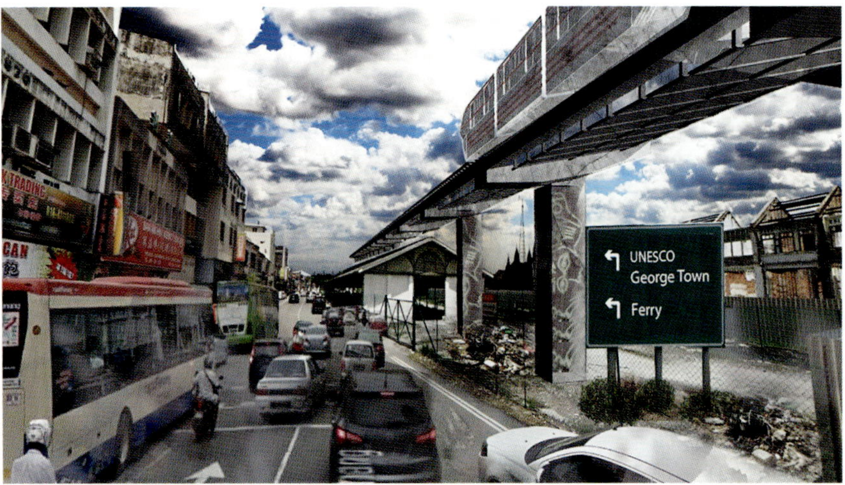

Figure 5. Visualisation of the proposed monorail line running along Siaboey. (Penang Heritage Trust)

Jerejak Island

The fourth example concerns the preservation of Jerejak Island, which lies just off the southeast coast of Penang Island. The ruins of a historic leper settlement from 1870, a tuberculosis station, and a quarantine station with structures from 1911, later used as a penal site, bear witness to the island's rich history. The sale of 80 acres of land by a government-linked company, and the subsequent approval of 1,200 housing units on that land, may have jeopardized a proposed joint UNESCO nomination for the historic leprosy settlements at both Jerejak Island and Sungai Buloh, the latter near Kuala Lumpur.

Penang Hill

The fifth example concerned the building of 200 hotel rooms on top of Penang Hill, even though the site straddled a water catchment area, and the larger Penang Hill site, extending to the National Park on the northeast of the island, was earmarked for nomination as a UNESCO Man and Biosphere reserve. Ironically the hotel project is a spinoff from the increase in tourism to which the UNESCO listing contributed.

Despite the passing of the State Heritage Bill in 2011, until today there is no proper inventory or protection for heritage buildings outside the World Heritage Site, with the exception of a few buildings already identified by the city council in the 1990s. We have a "Kampung Siam" outside the World Heritage Site, a "heritage village" where Menora was introduced to Penang; though the site was granted to the Thai and Burmese communities by Queen Victoria in 1845, today it is in a state of tension due to its lack of protection. In 2016, a bungalow on Runnymede, a site associated with Stamford Raffles, was demolished. At the end of 2018, four heritage bungalows at Peel Avenue were demolished. What is shocking is that these four bungalows were sitting on state land, and the state quietly sold the land without any condition that the new owner should preserve the bungalows.

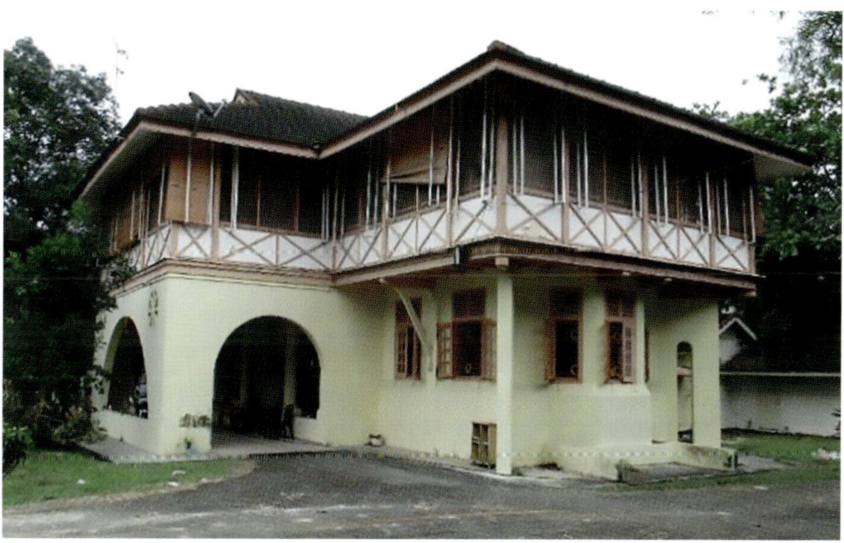

Figure 6. Heritage outside the World Heritage Site: state-owned colonial bungalow along Peel Avenue demolished end 2018. (Photo © Mark Lay)

Like environmentalists, heritage activists are also well-versed in the critique of wasteful and destructive development, to some extent familiar with the planning process and having eyes well-trained for seeing through the greenwash. As the state vision of physical development and tourism development in the small city-state of Penang became increasingly divorced from the state's own rhetoric of "Cleaner, Greener, Penang," civil society was increasingly mobilized to expose policy failure, and the lack of public consultation and monitoring capacity, particularly after the occurrence of the worst floods in November 2017, and also two landslides (in October 2017 and October 2018), alleged to be work-site related accidents, claiming a total of twenty lives.

HERITAGE AND ENVIRONMENT

Coming back to the concerns of the World Heritage Site, how are the concerns of heritage relevant to larger environmental issues? The George Town World Heritage Site in fact showcases the potential of a zero-carbon city, with the prospect of reusing old buildings embodying embedded energy and climatically appropriate design. One can indeed learn from such a compact walkable downtown, the socially inclusive mixed-use city, designed according to building codes and not zoning, a historic quarter where it is possible to live without cars.

The new urbanism is the old urbanism. We have neighborhoods that have grown organically around the civic area, the church, the mosque, the temple, where everything is within walking distance. We can introduce renewable energy and plant more trees within the World Heritage Site to make walking and cycling possible in climatic comfort. We have the potential of using cultural values in a sharing economy as a strategy of sustainable development.

All the years of fretting about the right type of window shutters and cornices have proved largely futile, and to many, narrow and elitist. Taking a step back, it seems more important for people to understand how to maintain aging buildings, repopulate the city, and restore mixed use. The economic viability of neighborhoods has to be predicated on affordable rentals, at least for housing. The enhancement of the public realm is another worthy strategy to pursue. During my one-and-a-half year stint from January 2017 to mid-2018 as a city councilor representing Penang Forum, I spearheaded a campaign to clear the blocked five-foot ways in George Town in order to improve walkability.

At the World Urban Forum of February 2018, I familiarized myself with the UN-Habitat's New Urban Agenda. Compared to the silo approach and bureaucratic language of the UN Sustainable Development Goals, the New Urban Agenda espouses a more holistic thinking and empowering language, though more urban-centric. The New Urban Agenda highlights the importance of social inclusion, the role of governance, and planning approaches that promote new urbanism, mixed use, a walkable/cyclable city, eco-mobility, green open spaces, public realm enhancement, extending to environmental and biodiversity conservation.

As heritage advocates, we are among those who interpret progressive global ideas for our local society. I have always felt that people in the heritage movement have a lot to learn from people in the environmental movement, who are much more advanced, holistic, and radical in their thinking about the important issues, particularly about climate change.

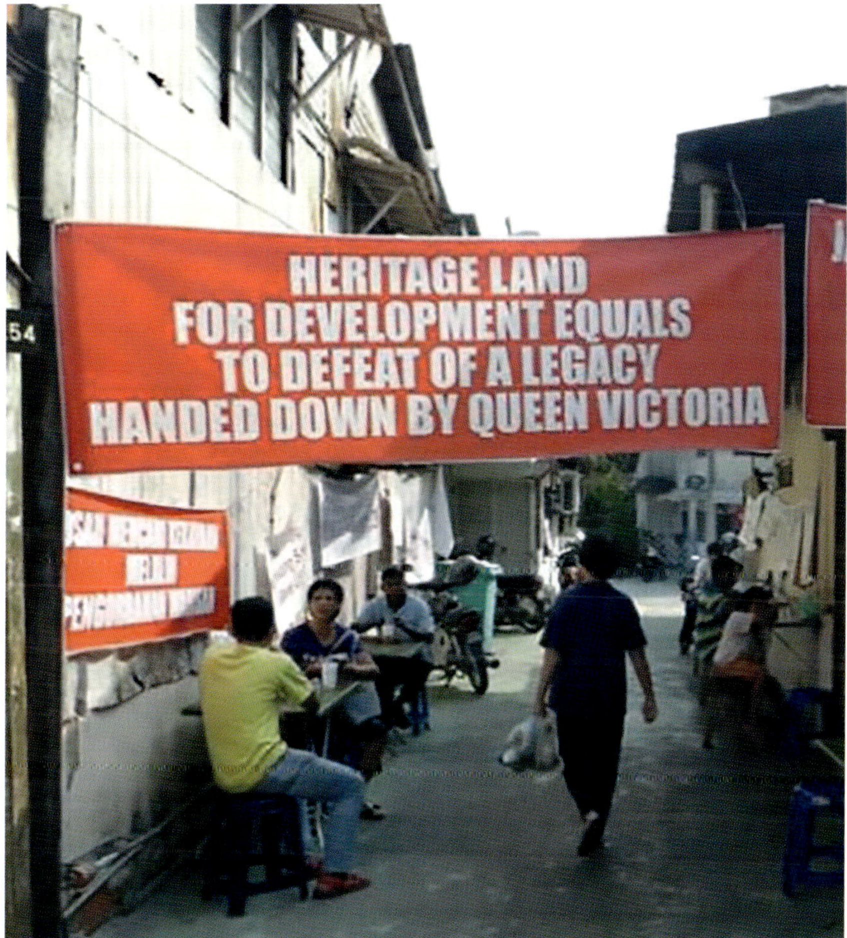

Figure 7. Protest against eviction by residents of Kampung Siam in Pulau Tikus, 2016. (Photo © SN Khoo)

The Western trajectory of the heritage conservation movement still remains a long-term strategy, but we also cannot ignore contemporary realities. We need to be more socially inclusive in what, how, and for whom we conserve. Informed by our understanding of cultural heritage, we can yet contribute to better ways of seeing and doing.

We need new ways to explain about heritage to young people. It's easier to get young people involved through environmental arguments rather than cultural arguments, partly because cultural arguments have to be customized for different groups while the environmental arguments are universal.

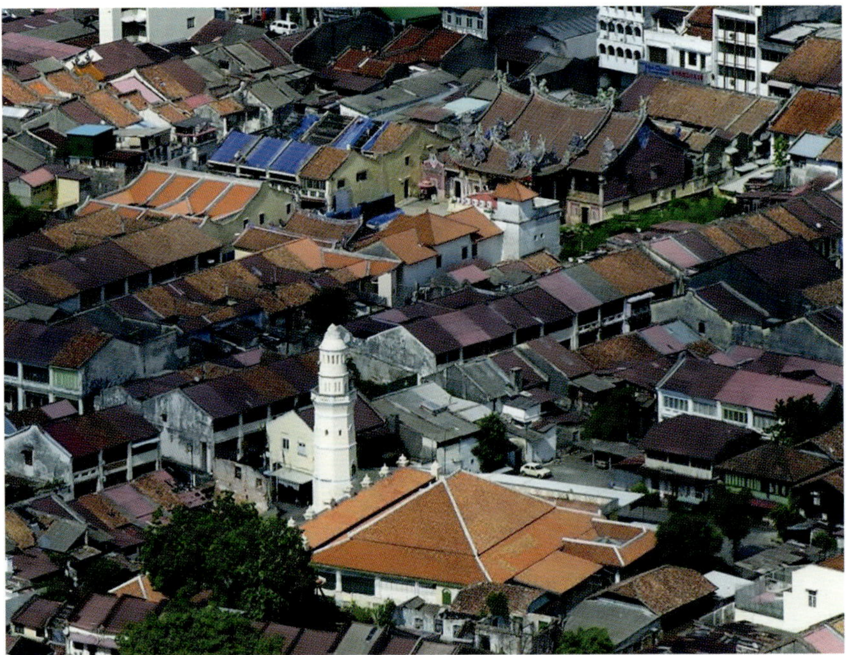

Figure 8. Penang roofscape, showing the urban grain of shophouse roofs, and the close proximity of mosque and kongsi in a multicultural historic milieu. (Photo © James Bain-Smith)

Heritage has been a very interesting conversation because we are talking about local genius and cultural identity. There are so many different aspects to cultural identity, and there are so many questions about what to conserve and how. The tangible or the intangible? This part of town or the hinterland, the environment around it? We try to have some sort of holistic thinking so that the conversation is not just about "high heritage" but also about livelihoods and how people perceive their cultural identity. The ongoing conversation about heritage makes us think holistically about nature, culture, and the places where we live.

People as the Last Defense in the Protection of Heritage: Recent Experience from Trowulan-Majapahit[1]

Catrini Pratihari Kubontubuh

People play a vital role in the protection of their own cultural heritage. This is particularly the case when it comes to space-related heritage. Besides the historical value attributed to a specific location, people find cultural significance in the place in which they live. Heritage is not merely about the past, but also very much about the present. The present-day valuation of such local heritage is what will be passed on to the next generation.

Taking the Majapahit Heritage Site in Trowulan, Java, as a case study, this chapter discusses ways in which local people are seeking to take ownership of their specific local heritage. It also illustrates just how hard it is to protect such heritage from the present-day challenges of rapid demographic growth and unregulated economic development. The chapter argues that although there is perhaps no "native" Majapahit blood in the present-day Trowulan population, the people who live in the former Majapahit royal capital still have a strong attachment to its history and the safeguarding of what they understand to be "Majapahit" traditions. These activities give them a significant role in the safeguarding of Majapahit heritage. Several present-day conflicts in and around Trowulan are caused by contestation over economic, sociocultural, political, and environmental issues. This chapter foregrounds these issues to highlight the challenges faced by the local Trowulan population in defending what they understand to be their unique heritage.

1. This paper is based on research for my doctoral dissertation, *Pelestarian Berbasis Kawasan dan Pengaruh Kontestasi: Situs Majapahit di Trowulan* (*Area-based Conservation and the Impact of Contestation: The Majapahit Site at Trowulan*), currently under preparation at the School of Architecture, Planning, and Policy Development at the Institut Teknologi Bandung, under the supervision of Prof. Dr. Ing. Widjaja Martokusumo, Dr. Denny Zulkaidi, and Prof. Peter Carey.

BACKGROUND

Each place has its own dynamics which contribute to change on the ground as it develops. We risk losing the rich and unique characteristics of a place, especially its architecture and built environment, when it is carelessly passed from one generation to the next. A space is no longer regarded as an empty space comprising just physical buildings and other material structures. Instead, it should be understood as a spiritual construction of memories and values. This meaning is related to a community's custom and local laws, and also involves local beliefs and a community's daily activities be they in the home, work place or wider neighborhood and community (Tuan 2008: 179). A particular space is therefore built by people both to express their thoughts as well as to conduct their daily activities. In so doing, these activities help to maintain the location's legacy passed down from previous civilizations. People find cultural significance in the place in which they live. And this remains the case, even though they experience change in their daily living conditions. This dynamic is part of what they understand to be their heritage. It transcends the historical value attributed to a particular place. This experience is indeed connected with immaterial values in the long sweep of history from a particular place's past to its current condition. People are an essential component of the rapidly changing context in which heritage exists. More and more they are moving to take ownership of their heritage to protect it from the contestation of increasingly challenging and hostile urban environments.

This experience might well be similar in other regions in Asia. This is especially the case when government agendas have a direct and indirect negative impact on cultural heritage sites. Heritage is often used and abused, promoted and destroyed, by governments to suit their own respective agendas. All too often cultural heritage protection policies in Asia are defined in a topdown approach by central governments. This leads to the neglect of the very people who claim ownership of the heritage. This chapter addresses the problems of just how and why heritage ownership can be claimed by local people. It also interrogates what the respective roles of stakeholders should be in protecting heritage, and how to redefine that heritage by understanding its inherent values in addition to its outward physical appearance.

HERITAGE CONSERVATION AND PEOPLE PARTICIPATION IN INDONESIA

The 2003 Indonesian Charter for Heritage Conservation clearly states that the definition of heritage in Indonesia consists of the "legacy of natural heritage and cultural heritage." This is combined with cultural landscape heritage known as *saujana*. Natural heritage comprises all forms of God's creation with its myriad forms and appearances. Cultural heritage includes all creativity, intention, and products from the over five hundred ethnic groups in Indonesia. Cultural heritage includes both tangible and intangible heritage. *Saujana* (cultural landscape heritage) is a mixture of natural and cultural heritage as it plays out in the context of time and space. These all manifest as national character and cultural identity. These are indeed very unique and differ in Asian countries from their equivalents in societies in the Western hemisphere. In this chapter, I will not just consider material and physical structures, but will also discuss immaterial and immanent values. I should also stress that I am not addressing cultural heritage as distinct from natural heritage, because in my view they are indubitably a unity.

The participation of people in safeguarding Indonesian heritage started in the 1990s and was marked by the establishment of various forms of community organization linked with heritage conservation. In 2000, a strong network began to be built in Bali through the Indonesian Heritage Conservation Network (Jaringan Pelestarian Pusaka Indonesia, JPPI). This encouraged the formation of the Indonesian Heritage Trust (Badan Pelestarian Pusaka Indonesia, BPPI) in 2004. BPPI, together with all conservation organizations and individuals from various regions in Indonesia carry out activities to promote heritage understanding and awareness, to preserve and utilize heritage, as well as to safeguard such heritage.

People participation rooted in their own individual initiatives will have a greater impact on public awareness than if such people-oriented participation is lacking. Nevertheless, the conflicts between economic interests, business ambitions, and heritage conservation create their own problems. Much irreplaceable heritage is degraded, damaged, destroyed, lost, or threatened through neglect, ignorance, incompetence, and mismanagement. For the most part this is done for short-term gain by special interest groups. Heritage is also not seen as an urgent need and does not rank amongst the nation's development priorities. The government's role in preserving, developing, and managing heritage is still far from optimal. In fact, it should be far more deeply involved in developing a "sense of urgency" regarding the importance of heritage protection.

On 25 October 2008, the BPPI initiated the establishment of the Indonesian Heritage Cities Network (JKPI) together with HE Joko Widodo, then mayor of Surakarta,[2] and the mayors of several other Indonesian cities. The network aims to enhance the policies pursued by local governments in integrating conservation aspects into their respective cities' development. Heritage conservation is not the responsibility of national and regional governments alone, but also requires the participation of people and the business sector.

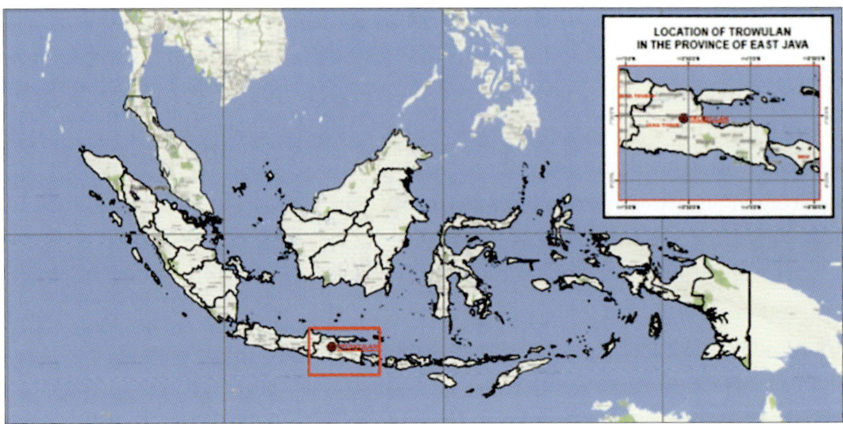

Figure 1. Location of Trowulan.

TROWULAN HERITAGE SITE

Trowulan has long been recognized as the former royal capital of the Majapahit Kingdom which flourished between 1293 and the early sixteenth century. Located in Mojokerto Regency in East Java (Figure 1), it counts more than sixty-five ruins in an approximate 92.6 square kilometer area. We know from Chinese imperial records that Majapahit was linked to international trade and diplomatic networks from as early as the first decade of the 14th century. Following the fall of Majapahit in the early 16th century, the site of the former royal capital in Trowulan has become progressively dilapidated. Today, most of the remains are either ruined or buried underground (Figure 2). With the development of the

2. Currently president of the Republic of Indonesia (in office, 2014–24).

colonial sugar industry in the late 19th century, the area that used to be the royal capital has been built over and destroyed by uncontrolled urban and agricultural development. Thus, the main present-day challenge is how to address the resulting problems and consequences attendant on this uncontrolled development. Specifically, how can heritage ownership be claimed by people? What are the respective roles of the various key stakeholders in protecting such heritage? And how to redefine such heritage by understanding its values over and above its purely physical manifestation as 'ruins'?

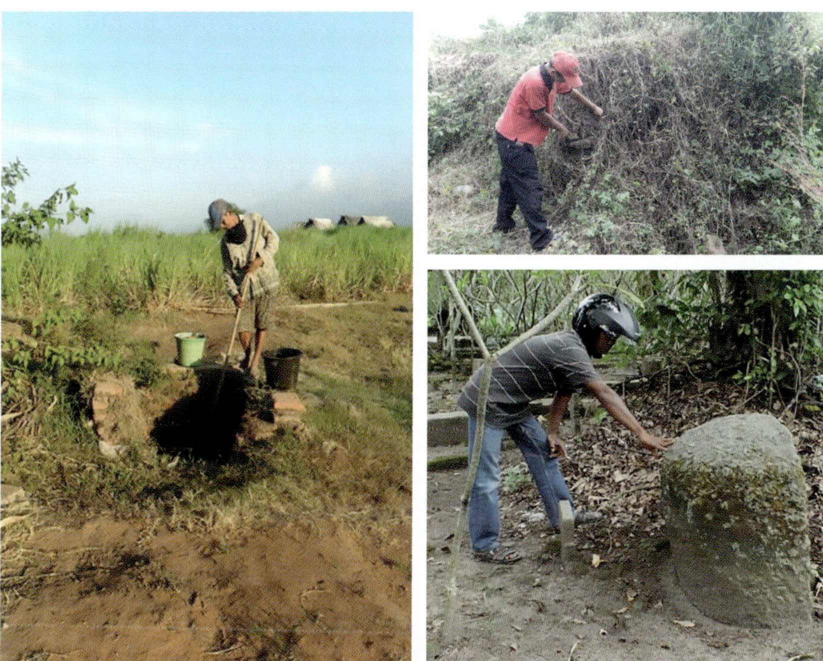

Figure 2. Remains found around Trowalan.

The Trowulan site has been the subject of professional research from as early as October 1815, when an initial survey was carried out by Captain-Engineer JWB Wardenaar (1785–1869) on the orders of the then lieutenant-governor of Java, Thomas Stamford Raffles (in office, 1811–16) (Gomperts, Haag, and Carey 2014). Other researchers include the colonial era Regents (*bupati*) of Mojokerto, RAA Kromojoyo Adinegoro (in office, 1894–1916), and his son and successor, RA Kromo Adinegoro (in office, 1916–33), as well as other key players such as the Dutch architect turned amateur archaeologist, Henri Maclaine Pont (1884–1971), during the last two decades (1922–42) of the colonial era. These colonial era researches were continued after Indonesia's independence in 1945 by Abu Sidik Wibowo (1936–85), a leading archaeologist and head of the Indonesian Archaeological Service (Dinas Purbakala) in Trowulan (in office, 1980–85), Ir. Kardono Darmoyuwono (1928–84), an Enschede ITC-trained geomorphologist, and Prof. Mundardjito, Head of the Archaeology Department (in office, 1970–72) and Vice Dean III of the Faculty of Letters, University of Indonesia (in office, 1972–76). The work of these men—and they were sadly all men—have recorded the changes in the demographics, land usage, and administration of the core areas where the former royal court (*kadaton*) and residences of the royal family were situated (Kubontubuh 2019).

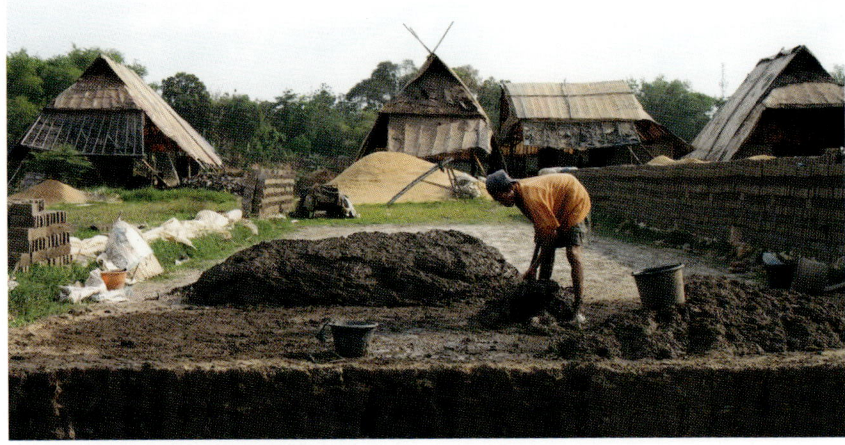

Figure 3. Brick making at Trowulan.

The grandeur of what was once Majapahit is almost nowhere to be seen at Trowulan today. This is a direct result of many individual acts of vandalism and wilful destruction. In fact, even after it was officially declared as a National Heritage Zone on 30 December 2013, the former royal capital has experienced many conflicts over economic, sociocultural, political and environmental resources. In an official decree (260/M/2013) signed by the Minister of Education and Culture of the Republic of Indonesia, Muhammad Nuh (in office, 2009–14), this stipulated some forty-nine[3] villages (*desa*) as forming the core conservation area and

3. According to study by Ramelan et al. (2015: 65) this number was independently reviewed by the Faculty of Humanities, University of Indonesia (2015) and corrected to forty-two villages, due to double mentions of five villages, and unknown names of two villages.

envisaged a continuation of the work of the previous New Order period (1966–98) when the national government had overseen restoration work on a number of temples, ponds, and archaeological relics in the Trowulan area (Mundardjito 1986). As in Western countries, these restoration works mainly addressed the physical aspect of the heritage objects themselves. The immaterial aspects and spiritual values were largely ignored. This was in line with prevalent practice and the culture of conservation work in Asia more widely during this period. As a result, many local people were unhappy and critical. They wished to maintain the site for their traditional activities, at the same time as becoming increasingly uncomfortable seeing these sites prioritized for short-term gain through their promotion as sites for local and national tourism. These local people felt they had no role as participants, and their voices were ignored. Yet such indigenous populations often act as watchdogs to ensure the protection of their own local heritage.

Trowulan's current inhabitants are seeking to take ownership of their heritage. Their experience illustrates just how hard it is to protect such heritage from the pressing challenges of the contemporary profit-fixated world. This move by the local population to take ownership of their heritage is all the more remarkable when we consider that hardly any native Majapahit blood flows in the veins of the present-day Trowulan population. Despite this absence of blood ties amongst the urban inhabitants of the former royal capital, contemporaries have a strong attachment to the place's history, and wish to do what they can to safeguard what they understand to be "Majapahit" traditions from modern-day encroachments. In fact, despite their DNA record, which indicates that the majority of present-day Trowulan citizens are newcomers, they still proudly insist in thinking of themselves as "descendants" of the "original" Majapahit population. Perhaps a tiny minority of their ancestors might have hailed from those who survived the fall of the kingdom in the early 16th century, or migrated to Trowulan in the golden age of the East Java sugar industry in the mid to late 19th century, when so many newcomers came to settle in the Trowulan area drawn by the opportunities of the Cultivation System (1830–70) and subsequent post-1870 Liberal Economic Period. Whatever their origin, the current generation is passionate about safeguarding Majapahit. Many work locally as sculptors, farmers, and even merchants, but, despite their diverse occupations, they nearly all have a strong attachment to the Majapahit legacy and a passion for nurturing local traditions. They have learnt a lot from their experience of threats and conflicts, establishing community groups such as "Gotra

Wilwatikta" (Family of Majapahit) to pursue their goals. Meanwhile, parallel organization and heritage NGOs such as "Save Trowulan," "Jaringan Pelestarian Majapahit" (Majapahit Conservation Network), and "Mojopahit Lelono" (Majapahit Trails) have all acted as watchdogs to overcome threats to valued archaeological sites. In so doing, they have gained strong support from the local media, particularly social media, which has spread information widely about their activities. They claim ownership of the heritage, but their limited capacity sometimes hinders their efforts to fight effectively for heritage conservation.

ECONOMIC, SOCIOCULTURAL, POLITICAL, AND ENVIRONMENTAL CONTESTATION

The conservation of a heritage site is not merely about preserving an archaeological object, but also about understanding and nurturing such intangible cultural heritage. Several present-day conflicts in and around Trowulan are caused by contestation over a number of issues which include the economic, sociocultural, political, or environmental as follows.

From 1960 onwards, the sites have been damaged by illegal excavation, treasure hunting, use of the land for producing traditional bricks (Figure 3), and new economic development without proper feasibility studies.

In 1980, construction began on the Balai Penyimpanan Arca-Museum over an old settlement site. Archaelogical researchers recommended a suspended building to protect the old settlement of "Permukiman Segaran" under the ground of this museum area. This advice was ignored (Figure 4). The construction of a building had already started, but was stopped half-way by the National Planning Board (Bappenas).

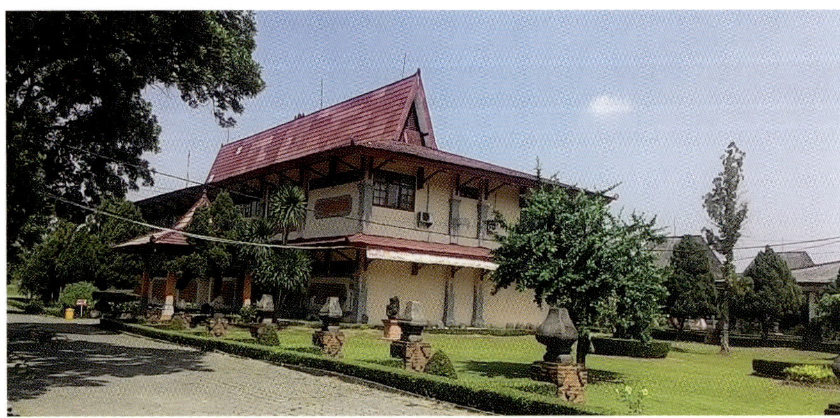

Figure 4. Trowulan Museum.

In 1983–85, an Archaeological Masterplan of Trowulan was drawn up, but never implemented by either the local or national governments because of political conflicts.

Between 1989 and 1997 there were several projects of academic study. The University of Indonesia's Field School of Archaeology excavated Segaran site V in 1989, made a surface and density survey in 1991–93, and reconstructed a "Majapahit House" on the basis of 1997–99 excavations. These projects resulted in different intepretations of the site and radically different recommendations on how it should be conserved.

In 2008, the Ministry of Culture and Tourism began constructing a Majapahit Information Center which provoked controversy because it was constructed on top of archaeological findings in the Segaran area. After protests by local communities and other stakeholders, which were widely aired in the local media, the project was halted.

In 2009, the then Minister of Culture and Tourism, Jero Wacik (in office, 2009–12) sent an Evaluation Team to inspect the damage caused by the Information Center project and recommend restoration work. A large group of researchers then worked on restoring the site to its former state.

The Evaluation Team recommended that government hold a public contest for the design of a building to protect the restored site. The contest was won by the Indonesian architect, Yori Antar, with an open air, suspended design (Figure 5). During implementation, however, the oversight was weak. The spec was downgraded by the contractor, resulting in poor-quality construction which deteriorated badly over a short three-year period.

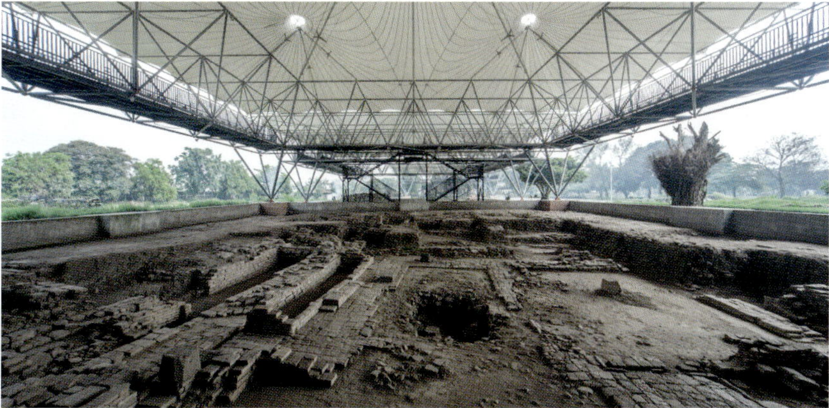

Figure 5. Open Museum designed by Yori Antar.

In 2012–13, the national government constructed an Open Museum named "Candi Kedaton" with a massive and invasive design that offended the local community (Figure 6).

In 2013, another Trowulan Masterplan was drawn up, and Trowulan was listed as a National Heritage Site, but the implementation of these two major policies was complicated because of political conflicts amongst key decision-makers.

From 2012 to 2018, the *bupati* (sub-province head) of Mojokerto played a criminally improper role in this field of conservation. In 2012 he gave a permit for a steel factory in the heart of Trowulan, and in 2017 he allowed artefacts to be moved from one site to another within Trowulan with cavalier regard for local sensibilities. In 2017 the local government also began to construct an art market without studying its likely impact on the Segaran Tank site. At the same time, illegal excavation and the sale of old Majapahit bricks continued unabated on the site. Local communities protested all these activities. The *bupati* was eventually arrested on corruption charges in 2018 and has recently received an eight-year custodial sentence.

From 2014 to 2016, the local government launched a "Majapahit houses program" to erect supposed replicas of the original "authentic" houses at the site (Figure 7). Local communities again objected, and most of them refused the grants offered by the local authority to adapt their own dwellings to this style.

At Trowulan, the archaeological remains of what was once the royal capital are scattered over a wide area. Such sites as old wells, and artefacts—in particular, pottery sherds—are still found on land owned by local people. Defining a heritage area by drawing a fixed borderline does

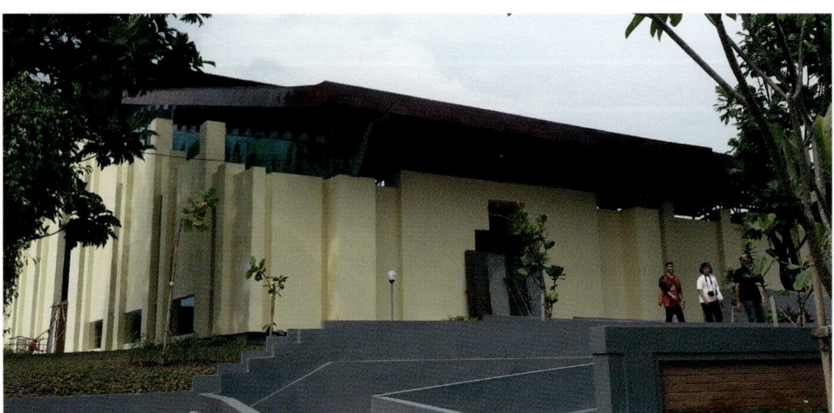

Figure 6. Candi Kedaton.

not always suit local circumstances. The construction projects proposed by local and national governments have all too often ignored the Trowulan site's unique character as well as the opinions of the local communities. Management of the site has to take account of the traditions and practices of the local communities, and their understanding of the site's intangible qualities (Smith 2006).

The economic, sociocultural, political, and environmental aspects of protecting the former Majapahit heritage will always be a work in progress, forever re-negotiated and contested. The local population is growing and becoming more urbanized. The usage of land is changing along with the changing nature of economic development. The conservation of the site has to take account of the site's unique character and also the needs and feelings of the local communities. At present, the understanding and practice of heritage management as cultural property is still dominated by the material-based approach. According to Wells (2010), the selection of buildings, structures, and places for conservation is based on the interrelated concepts of integrity, authenticity, and historical value. Nevertheless, as argued by Smith (2006), these concepts are traditionally predicated on preserving the object rather than conserving the meanings and values associated with that selfsame object. In other words, the goal is to benefit the object and not the people who value the object (Wells 2010). Thus, a breakthrough in the concept of heritage will be required to understand local values and culture, and to develop a people-centered conservation plan to address the dynamic circumstances of Trowulan's heritage derived from its former position as the Majapahit royal capital. People redefine their heritage by understanding its values as well as its physical appearance.

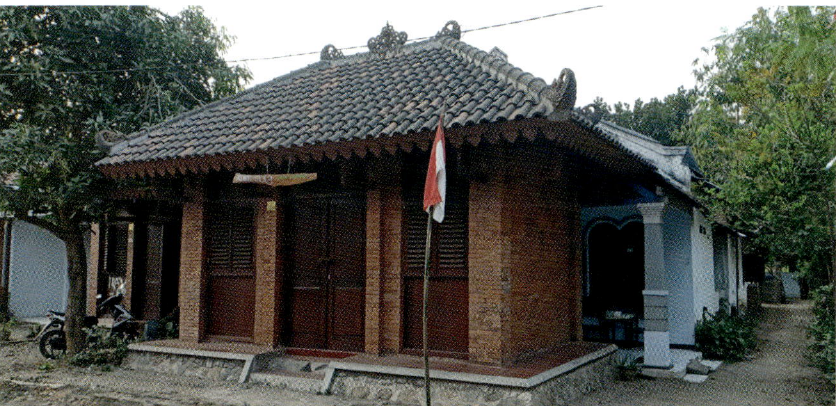

Figure 7. A "Majapahit House."

PEOPLE'S PARTICIPATION IN TROWULAN CONSERVATION

Conservation in Trowulan should no longer be simply limited to maintaining the authenticity of the historical remains, but should consider such intangible factors as "spirit," which are unique to each place. The effort to create a sense of place and to provide a deeper meaning for such a place is far more important than restoration of its physical form. People need to redefine their heritage by understanding its values beside its physical appearance. This can be done through the selection of the elements to be preserved, and by respecting the living traditions as practiced by the local population in their daily activities and ritual practices (Figure 8). Harmonious interaction beween the site and the people will develop their sense of place. The spiritual aspect of the place must be recognized alongside the economic, sociocultural, political, and environmental aspects. The meaning of the place must be shaped by a combination of artefacts and social interaction involving multiple parties' views and interests (Rukmi 2015).

Area-based conservation in Trowulan should reflect ideas about the quality of urban space as well as protection of significant physical objects. The resident population must be allowed, and indeed encouraged, to continue their local traditions thus enriching their physical space. Conservation should go beyond creating a visually harmonious relationship between the forms of old and new, and restoring heritage objects based on authenticity, to encourage people to participate and contribute an intangible spiritual and aesthetic element, thus ensuring the sustainability of the social, cultural, and environmental aspects of heritage conservation.

CLOSING REMARKS

It is not easy to integrate conservation as part of the political framework of modernization and development. Heritage conservation management requires commitment and broad participation from both government and people. With the increasing complexity of contemporary life and the dynamics of development, the conflict between conservation and economic development is becoming daily more evident. Promoting conservation does not mean ignoring the economic life of the people. Efforts to conserve heritage assets must open up the possibility of new economic opportunities. The design of conservation policies and projects must take into account the multiple contestations over economic, sociocultural, political, and environmental issues.

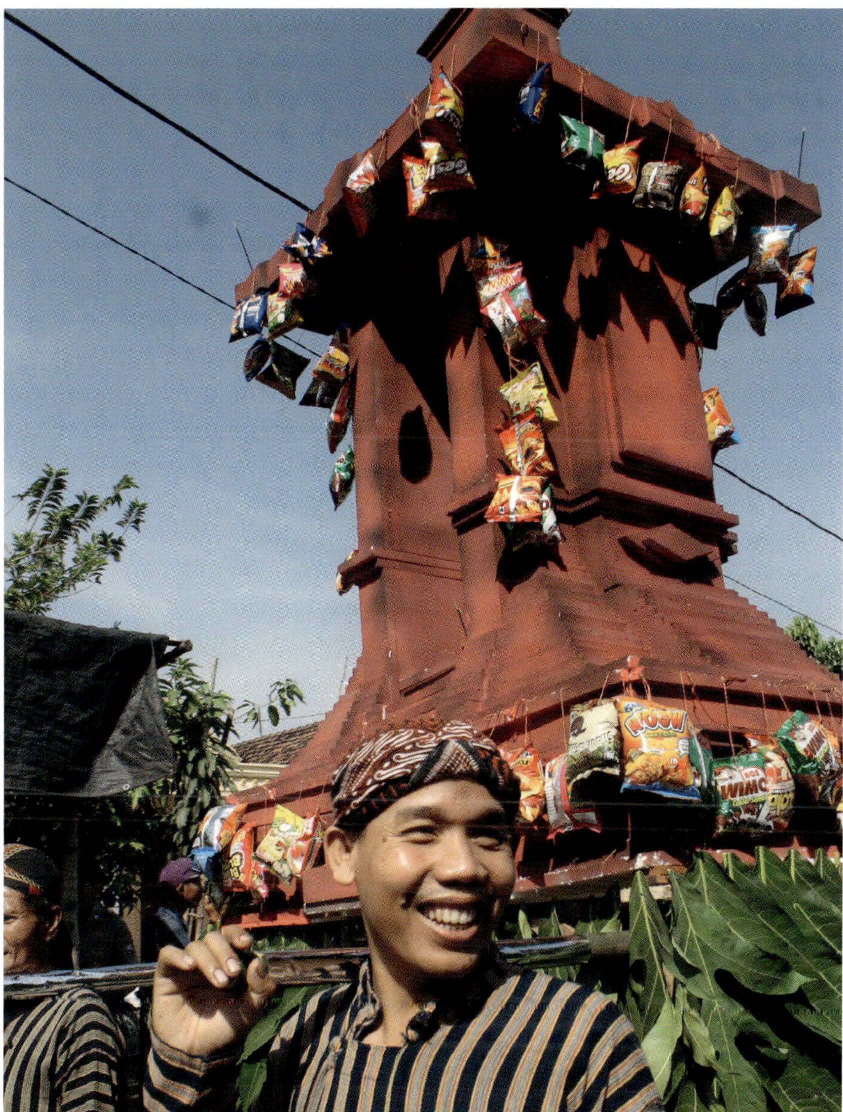

Figure 8. Local people participating in historic rituals.

The conservation of Trowulan's heritage should be based on the people's ownership of their heritage. The practice of the resident people's traditions adds color and spirit to the physical form of the heritage site. A sense of place can arise from negotiation among the economic, sociocultural, political, and environmental aspects of the site. The roles of government and grassroots communities are both important for protecting heritage. Heritage conservation in Asia, as mentioned in the Hoi An protocol (UNESCO Bangkok 2009), keeps changing and is constantly negotiated by stakeholders. There must be room for flexibility in the contestation among stakeholders. In recent decades, there have been controversies over ill-conceived interventions by various government agencies at Trowulan. The local people have been active in safeguarding their heritage in the face of such threats. Though most of the inhabitants of Trowulan are not themselves direct descendants of the original inhabitants of the Majapahit royal capital, they continue to practice rituals, processions, and ceremonies related to the site's supposed history. However ill-informed, such local activities should be taken into consideration when planning the long-term conservation of the site. Hopefully, this study can stimulate wider opinions and invite broader arguments on how to manage such heritage conservation by involving direct popular participation by local stakeholders. Based on the experience at Trowulan, we can conclude that people are the last defense of their heritage.

References

Gomperts, Amrit, Arnoud Haag, and Peter Carey. 2014. "The Archaeological Identification of the Majapahit Royal Palace: Prapañca's 1365 Description Projected onto Satellite Imagery." *Journal of the Siam Society*, 102: 67–118.

ICOMOS Indonesia, Minister of Culture and Tourism of Republic of Indonesia, The Indonesian Network for Heritage Conservation (JPPI). 2003. *Indonesian Charter for Heritage Conservation.*

Kubontubuh, Catrini. 2019. "Enigma Sejarah Jawa." In F. X. Domini B. B. Hera, ed., *Urip iku Urub. Untaian Persembahan 70 Tahun Profesor Peter Carey,* pp. 97–105. Jakarta: Kompas.

Mundardjito. 1986. *The Master Plan of Trowulan.* Jakarta: Ministry of Education.

Ramelan, Djuwita, Supratikno Rahardjo, Karina Arifin, Myrna L. Hunltley, Ingrid H.E. Pojoh, and Agi Ginanjar. 2015. "Model Pemanfaatan Kawasan Cagar Budaya Trowulan Berbasis Masyarakat." *AMERTA (Jurnal Penelitian dan Pengembangan Arkeologi),* 33, 1 (June): 1–76

Rukmi, Indira. 2015. "Nobility Space, Spatial Movement Construction in the Center of Majapahit Site, Trowulan." Unpublished PhD dissertation, University of Gadjah Mada, Yogyakarta.

Smith, Laurajane. 2006. *Uses of Heritage.* London: Routledge.

Tuan, Yi-Fu. 2008. *Space and Place, the Perspective of Experience.* Minneapolis: University of Minnesota Press.

UNESCO Bangkok. 2009. *Hoi An Protocols for Best Conservation Practice in Asia.*

Wells, Jeremy. 2010. "Valuing Historic Places: Traditional and Contemporary Approaches." *School of Architecture, Art, and Historic Preservation Faculty Publication 22,* Roger Williams University. Available at: docs.rwu.edu/saahp_fp/22/

Public Participation in Chinese Heritage Preservation: Shijia Hutong Museum

Matthew Hu

For the benefit of those who have not been to Beijing or are not familiar with *hutongs* in Beijing, please allow me to say a few words on its cultural significance before I move on to discuss my preservation practice.

Hutong generally refers to a narrow backstreet alleyway, mainly lined by courtyard residences on both sides, commonly found in many north China cities, including Tianjin, Kaifeng, and Datong. But the hutongs in Beijing stand out, simply because of their secondary role in the built environment of Old Peking. To glorify and to maintain the absolute power of the emperor, all the imperial palaces, offices, temples, and shrines were built in the city center, on a grand scale, decorated with high-quality building materials. All the hutong courtyard residences were forced to observe a strict hierarchy in terms of color scheme, materials, and size. This clear distinction has defined the built environment of Old Peking, and nurtured a very unique folk culture among its residents.

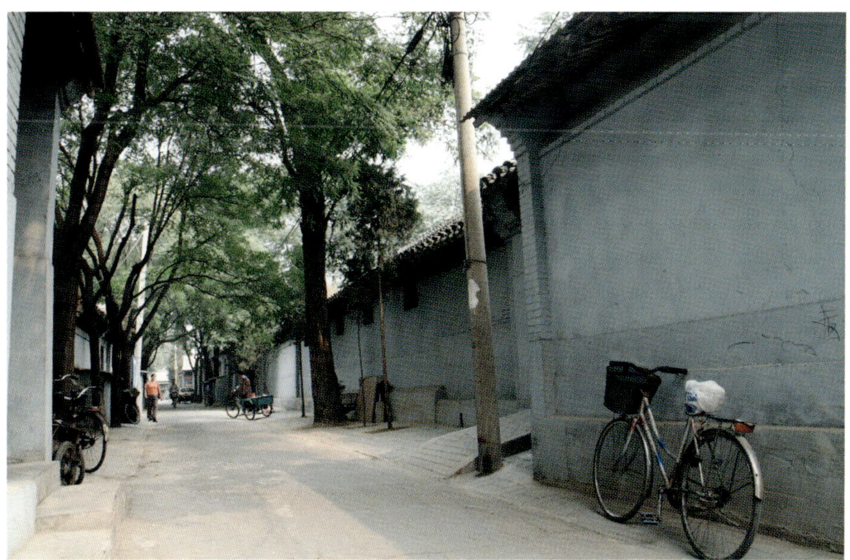

Figure 1. A typical hutong in Beijing.

The challenge we face today is that this holistic approach has been gradually abandoned and such clear distinction has become vague. A once complete and systematically planned and built old city has been torn apart over the past century. The remnants of the old pattern have become more and more rarely seen.

SHIJIA HUTONG MUSEUM TODAY

On 18 October 2018, I was invited by the local government to attend a celebration at Shijia Hutong Museum for the fifth anniversary of the launching of this modest hutong preservation project.

Largely thanks to the enthusiasm and professionalism of the museum staff and volunteers, this project has been very well maintained and managed, and has received a number of honors and recognitions from both the government and the general public in the past few years.

On Trip Advisor, for example, Shijia Hutong Museum ranked 144th out of 1,568 sites in Beijing. Also on Trip Advisor, the China National Gallery has 142 positive reviews and ranked 97th out of the 1,568 sites.

Other than the reviews and awards, the most touching compliments come from the visitors.

> What a wonderful and moving museum, documenting with detail and care, the precious history of this hutong. The stories of residents, of lives lived here, and the displays, brought this place to full life for me.
>
> And the kind gentleman caretaker, such a sweet man. We managed to communicate somehow! Thank you." (Janine Octarri, Azrieli School of Architecture and Urbanism, Ottawa, Canada, February 20, 2014)

> 历史的厚重感，在四合院中形成文化积淀，勾起我儿时的记忆。请告诉她，北京，我很想她。
> 看到泪流。
>
> The rich history has laid a very solid foundation in this courtyard, which brings back my childhood memory. Please tell her, Beijing, I missed her a lot. I can't help with my tears." (Mr. Li and his wife, March 1, 2014)

As you can see, this has created great resonance in the hearts of visitors.

Indeed, the most important reason for the success of this museum perhaps came from the public participation approach we took during the planning stage.

PUBLIC PARTICIPATION APPROACH

What would be the most important factor that has made this museum so successful in such a short period of time, you may ask. As the manager of this project on the ground from beginning to end, I had the rare privilege to witness the entire process. On reflection, I would contribute this unexpected outcome to the public participation approach that was taken, rather seriously, from the very initial stage of this project.

The two founding partners of the project were The Prince's Charities Foundation (China) (PCFC) and the Chaoyangmen Sub-district Government. The PCFC, together with its sister charities in the UK, not only produced the funding, but also the essential notions, methodologies, and skill sets.

During the entire process, we managed to engage with all important stakeholders from different backgrounds, who have strong connections with this project, and this was also gradually accepted by our local government partners, and became more and more known to the public.

The next question is: Was public participation a very popular approach to heritage preservation? The answer is yes and no.

Yes, because lots of people, government officials, scholars, entrepreneurs, and social workers, were talking about public participation in their speeches, their interviews, or their papers.

No, because not all public participation means authentic public participation, or generates positive results. At least, we did not see the fruits of such efforts, and thus we were not inclined to believe what we were told.

Considering the authoritarian approach to engineering social change normally used in China, it is difficult to imagine how much trends have changed since a decade earlier.

Back in 2006, in preparing the opening of the Beijing Olympics, a total of 1,474 courtyard houses were renovated with government funding of about one billion RMB. Although the campaign had an expert panel, there was only a dozen members, mostly in their 70s and 80s. Considering the speed with which these projects were conducted, from spring 2006 to fall in the same year, it was not feasible to ask these experts to supervise each and every regeneration project and still meet the target deadline.

The 1,474 renovated courtyard houses are all properties of the state (roughly 60 percent of Beijing Old City courtyard houses are state-owned), as back then, the policy did not allow state funding for renovating private property.

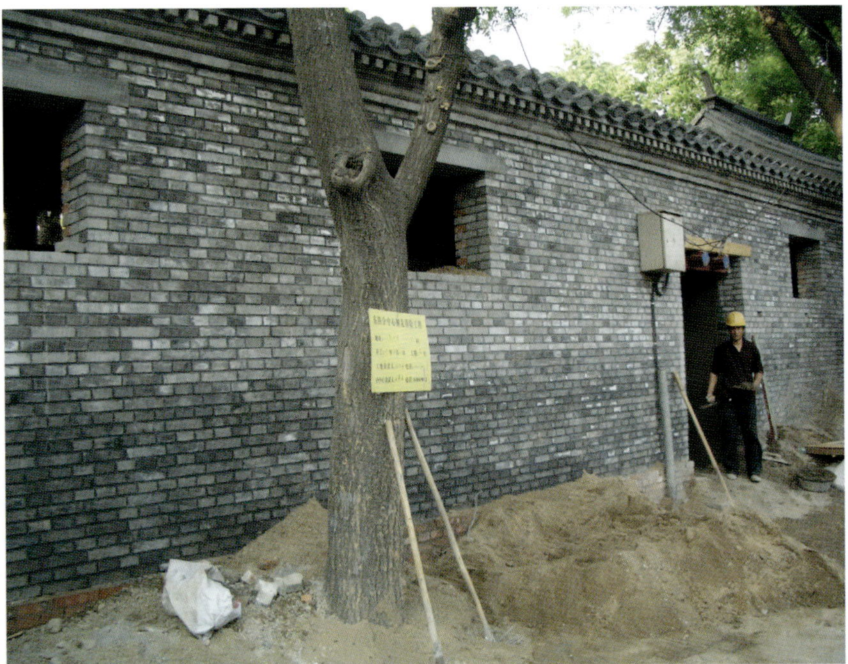

Figure 2. A "simplest" revnovation.

I had been to some of these renovation projects, and I saw some of the "simplest" ways of renovation, if I may put it in a "polite" way.

Let's do a simple calculation: one billion RMB divided by 1,474 courtyard houses means that each courtyard house received about RMB 678,426 for the renovation.

The size of each courtyard house varied from 150 to 1,000 square meters, with an average of 400 square meters by my estimate. Out of the 400 square meters, let's say 50 percent is the house, with the rest being open yard and passages, so the area being renovated was about 200 square meters. The cost per square meter was thus about RMB 3,392. Given the system through which this funding was allocated, perhaps only half of the funding was spent on the materials, labor, and management, meaning about RMB 1,696 per square meter.

Back in 2006, the best estimate for renovating a courtyard house to guarantee quality would be at least RMB 5,000 per square meter. In 2013, when we completed the Shijia Hutong Museum project, the cost of labor and materials had increased so the per square meter cost was about RMB 6,140. So you can imagine the quality of work of this renovation campaign.

In the past ten years, there have been no positive reviews of this project from the public. The state-run media carried only "press release" type of reports. I have heard nobody quoting this project as a model project for best practice when speaking about preservation.

BACKGROUND

Shijia Hutong Museum is a modest heritage preservation project piloted by The Prince's Charities Foundation (China) in 2010. The size of the land is only 1,200 square meters, and the built footprint is 700 square meters.

The location are very central, only about three blocks away from the Forbidden City, and 3.5 kilometers from Tian'anmen Square. In fact, the former resident of this courtyard house was a very senior official in the imperial court in the late 19th century. He bought this house because it was a short distance for him to go to work every day.

Each hutong is different in length and width, but in general, a standard hutong is about 700 meters long, and 7 to 9 meters wide, accommodating about 60 to 120 courtyard houses, again varied in size. On average, there are about two to three thousand residents in each hutong today, so it is like a small village or city community in many parts of the world.

The original idea of the Shijia Hutong Museum project came about in a rather serendipitous way.

His Royal Highness The Prince of Wales is an avid heritage preservationist. When he met with a group of Chinese businessmen led by the late Sir David Tang in 2006, he was most interested and concerned about the preservation status of heritage and tradition in China, although he had not made a trip to this part of the world yet.

The result of that meeting was the founding of The Prince's Charities Foundation (China), and the first thing that came to The Prince's Foundation's attention was the demolition of hutongs, which formed the basic city fabric of China's ancient capital.

In 2006, there were 1353 hutongs remaining in Beijing, according to an officially published report, which is about 45 percent of the roughly 3000 hutongs extant in the 1950s. Many of them were under threat because the real estate industry was excited by the prospect of a commercially successful Olympics.

Although there were thirty-three hutong preservation areas defined by the urban planning commission of the Beijing Municipal Government, these areas covered only 56 percent of the remaining hutongs, which meant the rest could disappear.

After decades of neglect during the planned economy, the hutong residences were mostly in a dilapidated condition. It was in the local governments' best interest to remove these "slum" areas, so that they could both save face and make way for economic gain.

The front page of many media, both in China and abroad, carried criticism of the ruthless demolition which ignored both the heritage value of the courtyard houses and the livelihood of the communities.

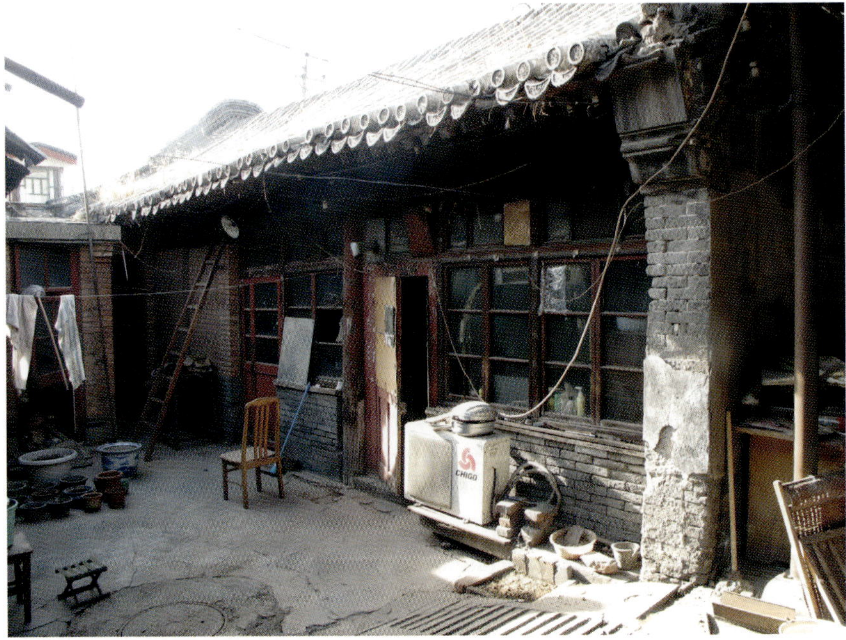

Figure 3. Dilapidated condition.

The challenge in the preservation of hutongs in old Beijing was huge. It only seemed natural that the future British king's foundation might be able to make a contribution with all the international best practices it had exercised around the world. The foundation's proposal was warmly welcomed by the Chinese government.

In the beginning, the Beijing Urban Planning Commission induced The Prince's Foundation to focus on Dazhalan'r, a hutong area of a little over 1.3 square kilometers, with 45,000 to 50,000 permanent residents.

Although Dazhalan'r was quite a large area with a very high population density and many complex social and economic issues, The Prince's Foundation was confident that it would be able to make a difference as long as it adopted a public participatory approach.

Yet the lead Chinese architect who was supposed to coordinate an opening workshop had absolutely no idea why this project mattered to the old man who sat at a street corner puffing all day, and why professionals and government officials could not decide for him. Partially because of miscommunication and partially because of deliberate resistance, only two "model" residents came to the workshop.

After this failed attempt to work shoulder by shoulder with the local communities, The Prince's Foundation still managed to produce a quality paper on some general principles and guidelines for hutong regeneration.

But for almost three years from 2007 to 2009, nothing happened with the Dazhalan'r project on the ground. As a result, The Prince's Foundation turned their attention elsewhere.

By the time I joined the Prince's Foundation in late 2009, my first task was to find a site that would be small enough to put our hands around, but significant enough to make a statement.

Luckily, with three-year's experience working for the Beijing Cultural Heritage Protection Center, I already had a number of strong connections in the preservation circle. So I asked a number of friends to contribute their suggested sites, establishing No. 24 Shijia Hutong as an option.

NO. 24 SHIJIA HUTONG

There seemed to be no site more ideal than No. 24 Shijia Hutong.

As mentioned above, it is about 1,200 square meters in size, so the total budget would be manageable for the Prince's Foundation. It is also located in one of the core preservation areas, which would make it easier to test the public participation approach without having to worry about a threat of demolition.

The property is owned by one of the fifty-six sub-district governments in old town Beijing, and the local government was very supportive to this project. This courtyard house had been left unoccupied, after many years as a community kindergarten, thus we did not have to worry about moving anyone out. The family of the former owner of this courtyard residence has a legendary history which left a very good foundation for story-telling. There is even a very good China–UK connection as this family had moved to the UK in 1946.

But, most importantly, the local community was very well organized and enthusiastic about community affairs.

The Prince's Foundation has a way of organizing workshops, which is called EbD, meaning Enquiry by Design. Enquiry is more important than Design.

From March to August 2010, we organized a number of rounds of workshops with almost all the important stakeholders of this project, including over a hundred local residents, all the four hotel owners or managers on this hutong, the deputy headmaster of the local primary school, the party secretary of the local traffic police bureau, and representatives from the district urban planning, infrastructure, and construction commission.

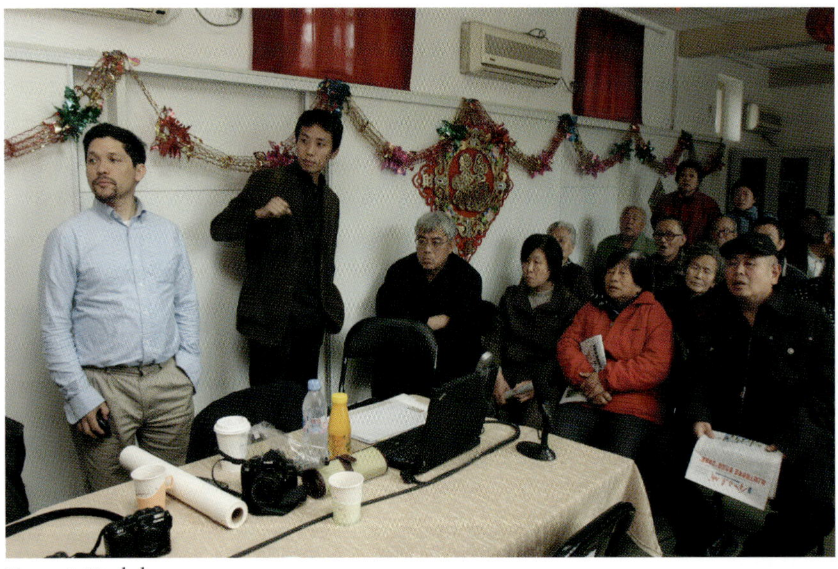

Figure 4. Workshops.

Outside the workshop, we also made many field trips to visit other successful regeneration projects, both public and private, to see what merits they were known for.

Regular communications with the local government were essential in securing the continued support of our "client," as during the four years this project was implemented, the party secretary or No. 1 of the local government changed three times.

The result was a full understanding on the interest of all parties involved, and then a master plan that consolidated all the reasonable and feasible requirements of the various parties.

The process was not as simple as it sounds.

When we tried to get hold of the party secretary of the local traffic police, it turned out to be extremely difficult.

Since the mid-1990s, the auto industry took off, and China is quickly embracing a modern life on four wheels. Beijing's one-millionth car appeared in 1997, and by 2009, Beijing had 4 million cars. Thus the pressure on transportation management became extremely important. The local police could not care less about the traffic in a tiny hutong, since their primary goal is to make sure that Chang'an Avenue, Jinbao Street, and a few key junctions near Shijia Hutong function normally. Even the slightest traffic jam in any one of those spots is catastrophic, so they would rather sacrifice the comfort of Shijia Hutong and allow it to be used as a diversion sub-road.

And the deputy principal of Shijia Hutong Primary School was another tough player in the game. Given the importance of the school in Beijing, it had grown to an unbelievable size by 2010. Although there were only two grades in the school campus located on Shijia Hutong, each grade had over a thousand students. To make it worse, since Shijia Hutong is only seven meters wide on average, the lane has to be one-way, running from west to east. The school is located at towards the west end of the lane, but all the school buses have to exit the hutong at the east end. One of the main responsibilities of this deputy principal is to make sure that all the 2,000 students are able to leave the school within a reasonable 45 minutes each school day.

Thanks to the support of the local sub-district government, after a lot of hassle of course, we were able to invite both of them to come to the workshop.

But the embarrassing thing was that the party secretary of the traffic policearrivedwithanopenacknowledgementthathewasverybusyandmight have to leave in half-an-hour, and the deputy principal arrived rather late.

As the chief architect from the Prince's Foundation started his talk about the vision of this project, as well as the public interest it had for the future, the party secretary sat down and started to take interest. The deputy principal also nodded his head all the time. After the introductory session, they each began to ask very good questions, then got into a heated debate, as each seemed to think the other had created great difficulties for his own job. Our chief architect listened to their comments and started to make revisions to the master plan on a flip chart, with multiple layers of tracing paper showing the different approaches of each suggested solution.

The fact that we managed to get everyone sitting around one table helped. When the two got stuck over a point, other stakeholders would jump in to make a few comments, which were normally more objective. Although neither of them was fully convinced, they did learn to restrain their own temper.

So both the party secretary and the deputy principal managed to stay till the end of the conference, which lasted for three hours.

When leaving, they came to us and thanked us for organizing such an interesting workshop, creating the opportunity for them to share their concerns and frustrations towards each other which they had for years.

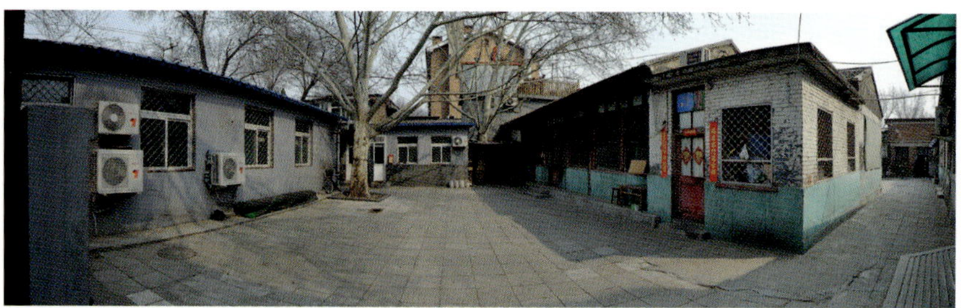

Figure 5. Shijia Hutong No. 24, before . . .

CONSTRUCTION AND EXHIBITION CURATION

Before we reached the implementation stage of this project in April 2011, we spent nearly one year dealing with all sorts of permits and paperwork for various government offices. We made use of the time immersing ourselves in the community to understand the parameters of this project.

Although the initial master plan was for the entire hutong, which had over eighty courtyard houses on both sides, with suggestions on almost all essential aspects of the built environment, we decided to begin with courtyard No. 24. The reasoning was obvious. We had no control over the entire hutong, which is far more complicated when it comes to any simple changes and interventions. Plus, we had the confidence that a good exemplary project would generate impact in the end, and would bring changes to the community.

At the stage of construction and exhibition curation, the public participation took a different form, more or less like the focus group approach in social studies.

The design of the entire project has nothing special in terms of its outlook. We have tried to keep to the traditions of Chinese wooden buildings, but the critical thing is how to keep the traditional features while at the same time increasing the energy efficiency and comfort.

To achieve this goal, we invited experts to our sites, ranging from an architectural archaeologist to a geothermal expert. More importantly, we invited architects and ordinary home-owners to come to our place and give comments and suggestions. We revised our plan numerous times on site and found many ways to make small changes, improving the quality significantly.

A similar procedure was followed during the exhibition curation phase, although here the funding was provided not by the Prince's Foundation

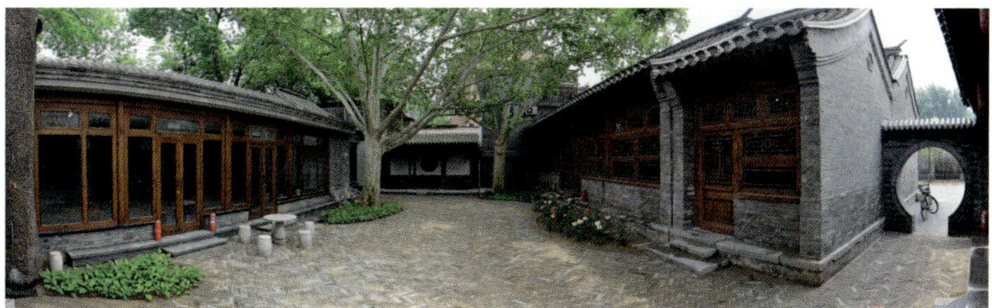

. . . and after.

but by a government agency, which we were more than happy to see. We still took an active role in providing all the contacts and materials we had gathered when talking to various stakeholders, including the descendants of the Ling family who had owned this property until 2000.

All the hard work paid off when the museum was opened and received almost immediate recognition from both the leadership of Beijing and the general public. The party secretary and the mayor of Beijing each paid more than one visit, and the general public came, leaving a lot of very warm comments.

At this stage, we can feel relieved as we had spent the donors' money to not only preserve a courtyard house in the authentic traditional way, but had also laid a very good foundation for various community-based activities.

The Shijia Hutong Museum has recently completed another training program, partnering with the Shijia Hutong Primary School, for a group of second grade students. The program is called "Junior City Planners." Parents seem to be as excited as their kids after the tour of the museum and the training sessions.

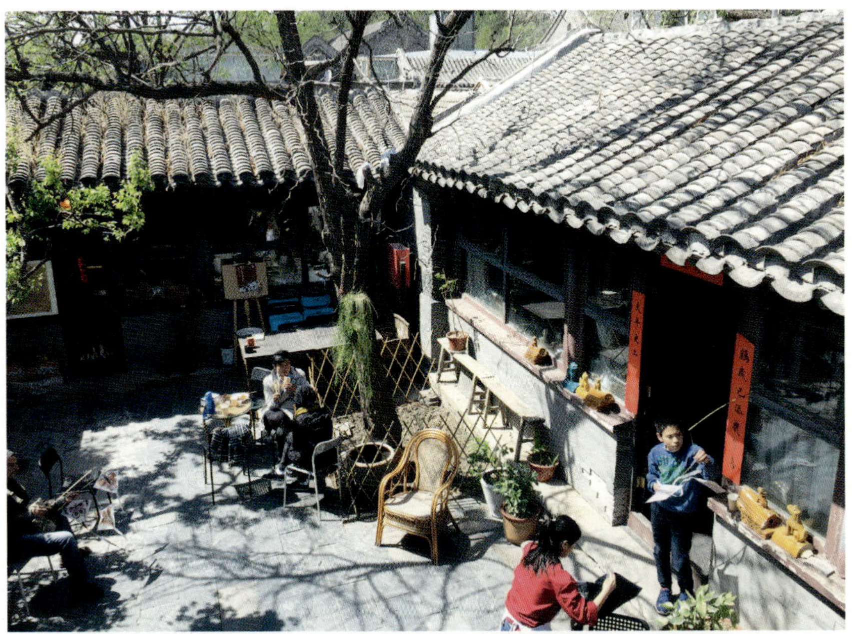

Figure 6. Activities in the courtyard on a summer afternoon.

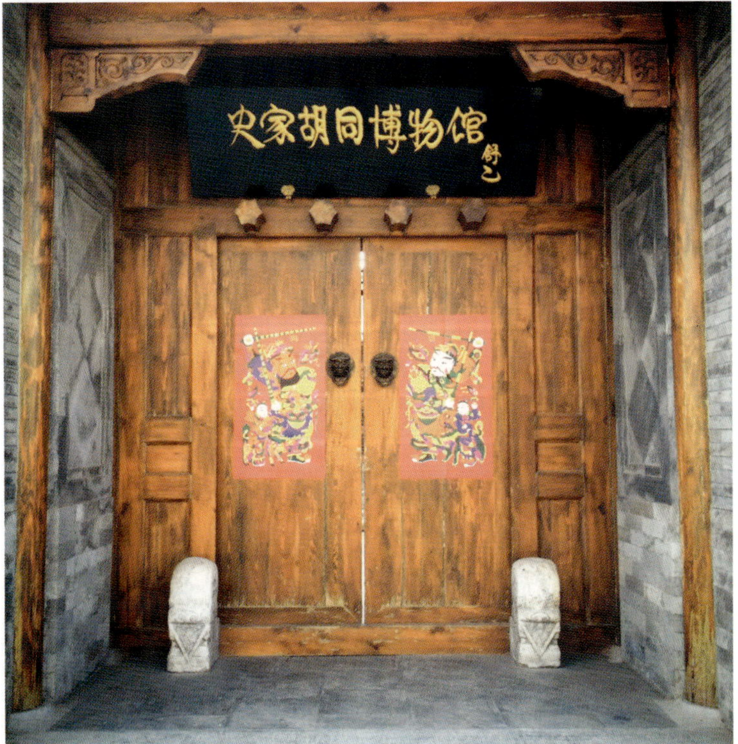

Figure 7. The main entrance.

CHANGE IN THE WIND

Around the same time that we were preparing the Shijia Hutong Museum project, the Xicheng District Government, one of the two district-level governments which manages the Old City of Beijing, started to adopt a new approach.

In 2009, the first Beijing International Design Week was launched by the municipal government. The initial purpose was to uplift the quality in the design industry, including graphic design, product design, as well as architectural and even urban design. But the organizer of this first Design Week was one of the government agencies who had no genuine interest to move things forward, so there wasn't much impact.

Due to the failure of this first Design Week, the government funder looked for help from a private curator, Alex Chan, who was a second-generation immigrant from China to the US. Alex was always interested in hutongs, and somehow the government funder got to know him, and got him involved in the same area it once had delegated to The Prince's Foundation, namely the Dazhalan'r area.

It happened like this. A new state-owned company had been founded, Guang'an Holding, and put in charge of the regeneration of the Dazhalan'r area. During past facelift campaigns, each hutong area had to be completely cleared so the land could be used for commercial real estate development. If someone decided to be the "Nail House," meaning a home whose resident refused to leave and make way for new construction, the government had to pay a higher compensation to make them move. When Guang'an was founded, the policy environment was much more benign. The ultimate purpose of the development in Dazhalan'r area was not a complete transformation, but rather a gradual, organic adaptation, which the government officially termed "micro-circulation."

Under the "micro-circulation" guideline, Guang'an Holding pays every hutong resident, mostly tenants in public housing, a standard amount of compensation, with no room for "bargaining." Those who don't want to move are entitled to stay, although some might be prompted to move to another courtyard house with similar living space, so the completely evacuated courtyards could be refurbished and rented out to cultural creative industry practitioners.

By the time Alex Chan stepped in for the second Design Week curation, he talked to Guang'an Holding, and was allowed to make use of all the evacuated spaces in the Dazhalan'r area for various curated exhibitions, from fashion to handicrafts, from oral history to photo journeys, from multimedia display to installations.

Also because of Alex's connection in the expat community, this Design Week was perhaps the first authentic International Design Week, which attracted the attention of a lot of old China hands. By the time I paid a visit to Dazhalan'r that week, I could see that a very high percentage of the pedestrians on that street or in the nearby hutongs were from a totally different social circle to those who would normally appear in the old town of Beijing. This tremendous interest brought new life to the area, and brought us new hope as well.

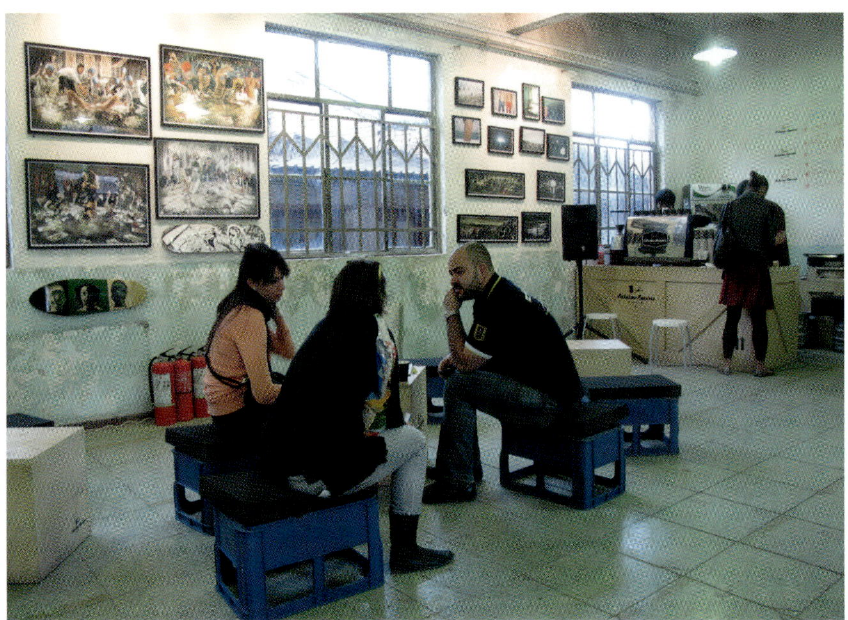

Figure 8. Dazhalan'r Design Week.

Almost ten years after the second Design Week, this area had gradually been transformed. More and more young designers, both Chinese and foreigners, have set up their experimental shops and studios in the area. At the same time, many locals are still enjoying their old lifestyle. The two had merged harmoniously in the same neighborhood.

Inspired by the Dazhalan'r experience, the Baitasi area became another popular destination for the most dynamic and creative group in the city.

Baitasi is the Chinese name of the White Dagoba, a Buddhist sacred site built by a Nepalese architect who traveled to China during the rule of Kublai Khan. Compared to Dazhalan'r, this area is equally densely populated, and rich in history. All the hutongs are zig-zagging, forming a maze behind a few major streets.

Encouraged by the experience with Guang'an Holding, the Xicheng District Government formed another company called Tianheng Holding to deal with the complex social and economic issues. Same approach, same policy, and same public participation.

I have personally talked to artists and architects from many different nationalities, including French, Belgian, and German just to give a few examples. There are no data on how many new businesses have moved into the hutong areas, but you can feel it when you walk into every hutong.

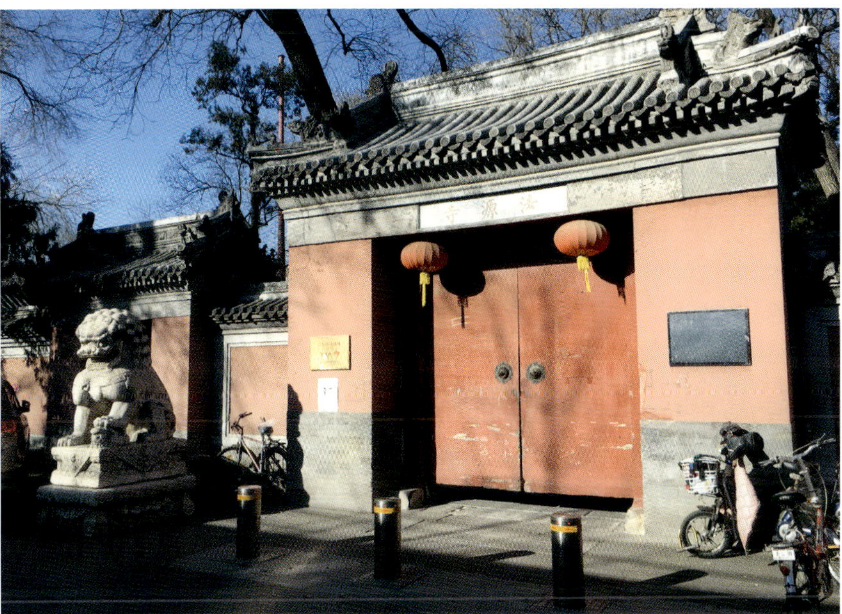

Figure 9. Fayuan Temple.

Very recently, there is a third area in Xicheng District, the Fayuansi Area, near Fayuan Temple. The history of the temple can be traced back to the Tang Dynasty. The second Emperor Li Shimin declared war on Korea in the 7th century, and this temple was founded to commemorate the warriors who died in that war.

Fayuansi is still a thriving temple, with a lot of heritage inside. The community is shrinking every day, so the same "micro-circulation" approach is perhaps the best approach to enlist help from the public.

There are also bad examples. The Xianyukou Development Project, to the southeast of Tian'anmen Square, began in 2005, and is now mired in a financial mess because of many bank loans. On the site of old houses that were demolished now stand newly rebuilt courtyard houses, which in reality are made of concrete and steel. Very few businesses want to move in as there is no real attraction for visitors other than groups of soulless bronze sculptures trying to tell the glory of the past. If you take a walk at night, this might seem like a perfect place for making ghost movies.

And this is the "masterpiece" of the Chongwen District Government, which later merged into the Dongcheng District.

SPLASH AND RIPPLES

Other than the above projects, further interesting initiatives are happening in and around the Shijia Hutong Museum.

Right after The Prince's Foundation handed the museum project back to the landlord, the Chaoyangmen Sub-District Government of Dongcheng District, we introduced the Vanke Foundation to this community. The Vanke Foundation, established by the China Vanke Company, has a mission to promote a green and sustainable community lifestyle.

Building on the community work initiated by The Prince's Foundation, Vanke introduced a Mini Vegetable Garden Project into this community. Vanke provides vegetable seeds, proper training, tools and, most importantly, a competition to encourage the community to use their skill sets. In exchange for the seeds and tools, the local residents' responsibility is to provide wastes for recycling, separated in a standard efficient way.

At an annual conference with participation of the local residents, everyone praised the project. Thanks to this simple yet effective approach, enthusiasm for a community-building approach was well sustained, laying a solid foundation for more community engagement activities.

Around the time that the Vanke Foundation was implementing its three-year program in the community, the Beijing Municipal Institute of City Planning and Design (BMICPD) also completed a new Conservation Plan for the Dongsinan Historical Preservation Area. As mentioned, there are thirty-three historical preservation areas in the Old City of Beijing, and a detailed Conservation Plan was drafted for each area for the years 2010 to 2014.

In the past, a plan could be an empty plan because the vision did not really match the reality. Unless there was a serious issue, such as the demolition of some heritage buildings, the authorities would not step in to interfere. But luckily, Dr. Feng Feifei, director of the City Design Department of BMICPD, and many of her colleagues were both very curious and serious about the future implementation of this Conservation Plan.

Encouraged by the successful launch of the Shijia Hutong Museum, the Chaoyangmen Sub-district Government founded a community-based non-profit organization called Shijia Hutong Heritage Preservation Society (SHPS). As this was a community-based non-profit organization, the local government could not allocate any of their staff to run it. Moreover, none of its staff had any experience running such an organization.

Dr. Feng brought in her team, and among them Ms. Zhao Xing arose to be a perfect candidate for the secretary-general of SHPS. As an experiment, Dr. Feng and her department wanted to create a new mechanism in the hutong communities through a system called Community Planner. The community planner for each community is a professional planner from the municipal government, responsible for introducing the Conservation Plan, and at the same time, assisting the local community to implement the plan under the existing community governance.

As the main think tank and design arm of the Beijing Urban Planning Commission, BUPCDI was responsible for the urban development design of the entire municipality, which is 16,800 square kilometers in area (about half of Belgium), but its key challenge is the preservation of the Old City of Beijing, 62.5 square kilometers in size, as it is not only regarded as an outstanding example of city design throughout human history but also has many social and economic challenges that have not been thoroughly addressed.

Given the challenge, the director of the City Design Department of Beijing Municipal Institute of City Planning and Design , Dr. Feng Feifei, was very much interested in the Shijia Hutong Museum project from the very beginning. She was thinking about how best to regenerate the Old City communities without cutting them off from their rich cultural and historical heritage.

In fact, both Dr. Feng and her staff had actively participated in the EbD workshop that The Prince's Foundation had run back in 2010. And since then, they have gradually moved in and started to take a more active role in keeping the momentum going.

The deputy director of Chaoyangmen Sub-district Government, Mr. Li Zhe, is a great fan of Old Beijing history, and with this passion, was strongly motivated to work with Dr. Feng and Ms. Zhao on the operation of SHPS.

The municipal government also took concrete measures to implement the guidelines of Old City preservation by setting up a dedicated government fund supporting pilot preservation projects.

So with Shijia Hutong Heritage Preservation Society as an independent platform, with Dr. Feng's team as professional project managers, with Mr. Li Zhe's support in securing funding, a wider public participation approach was exercised in and around Shijia Hutong Community.

In 2014, one year after the Shijia Hutong Museum was opened, another small yet important pilot project began, called "Regaining Public Space in the Courtyard." After the 1976 Tangshan Earthquake, which severely affected Beijing, many people started to build temporary housing in the courtyards, by removing trees and flowers or taking over children's playgrounds. This temporary housing was retained and used as extra living space when children grew up. Little by little, a once beautiful courtyard was changed into a Da Za Yuan, or big messy courtyard.

As China went through a very aggressive Socialist period, when almost all properties in Old Beijing became state-owned by the mid-1960s, courtyards that had once been private came to be shared by many different families. The space outside a courtyard, mainly on the hutongs, is considered public space, where the government is responsible for maintenance, while each house inside a courtyard is private space, where the occupying families look after maintenance and renovation. However, the space that was shared inside a courtyard was ambiguous space, and went largely neglected.

So what was once a lovely garden might become a dump for piles of abandoned furniture, unused building materials, or simply waste that nobody cared to take outside the yard. To make matters worse, a courtyard might not have any light in the yard, as nobody felt responsible for paying the electricity bill.

To address these issues, Dr. Feng and Ms. Zhao Xing mobilized their resources and brought in more volunteers from the Central Academy of Fine Arts and the Beijing University of Technology, two institutions that have an architectural or urban planning department which needs good field research opportunities. In this case, the teachers and students were excited to find out that they actually had a chance to implement their ideas, no matter how small their project was.

Ms. Zhao Xing had two roles in this project, as the community planner and as the secretary-general of SHPS. This is a very unique position for moving forward such a project. Although very small, this project is very significant as a milestone breakthrough in how the hutong communities were managed in the past.

Zhao Xing described the process in five steps: 1. field trip to understand the courtyard; 2. community participatory design process; 3. community mobilization; 4. project implementation; and 5. post-construction maintenance. As a designer and planner, everyone participates in the first, the fourth and the fifth steps, but not very many are involved in the second and third—as you can imagine how difficult it is talking to a group of neighbors who might have a lot of history behind them.

There is one good example of how they solved problems. For those courtyards that did not have any outside lamp, the designer suggested placing a solar-powered lamp in the yard. As the yard is often used to store belongings that are temporarily not in use, the designer combined the design of this lamp with a stainless steel chest. One stone, two birds. A perfect solution to improve the quality of life while not causing new troubles for the neighbors.

Very recently, the local vegetable market had a major facelift, largely taking the same approach, implemented under the platform of Shijia Hutong Heritage Preservation Society.

In all the above examples, public participation played a very important part, which had a significant impact.

All the efforts paid off when the Chinese Ministry of Construction nominated the Shijia Hutong Museum for a China Human Settlements and Environment Award.

CONCLUSION

Frankly speaking, Shijia Hutong Museum project succeeded for many reasons. The most important reason other than the public participation approach was the deep love and respect for the culture of Old Beijing. We all need a place to remember our past, and realize our own cultural identity.

But this does not undermine the importance of the approaches taken by the funder, the project manager, the local government, and the current museum management team.

If I have to summarize my experiences into a few tips, I will focus on two: First, it is of primary importance to give full respect to the local culture.

Most Asian cultures embrace a "top-down" approach, and give little room for any "bottom-up" movement. In China this is perhaps especially true, since we have had such a long history of effective authoritarian administration.

We took on this project with great care and sensitivity, always taking one step backwards when our local government partners had any concerns, and always showing our sincerity, flexibility, and patience. After we had signed the agreement, our local government partner took almost three months to get back to us with their counterpart signature. We have our frustrating moments of course, but we tend to view these from a cultural perspective, and offer to listen and learn when we have any disagreement.

Second, the local government in China has great resources, so we always work closely with the local officials for a "bottom-up" discussion. Once you secure the trust of the local officials, they will be allies who can set up local community meetings for open discussion, where our role is to lead the discussion to a constructive outcome. The story of the local traffic police above is a very good example.

I could add more tips, but without these two no others will work. In fact, I have observed that other examples across China, including the Brickyard Hotel regeneration project in Huairou District, Beijing, and the Linden Center in Dali County, Yunnan, have followed the same principles, which gave me a lot of reasons for hope.

We hope, and we firmly believe, that there will be more such examples on how these hutong communities and courtyard houses can be improved and regenerated in the future.

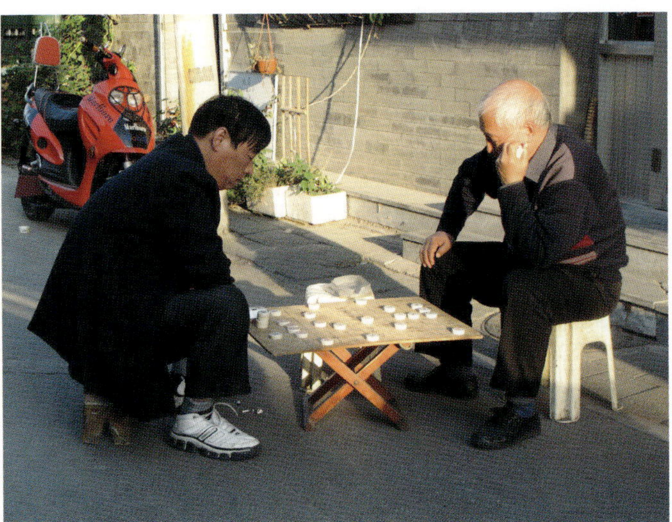

Figure 10. Local residents in a hutong.

Nurturing Cultural Entrepreneurship for Intangible Heritage Protection: Cambodian Traditional Performing Arts

Jean-Baptiste Phou, Frances Rudgard, Kai T. Brennert[1]

In the aftermath of the Khmer Rouge regime, which had specifically targeted artists and intellectuals, arts and culture in Cambodia were in a critical condition with several traditional forms in danger of disappearing. Cambodian Living Arts (CLA) was founded with the main objective of preserving and transmitting the intangible cultural heritable of Cambodia to the next generations. After a successful decade of running "schools without walls" across the country, CLA engaged the artists in a transition process to become self-sustainable organizations, performance troupes, and classes. Major socio-economic challenges for artists remained a threat to cultural heritage preservation, however. To offer fair and safe employment opportunities to artists, and to develop both the market and audiences for the performing arts in Cambodia, CLA started a cultural enterprise in 2013. Whilst keeping the arts alive through regular performances, issues such as economic viability, dependency of artists, "folklorization" of traditional art forms and reaching only a limited number of beneficiaries had to be navigated. Learning from all these experiences and taking into account the current economic and social-cultural context, CLA initiated the "Artist Incubator Project" in 2018. The creation of a "new traditional" show with recognized art directors was designed to not only provide employment to artists but also to equip them with the artistic and professional tools to become the next cultural entrepreneurs of Cambodia.

In 1998, Arn Chorn Pond returned to his birth-country, Cambodia, and initiated a project to support performing artists who had survived the Khmer Rouge regime, to start teaching children in their communities. This cause was dear to his own heart for multiple reasons, including his

1. The authors would like to acknowledge the current and former staff members of Cambodian Living Arts who were instrumental in the implementation of the projects described here, and organizations that supported them: Chhuon Sarin, Yon Sokhorn, Eam Solinda, Sun Sopheak, Ros Rotanak, Sophie Mensdorff-Pouilly, Roeun Rina, Song Seng, as well as Air Asia Foundation, and Common Sense Fund.

own family's history as artists, the role of music in healing his trauma after the Khmer Rouge regime, and the relationship he built with his Master teacher, Yoeun Mek, during their time playing for survival in a Khmer Rouge prison camp (McCormick 2012). Master Mek was one of the first four teachers Arn's project worked with, and was one of the chief inspirations for the project that has since grown to become the NGO Cambodian Living Arts (CLA).

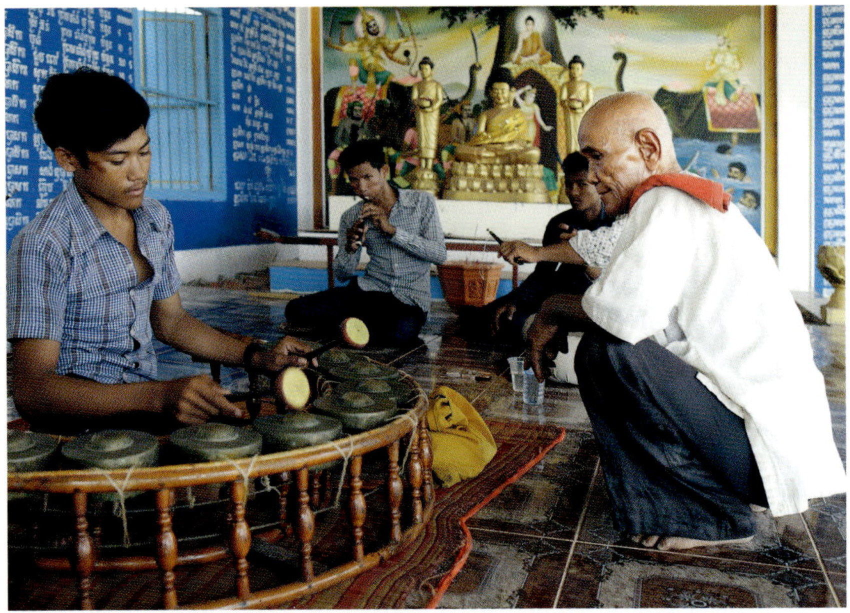

Figure 1. Master teaching gong in a pagoda. (Photo © Cambodian Living Arts)

Over the next decade, those first four classes grew to become a network of twenty-seven classes in nine provinces around Cambodia, teaching twelve performing art forms to approximately 1,000 children in villages, pagodas, schools and NGOs. Throughout that time, the focus was on heritage protection. In addition to supporting and managing the classes, CLA also organized festivals and conducted archiving projects to promote and preserve endangered performing art forms. The organization's vision was to stimulate a cultural renaissance in Cambodia by 2020.

In 2010 and 2011, CLA conducted a strategic review of its work and the contemporary context of Cambodia. By that time, many social and economic changes in the country created new living realities, and thanks to the work of many individuals, national and international NGOs, as well as the government, the art forms themselves were less at risk. The key strategic questions for CLA became:

> If the classes were still reliant on the hands-on management and funding from CLA, then could the mission to revive the art forms truly be considered achieved?
>
> What was needed to ensure that young people who had trained in these art forms were able to continue their involvement in the arts as adults?
>
> If a vision of a widespread "renaissance" of the arts were to be possible, then how would that be catalyzed?

The answers to these questions repeatedly returned to entrepreneurship—both in the commercial sense of the term and the energy and leadership of individuals driving forward cultural initiatives. The strategic direction of CLA from 2012 onward identified two priorities of entrepreneurship and sustainability. CLA needed to change its approach from doing hands-on work to taking a role as a facilitator.

The rest of this chapter focuses on case studies of two aspects of CLA's program that drew from this strategic direction and challenges faced in the process.

CLASS TRANSITION PROJECT: COMMUNITY-BASED ENTERPRISES

In September 2012, CLA took all the masters, teachers, and lead students from the sixteen classes involved in its community arts program at that time for a reflection and planning workshop. The main question for discussion was "what would be needed for the classes to be able to sustain themselves independently of CLA?" The expectation in advance of this session was that artists would identify issues such as realigning their classes with places such as schools or pagodas that would supply a reliable stream of students, or starting to charge students nominal fees. For some of the classes this was the case, but unexpectedly about half of the artists said that when they looked to the future, their vision was not to continue running classes but to create a financially sustainable performance troupe that would provide work to its members.

In response to that retreat, the CLA team developed specific tools and approaches to work with each group in order to address their specific needs. For those who wanted to continue as classes, we worked with their leaders to look for partnerships and approaches that would enable the classes to sustain. One of the very successful examples of this was the *smot* class in Kampong Speu province, which successfully integrated into the local high school curriculum, drawing 40 to 60 students each year (Grant 2017) and has since expanded to be taught in three grades, tripling the number of students.

For those who wanted to develop their artists to become a troupe, we created an assessment and planning tool to guide the process. The tool was developed with input from various resources and theories (Leung 2009; Bhattacharya 2011; Isar 2013), and created with CLA's specific target groups in mind. The hope was that if the tool and the approach was effective, then it could be used in future to nurture more small enterprises.

The assessment covered ten areas: artistic skills and knowledge; production materials; training and transmission; leadership and management; creativity; promotional materials; marketing channels; audience and market; sustainable revenue; and production quality.

The initial assessment was completed as a collaborative process between the artists and the CLA team, to identify strengths and weaknesses, and from there to identify priorities and develop an action plan. The model was tested with six classes who wished to become small cultural enterprises: Yike Amatak, Dontrey Mongkol, Community of Living Chapei, Children of Bassac, Wat Bo Shadow Puppet Troupe and Sounds of Angkor. In two cases, the group was already operating as an income generating entity. In one case, the approach did not make a difference to the troupe's operations, in another it led to the formation of an independent troupe built by the first generation of that class. Some more specific examples are described as follows:

> Children of Bassac / classical and folk dance: The generation of lead artists and students learned skills to manage their own leadership structure, financing and marketing, and ended up creating an independent troupe of their own, making space for a new generation of members of the original troupe.
>
> Community of Living Chapei / long-neck guitar and storytelling: This class decided to form an association, based on membership and participation. This was an innovative action, and today that troupe is thriving, with activities such as teaching and performances that generate revenue to support its basic expenses, as well as wider marketing and promotion outreach

that has inspired young people throughout Cambodia to develop interest in the art form of chapei dang veng. The group is now recognized by the government as a key actor in the sector.

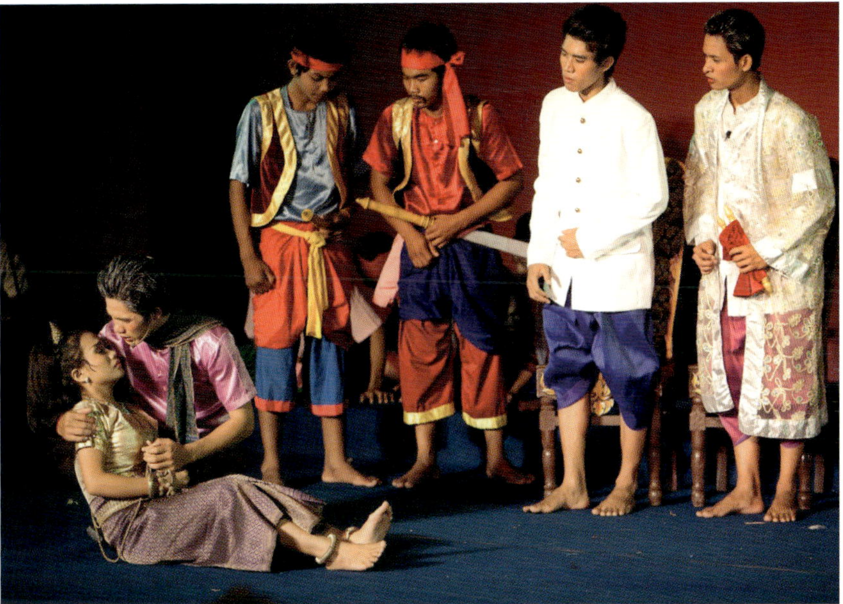

Figure 2. Yike opera Mak Theung. (Photo © Cambodian Living Arts)

Dontrey Mongkol / ceremonial music: This group developed a name and branding for itself and developed a specific strategy to find paid performances among the local community, including the nearby pagoda and families in the area. In addition to the troupe, the leader built a small classroom on his own land in order to ensure ongoing transmission of the art form.

Yike Amatak / yike opera: In order to sustain the class, the troupe leader decided to find ways that the troupe could earn money which would subsidize the class costs. This included ensuring the troupe could offer performances that had more market demand, for example, traditional dance.

While the outcomes were good, what was most interesting in the assessment and planning process were the greatest challenges and successes identified as both were found in the segment termed "management and leadership." In all cases, this was identified as the top priority for development in each group as there was a lack of clarity in who made decisions for the troupe, how work was shared among members and who had responsibility for what areas. Addressing this element took much more time than anticipated by CLA. The anticipated successes also rested on having someone in the group who had a vision of what they could achieve and the ability to motivate others to work towards it.

At the end of a three-year period, CLA has ceased providing hands-on support to all the classes. Today, of the 16 classes, four no longer practice, six are still running classes independently of CLA, and six are working as troupes which earn income that contributes towards sustaining their activities. Additionally, CLA provides pensions and medical support to all Masters that have previously been part of its programs.

CREATING EMPLOYMENT OPPORTUNITIES: CULTURAL ENTERPRISE

In parallel to working with the original classes to support their transition through entrepreneurship, CLA was also looking at ways it could improve economic prospects for artists beyond its own classes, including graduates from the Royal University of Fine Arts. How to survive and thrive?

Making a living as an artist in a very young and small market is difficult. The overall economic situation of the country did not allow for many employment opportunities for artists. The few jobs that people did get were less favourably paid and many artists had to either give up their artistic profession or work additional jobs to make ends meet. In short, the artist profession was not financially attractive, opportunities were few and support little. To address these challenges and preserve the intangible cultural heritage of Cambodia in the long-run, Cambodia was in need of enterprising innovation to create employment opportunities for artists that addressed issues of cultural, social, and economic sustainability.

To illuminate the challenging economic situation many Cambodian artists find themselves in, it is important to look at three contributing factors: 1. market size and opportunities; 2. employment situation and conditions; and 3. government support:

1. In 2012, Cambodia had only seven venues that were presenting performing arts productions (Cusimano et al. 2014). Additionally, many performances are free of charge for guests, which ultimately impacts the economic value that people attach to a cultural product.

The absence of culture and arts education in public school curricula (ibid.) adds to a lack of knowledge among the general public about much of Cambodia's intangible cultural heritage. With the exception of weddings, funerals, and other ceremonies, the local market for traditional performing arts is thus rather small and employment opportunities rare.

2. A country-wide employment study on artists from 2013 and 2014 (Cambodian Living Arts 2014) revealed that artists earn an average of USD 21 per performance, for which they put in an average of three hours work (excluding rehearsal and training which is typically unpaid). On average, theater actors, dancers, and musicians receive only USD 75 income per month from their work, depending heavily on weddings, tourism, and festival seasons. One third of all artists have at least one additional job to make ends meet, the majority of which includes manual labor. An entry-level garment factory worker was earning USD 100 at the time (International Labor Organization 2014), highlighting the artistic precariat in Cambodia.

3. With the exception of the National Arts Fund, which was approved in late 2017 but whose size, governance, and criteria are still under design, the Cambodian government does not provide any subsidies or grants to artists. Rather, the Ministry of Culture and Fine Arts employs a pool of their own artists and offers pensions for a few select *living human treasures* (UNESCO Office in Phnom Penh 2013). Becoming a ministerial artist requires a formal degree from the Royal University of Fine Arts, rendering only 11 percent of artists eligible (Cambodian Living Arts 2014).

These are just some of the aspects that illustrate the challenging situation of employment opportunities, support frameworks, and financial viability of the artist profession in Cambodia. Catherine Grant's article "Socioeconomic Concerns of Young Musicians of Traditional Genres in Cambodia: Implications for Music Sustainability" (2016) further describes how these challenges pose a threat to the vitality of these aspects of intangible cultural heritage. The sector is in need of entrepreneurial solutions to alleviate these shortcomings and create sustainable employment for themselves.

As illustrated by Rudgard and Prim (2018), Cambodian Living Arts decided to react to this situation by creating more and fairer opportunities for the employment of artists. By producing a regular performance with the goal of becoming a self-sustaining cultural enterprise, CLA aimed to keep the featured art forms alive through regular performances in the public domain, to provide artists with regular income for financial stability of the artist profession, to develop local audience and build a market for performing arts, and to tell a story of Cambodia and its rich and diverse cultures. In 2010–11 and 2011–12 an irregular performance was piloted before making the decision to significantly invest into this venture to achieve increased sustainability of the intangible cultural heritage of Cambodia. CLA secured a seed grant from AirAsia Foundation, which focuses on social enterprise and was interested in the project because of its goal to be financially self-sustaining.

A part of the grounds of the National Museum of Cambodia was leased and a 150-seat outdoor theater constructed that is large enough to host a music ensemble and full dance company on stage at the same time. Other activities of this initial two-year period of fully subsidized operations to produce visibility and gain market share included the development of a coherent one-hour performance and extensive marketing efforts.

In 2012, the first season of regular performances in the new theater started. Several changes to the pilot seasons were made to address economic, social, and cultural sustainability of the program. Rudgard and Prim (2018) describe how performances were now running all year round with six shows per week during high season and three to four nights a week during low season. This decision was necessary to satisfy hospitality partners and tour operators in the tourism industry who needed to include a regular visit to the show in their itineraries. Economic sustainability of the operations heavily depended on income from tourists. To offer a diversity of products but also to be able to showcase a variety of art forms and tell different stories, performances of three different art forms by three different troupes were programd. In order to achieve the cultural and social mission of Cambodian Living Arts, attracting Cambodian visitors was another main goal. A two-tier pricing system was introduced with significantly lower ticket prices for local visitors.

As implementation of the cultural enterprise continued, new challenges arose concerning capacity development and profitability. Several artists saw the performances as yet another income source they were hired to do and continuously pushed for more artists to be on the payroll. To realize its role not just as employer but also as capacity builder, CLA attempted to work more closely with the troupes. While such capacity development is deeply embedded in CLA's mission, profitability of some of the presented art forms were forcing the program to partly compromise its ambition to showcase the diversity of Cambodian arts and culture on a regular basis. The dance performance greatly outperformed the opera and music theater performances in earning capacity. When dance was selected as the only art form on the program, sales increased by 35 percent. CLA committed to using the theater for other uses to present and promote diverse Cambodian arts through commissioned performances, workshops, and festivals.

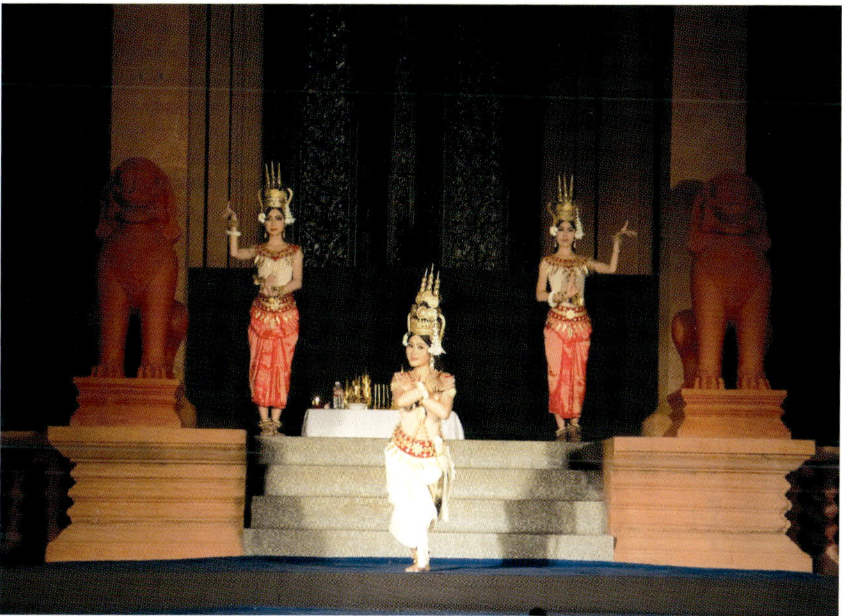

Figure 3. Dance on the stairs of the National Museum. (Photo © Cambodian Living Arts)

By contrasting these two entrepreneurship-related projects, the challenges of an institution wanting to meet cultural, social, and economic goals at the same time become apparent. In the first case, where CLA worked to support community groups to achieve their own economic and cultural goals, adhering to core values and principles created only little tension between the aims. In the case where CLA aimed to address socio-economic challenges in the arts ecosystem through actively nurturing cultural industries, the tensions grew. In order to find a balance and to acknowledge changes in the socio-economic development of Cambodia and its arts ecosystem, CLA has constantly been reviewing and innovating its regular performance platform. The final section of our paper elaborates on the most recent developments to this project.

THE ARTISTS INCUBATOR PROJECT: CULTURAL ENTREPRENEURSHIP

After five years of running the Traditional Dance Show with sub-contracted performance troupes, CLA realized that there were still several, deep-rooted challenges that need to be addressed to make the triple-bottom-line work. While the original intention of the project was to have the show act as a platform where young artists could gain professional experience, troupes were led by individuals, who not only determined who was hired but also under what working conditions. These troupe leaders also came with an established repertoire that they were reluctant to change or deviate from. This resulted in troupe leaders adding scenes that required additional performers who only appeared once or twice on stage, effectively lowering the overall income for each troupe member. In order to implement sustainability measures according to the CLA's values and to be more involved in the curation of the artistic content and narrative to correspond with the organization's mission, CLA started to test a radically different approach.

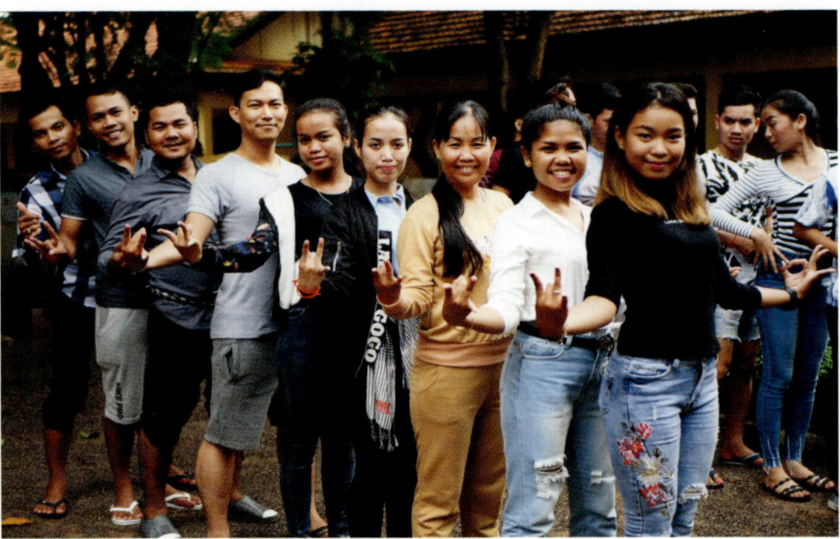

Figure 4. Dancers from the incubator troupe during a team-building workshop. (Photo © Cambodian Living Arts)

The new approach is called the *Artist Incubator Project*. The philosophy of the project is to create a quality performing arts show that celebrates and at the same time keeps the intangible cultural heritage of Cambodia alive while offering professional development opportunities for artists through a full-time two-year program designed to build foundations for future cultural entrepreneurship. The new model aims to create better working conditions as well as stable, fair, and safe employment. CLA is committed to offering a supportive environment where professions in the arts are given the same value as other professions. Entrusted with rights and embedded in a clear leadership structure, artists are expected to adhere to certain obligations, such as professional working ethics, regularly attending training and rehearsal, and valuing each other's differences. The objectives of the project do not stop at providing employment opportunities that generate income to reinvest into the artist profession. There is also a capacity building platform that nurtures the personal and professional growth needed to be well-rounded artists. Activities included in the incubation period featured training for both artistic and non-artistic aspects, such as teamwork, contract negotiation, creative workshops as well as artistic skills. The process itself reflected the values of the project. While these training modules have been developed and taught by CLA since 2014/15,[2] the incubator project allowed us to integrate these into the professional working and performing experience of the artists.

While in nationalist contexts, heritage and arts are often instrumentalized or in public settings often taken for granted, few people think about what it takes for artists to get to where they are and do what they do. The project's vision is that by equipping these artists with the tools to sustain themselves, the arts they practice can live on as well.

Cambodian Living Arts' Incubator Project objectives read as follows:

1. To empower the artists to fulfil their potentials through capacity building platform and within uplifting employment opportunities. With the tools provided, we hope that artists become responsible individuals, be the master of their own life and able to make a living out of the art career professionally.

2. To raise the quality and produce creative content that better tells the story of Cambodia, a story that touches the heart and enriches the experience of Cambodian arts and culture. Income generating from this will be the re-investment into CLA's dedicated programs.

---

2. Following the aforementioned research survey conducted in 2014, CLA designed a series of six one-day training modules targeted at addressing some of the most common skills gaps among artists, for example budgeting, marketing, professionalism, contract negotiation, and teamwork. These were offered as public trainings for two years, and in 2018 CLA worked with the Secondary School of Fine Arts in Phnom Penh to integrate these into their core curriculum.

3. To create a more fair and dynamic performing art market given access and chance to more artists with transparent audition process, generating emulation and inspiration.

Under the auspices of a hired artistic advisor, Prince Sisowath Tesso, who also assists Princess Buppha Devi in running the Royal Ballet of Cambodia, and a creative director, *neak kru* Voan Savay, who is one of the Royal Ballet's former star Apsara dancers, a selection committee was formed in November 2017. Joining hands with an independent artist and a professional trainer, the first public audition of this scale was organized in Cambodia, breaking with the tradition of individual-led troupes: from among the more than seventy applications, most of whom hailed from the national arts institutions, the Royal University of Fine Arts and the Secondary School of Fine Arts, thirty dancers and musicians were selected to become the first cohort of the Artist Incubator Project, including some former independent artists and graduates from non-governmental arts schools. From November 2017 until April 2018, a full audition, show conceptualization, artist training and harmonization, and performance production took place as the initial phase. However, the project had to face several unexpected challenges:

1. One of the underlying assumptions was that a fair and stable income would be a sufficient incentive for artists to fully commit to the project. In reality, however, many artists were still trying to juggle multiple gigs, resulting in missed rehearsals and training, and constant late appearance. Such disregard of working hours but also behavior such as cancelling appointments without notice and not being reachable had the project react in two ways. All artists received training how to be a professional, reliable artist and were encouraged to fully commit to this paid job with fixed working hours. Artists were also introduced to a sanction scheme that would apply if contracts were breached. Such methods were necessary to ensure the functioning and thus profitability of the undertaking but also ensured motivation among the hard-working, committed members of the incubator project.

2. Another challenge was strongly rooted in culture: leadership. Traditionally, Cambodian arts are transmitted orally and build on a strong and loyal master-student relationship. The project did not anticipate that a lot of artists would initially reject the idea of

working with new artistic directors. Despite the high status of *neak kru* Savay and Prince Tesso, they needed to impose their leadership to be respected and even listened to by the artists. According to the plan, a troupe leader from among the artists would emerge and could be trained after the set-up training phase with these experienced individuals. Interestingly, once the bond had been established, artists resisted the idea of a troupe leader that subsequently led to the re-hiring of the artistic director so that the performance quality would be maintained or improved.

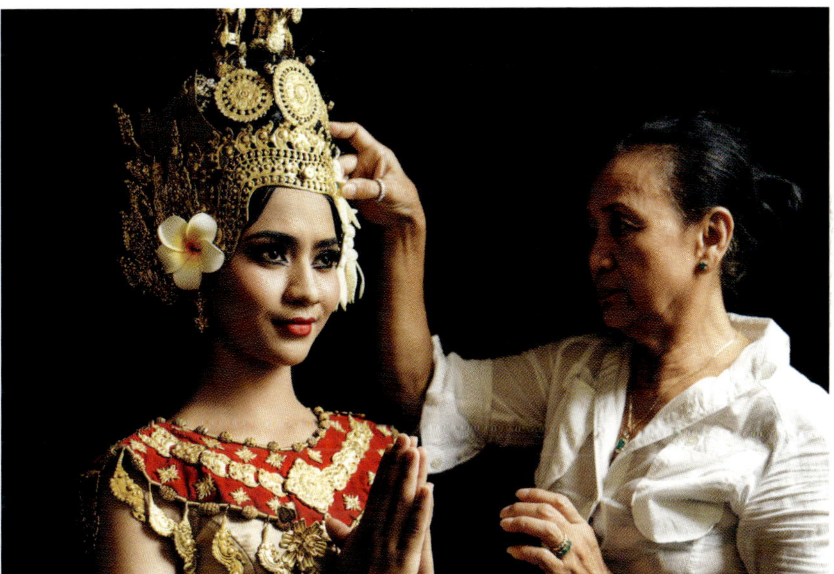

Figure 5. *Neak kru* Voan Savay adjusts a dancer's tiara. (Photo © Cambodian Living Arts / Sam Jam)

3. Another issue raised by the artistic director was the lack of consistency among the performers. Having been trained in different schools and provinces applying various different styles and techniques, artists were at very different levels when they first came together. It took the artistic director a lot of time to harmonize the troupe and adapt training agendas to fill significant gaps for them to be fully professional and coherent on stage. It was decided that the first of the two years of the incubator project would be dedicated to artistic development, featuring monthly workshops in stage presence, interpretation, expression, make-up, and other skills. The second year would be focused on professional development with the aim to build entrepreneurial capacity.

Despite all these difficulties, a one-hour show with thirty performers was produced that met artistic expectations of all the stakeholders involved. The program was still a selection of classical and folk dances, but now they were linked through an element of storytelling. It was important to celebrate the essence of each dance and also make it accessible to a non-specialist audience. Although there has been occasional criticism that the main audience of the production is tourists, CLA does not see this as a major problem. Cambodian culture is being shared in a respectful yet entertaining way to audiences who are eager to experience it. At the same time, CLA is adhering to its objectives of creating social, cultural, and economic value for the artists, Cambodia, and its intangible cultural heritage. Cambodians have consistently occupied 10 percent of the audiences, and there are plans to grow that proportion in the next three years. It is complementary to CLA's many other programs that do not seek to earn any income. Perception of the performance has been excellent as reviews on social media and the press show (e.g., Libson 2018, Say 2018).

Economically, the project has also produced positive first results. Thanks to this new model, production costs were lower compared to the previous year while still providing better salaries to the artists, making the show profitable already in its first year. Individual salaries per month rose to USD 400 for full-time performers and USD 250 for part-time performers, which is very competitive compared to the average income of performing artists and even laborers in the garment industry.

One of the main lessons learnt for CLA was not to be afraid to reform an existing model, not only internally, but also locally. With a current situation where most troupes are already formed, and a lot of professional dancers are part of the Department of Performing Arts (Ministry of Culture), it was very difficult to start a new troupe. Many viewed this as a threat to the way things were already operating, not wanting any structural change to keep their monopoly. With the current troupe, improvements in artistic skills, as well as positive changes in the attitude and professionalism of individual performers, have already been witnessed. There has also been a visible social impact as artists have become a lot more independent, and, for example, opened bank accounts for the first time to receive their own salaries. With the regular income provided, many artists are able to sustain their livelihood, support their studies, and bring additional income into the household.

Currently, the position of artistic director for this project is outsourced. However, in the long-run, the project aims to nurture its own well-trained people assuming roles such as choreographer, troupe leader, and artistic director. As the artist incubator project will be working with new troupes every two years, some individuals of the first batch are expected to take on leadership roles in the next incubator project, ensuring the transmission of experiences and institutional knowledge. CLA hopes that this project will become a model that is useful for other actors, and that it will be customized and replicated.

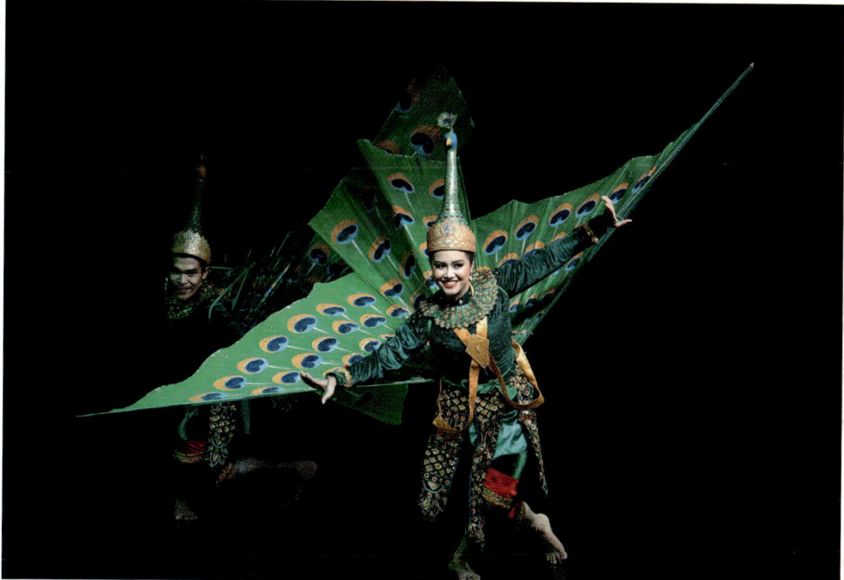

Figure 6. Peacock dance. (Photo © Cambodian Living Arts / Lamo)

As these projects and their evolution illustrate, entrepreneurial energies are essential for heritage preservation in CLA's model. It is important to complement the work of governments in safeguarding and promoting intangible cultural heritage by nurturing and releasing entrepreneurial energies from individuals and associations in the private and third sectors. Yet, such entrepreneurship strategies for heritage preservation must always be sustainable in nature and address not just the economic but also the social and cultural needs of the communities affected.

References

Bhattacharya, A. 2011. *From Art to Livelihood to Village Tourism*. UNWTO Seminar on Tourism Ethics for Asia and the Pacific: Responsible Tourism and its Socio-Economic Impact on Local Communities. Bali.

Cambodian Living Arts. 2014. *Training and Employment Needs Assessment on Cambodian Performing Arts Sector*. Phnom Penh.

Cusimano, E., Chhay, C. and Coupez, P. 2014. *UNESCO Culture for Development Indicators: Cambodia's Technical Report*. Paris.

Grant, C. 2016. "Socio-economic concerns of young musicians of traditional genres in Cambodia: implications for music sustainability." in *Ethnomusicology Forum*, Volume 25, 3: 306–25.

Grant, C. 2017. "Social shifts and viable musical futures: The case of Cambodian smot." In *Ethnomusicology: A Contemporary Reader*, Vol. II, pp. 97–110. London.

International Labor Organization. 2014. *Wages and working hours in the textiles, clothing, leather and footwear industries: Issues paper for discussion at the Global Dialogue Forum on Wages and Working Hours in the Textiles, Clothing, Leather and Footwear Industries.* 23–25 September. Geneva.

Isar, Y. R. ed. 2013. Creative economy report 2013: Widening local development pathways. Third and special edition, United Nations Development Program; United Nations Educational, Scientific and Cultural Organization. New York.

Leung, I. S. 2009. *Future Forward: Understanding the Support Structure for Traditional Performing Arts in Penang, Malaysia A research project of Reka Art Space 2009*. Kuala Lumpur.

Libson, Q. 2018. "Bringing Khmer dance down to earth. How a new incubator program is helping classical dancers with the practical side of their craft." *Phnom Penh Post*, 13 April, available at: www.phnompenhpost.com/post-life-arts-culture/bringing-khmer-dance-down-earth, accessed 27 November 2018.

McCormick, P. 2012. *Never Fall Down*. New York.

Rudgard, F. and Prim, P. 2018. "Negotiating cultural industries: a case study from Cambodia." In L. Lim and H. Lee, ed., *Routledge Handbook of Cultural and Creative Industries in Asia*, London.

Say, T. 2018. "Khmer ballet star uses traditional motifs to create new dance performance." *Khmer Times*, April 13, available at: www.khmertimeskh.com/50302209/khmer-ballet-star-uses-traditional-motifs-to-create-new-dance-performance/, accessed 27 November 2018.

UNESCO Office in Phnom Penh. 2013. "Nomination of 17 Masters of Living Human Treasures." February 13. Phnom Penh, available at: www.unesco.org/new/en/phnompenh/about-this-office/single-view/news/nomination_of_17_masters_of_living_human_treasures/, accessed 27 November 2018.

Participation in Conservation: An Example from India

Gour Mohan Kapur

> "The Heritage of the Past is the Seed that Brings Forth the Harvest of the Future." Inscription on the base of the Statue of "Heritage" at the US National Archives Building, Constitution Avenue, Washington.

The discovery in the 1920s of the Mohenjo Daro and Harappan sites from the third millennium BCE brought to light the hidden treasures of the Indus Valley civilization. But the local population was not particularly involved in this exercise, and did not show great enthusiasm about having one of the great archaeological wonders of the world nearby. Such was the indifference to the value of this priceless heritage that civil contractors removed bricks for constructing railway quarters in the vicinity and for use as ballast while laying railway tracks nearby. Of course it speaks volumes for the brick making technology which our ancestors had.

Many people in India have many other priorities in their lives, such as hunger, health, habitation, education, and employment, before they can consider looking after their heritage and culture. This is reality and must be accepted. However, even in the section of the population which should be expected to be more concerned with these issues, the percentage of concerned citizens is rather low. Yet the role of an active citizenry is vital for heritage protection. This chapter describes an example from India: the Indian National Trust for Art and Cultural Heritage (INTACH). The chapter first traces the history of heritage conservation in India from the colonial era through to the influence of UNESCO. It then turns to the record of legislation on heritage in independent India, showing that the legislation has added local elements to the colonial legacy, but that the implementation has been inadequate in the face of threats, especially from urban development and tourism. The final section presents INTACH's work in Calcutta (Kolkata since 2001), and the conclusion emphasizes the importance of participation in the conservation of heritage.

HISTORY OF HERITAGE CONSERVATION IN INDIA

The colonial legacy

Western concepts of preservation and conservation were introduced by the British, such as the Indologist Sir William Jones who founded the Asiatic Society, James Prinsep, and Alexander Cunningham who deciphered ancient Indian scripts leading to a deeper understanding of Indian culture, and Lord Curzon (Viceroy of India 1899–1905) who was instrumental in setting up the Archaeological Survey of India under John Marshall. Many Indian luminaries were also involved.

Heritage legislation was introduced during the colonial period. It is not surprising that the definition of heritage and its categories were influenced by the colonial experience and subsequently guided by international charters. Most of the definitions equated heritage with the built heritage or artefacts from the past. Material aspects were paramount in defining heritage. Intangible aspects were rarely incorporated. The colonial definition, as incorporated in the law, also reflected the perception that heritage had to be old or ancient. Accordingly, heritage places and objects were equated with monuments, relics, or antiques. Most colonized nations followed this trend even after they achieved independence. It is only later that the perceptions, lifestyles and cultures of the indigenous populations have to some extent been legally recognized. Most Western-driven legislation still in use in the post-colonial era takes little cognizance of community interests, aspirations, and belief systems which were the customary laws and practices of indigenous communities, especially for the protection of heritage places such as sacred groves, streams, rivers, shrines, temples, tombs, palaces, and mausoleums. The concepts of authenticity and integrity in the Indian context take on a different connotation when applied to cultural heritage and must accommodate the form, function, tradition, and techniques associated with the cultural landscape or monument.

The majority of India's architectural heritage and sites are unprotected. Many unprotected heritage sites are still in use, and the manner in which they continue to be kept in use represents the living heritage of India. This heritage is manifest in both tangible and intangible forms and, in its diversity, defines the composite culture of the country. Beyond its role as a historic document, this unprotected heritage embodies values of enduring relevance to contemporary Indian society, thus making it worthy of conservation.

This living heritage also has a symbiotic relationships with the natural environment within which it originally evolved. Understanding this interdependent ecological network and conserving it can make a significant contribution to improving the quality of the environment.

The UNESCO era

Conservation in India is heir not only to Western conservation theories and principles introduced through colonialism and later by the adoption of guidelines formulated by UNESCO, ICOMOS and international funding agencies, but also to pre-existing indigenous knowledge systems and skills of building. While the Western ideology of conservation advocates minimal intervention, India's indigenous traditions favor the opposite.

UNESCO, especially with its World Heritage program, has certainly brought about a resurgence in the heritage conservation and awareness movement.

While we have emulated and adopted the scorching pace of economic growth of developed countries of the West in the name of liberalization and globalization, we have unfortunately not emulated the environmental and heritage conservation policies of the West in practice and implementation. India is rich in heritage, both tangible and intangible. In fact, it is possible that we suffer from a "problem of plenty," fostering neglect and apathy. While in the West it is said a new museum comes up every fortnight, in India a heritage building is demolished in the same period, mainly in the large cities like Kolkata and Mumbai.

The threats

There has been a constant conflict between heritage protection and large-scale infrastructure projects in India. Also, there is considerable impact on cultural heritage at the local level through urban development. Old parts of major cities are disappearing and being replaced by modern construction which destroys heritage sites. Pressure from political interests, developers, and the real estate lobbies also leads to destruction of heritage. Entire habitats and villages go under water through the construction of dams and reservoirs. Because of the sheer size of the country, it is extremely difficult to police India's vast and diverse heritage. But, unless and until the central and state governments are willing to enforce the existing heritage protection laws, in the face of lobbying and corruption, heritage will remain at risk. The community can play a major role in assisting the government in its endeavor provided it is made aware and given necessary education of the importance of conservation and preservation. It may take time but it is absolutely imperative that the community is also involved in safeguarding heritage. They are the ones who will ultimately be the protectors at the local level.

Tourism is a double-edged sword. If not properly managed and controlled, it can cause more damage than gain. Tourist flows that exceed the carrying capacity of a site can cause irreparable harm. The central square of a tourist town all too easily changes from a place for daily life to a tourist market, causing conflicts between the ordinary life of the locals and needs of mass tourism. Originality and traditional ways of life disappear because the town becomes a tourist attraction. Many cities in India have already lost their cultural identities because of this.

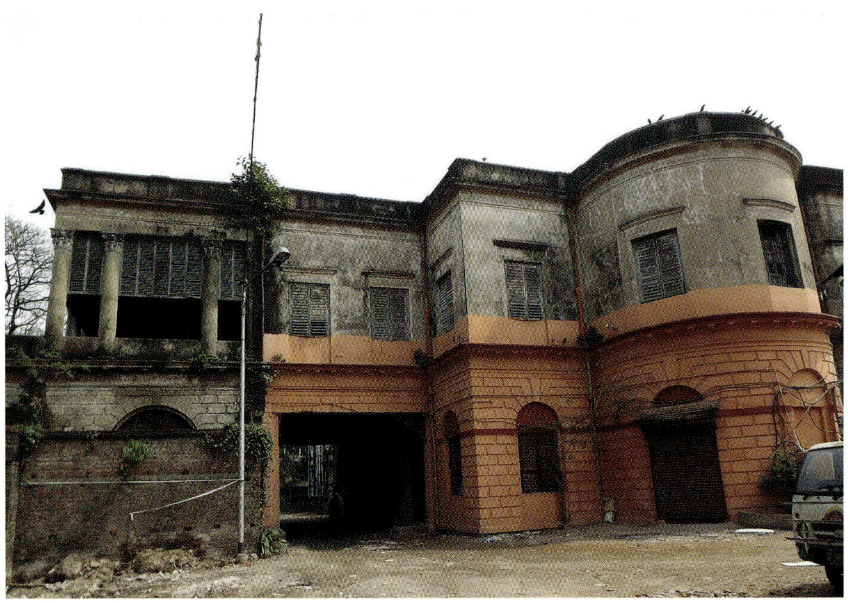

Figure 1. Belgachia Villa; Indo-Italian, almost in ruins.

HERITAGE LEGISLATION IN INDEPENDENT INDIA

Do we in India really value our heritage?

The answer to this is not a simple yes or no. While both the government and public are definitely becoming more aware of the need to conserve heritage, be it built heritage like monuments and buildings, environment, material heritage like art and artefacts as well as intangible heritage like culture and traditions, there is a sizeable part of the population whose priorities are different. They need to be sensitized to the fact that the heritage we speak about belongs to them and hence they need to protect what is rightfully theirs. Organizations like INTACH are playing a very important role in not only creating this awareness but also documenting both tangible and intangible heritage. While taking pride in the past is certainly a factor in this awareness, there is also the realization that there is great value in heritage which can be an engine for economic growth of the nation as a whole. This is primarily why it has become increasingly important to preserve heritage.

However, the unprotected built heritage in India is threatened by many factors including environmental pressures, uncontrolled urban development, communal conflicts, poverty, lack of political will, low levels of funding, inadequate expertise and equipment, and lack of inventories and documentation. Of course the conflict between development and conservation remains an important factor in this threat, especially since the clear demarcation of conservation areas is lacking. Heritage impact assessments for building activity in prohibited/protected zones exist for only centrally protected monuments. There is no concept of cultural impact assessment.

The question of whose responsibility it is to look after heritage remains a grey area. For many, heritage is somebody else's problem, somebody else's responsibility. They think it is the government's job to look after heritage, and their job is to look after themselves and their immediate future. This is despite the fact that the Constitution had addressed this issue (see below). Of course, heritage is an area where a large number of disciplines are involved, including politics, administration, archaeology, conservation, architecture, environment, planning, anthropology, ethnography, sociology, economy, and law. Most importantly, the "common man" is involved and has a say. India does have a well-developed legal and judicial system and court interventions have often been instrumental in righting wrongs brought to light by public interest litigation launched by conservation activists. But the implementation down the line by those empowered to protect heritage leaves a lot to be desired. Multiple government institutions and departments in areas such as education, tourism, information and cultural affairs have inadequate resources, both financial and human, and do not work as a team, but pull in different directions leaving heritage unprotected or poorly protected.

The Indian Constitution

At the conclusion of *Making of India's Constitution*, retired Supreme Court of India Justice Hans Raj Khanna wrote:

> If the Indian constitution is our heritage bequeathed to us by our founding fathers, no less are we, the people of India, the trustees and custodians of the values which pulsate within its provisions! A constitution is not a parchment of paper, it is a way of life and has to be lived up to.

The founding fathers of the country recognized the importance of preserving India's rich and diverse heritage, which is why this aspect was enshrined in the Indian Constitution promulgated on January 26, 1950. Among other duties for Indian citizens, Section 51A lays down the following:

> To value and preserve the rich heritage of our composite culture;
>
> To protect and improve the natural environment including forests, lakes, rivers and wildlife, and to have compassion for living creatures.

While the founding fathers of the nation had taken into consideration the richness and diversity of our culture, over the years in spite of a plethora of laws in place, we have not done justice to our duties as citizens because of various factors which are discussed in the following paragraphs.

Heritage legislation in India

Why do we need legislation to protect what belongs to us? We do not require laws to protect and preserve our personal possessions but the concept of collective ownership for something such as heritage is still alien to us, hence the need for legislation.

Without legislation there can be no preservation. Legislation is the cheapest and most cost-effective method of heritage protection. There is a lot of excitement when a palace, church or great building in saved and restored, but we forget the larger picture which is that restoration preserves only a few sites at tremendous cost and effort. But what happens to the thousands of other historic sites? They are totally unprotected and, in the absence of legislation, subject to destruction. Legislation cannot restore a building without cost. But it can do much more: it can stop the bulldozer. Legislation is equally applicable for the protection of tangible as well as intangible heritage.

Heritage legislation in India has drawn considerably from the colonial and Western thought on this subject. Many adaptations have been carried out keeping local conditions in mind.[1]

The Ancient Monuments and Archaeological Sites and Remains Act, 1958, has recently been amended in 2010 with strict rules in place for building and renovation activity in the vicinity of protected monuments. The Act states that no building activity is allowed in the "prohibited zone" within 100 meters from the notified limits of the monument. The next 2000 meters beyond this zone is the "regulated area," where some building, repair, and restoration activity is allowed with permission from the competent authority which consults with the National Monuments Authority for their expert opinion.

As India has a federal structure, the laws pertaining to heritage conservation are a state subject and have to be enacted at a local level. In spite of repeated requests by the central government and civil rights activists, not many states have enacted heritage protection rules. Cities such as New Delhi, Hyderabad, Mumbai, Jammu and Kashmir, and Kochi are among the few where protection acts are in place in various degrees. The Calcutta experience has been more active because the city has a legacy of colonial architecture which the local population values quite passionately.

India is a vast country with heritage at every corner. It is extremely difficult for the government to keep an eye on all of it. Hence, the involvement of local people in the conservation and protection of heritage is of paramount importance.

INTACH'S ROLE IN HERITAGE AWARENESS CREATION

To invite citizens to become part of a nationwide movement for heritage conservation, in 1984 the Government of India founded the Indian

1. Vastu shastra (vāstu *śāstra*) is a traditional system of architecture which literally translates to "science of architecture." These are texts that describe principles of design, layout, measurement, ground preparation, space arrangement, and spatial geometry. They incorporate traditional Hindu and in some cases Buddhist beliefs. The designs are intended to integrate architecture with nature, the relative functions of various parts of the structure, and ancient beliefs utilizing geometric patterns (*yantra*), symmetry, and directional alignments. Vastu-Vidya (literally, knowledge of dwelling) is a collection of ideas and concepts for the organization of space and form within a building or collection of buildings. Ancient Vastu shastra has principles for the design of temples, houses, towns, cities, gardens, roads, water works, shops and other public areas. During the colonial period, this knowledge was ignored. Today some believe it to be mere superstition.

National Trust for Art and Cultural Heritage (INTACH) as an autonomous organization with its own Memorandum and Articles of Association.[2] Government provided the initial funds, and occasional subventions, while further funds are raised by donations as well as through conservation and restoration projects on built and environmental heritage. The vision was to create a membership organization to stimulate and spearhead heritage awareness and conservation in India. An advertisement was issued in all national daily newspapers, reading as follows:

> WANTED: AN ARMY OF CONSCIENCE-KEEPERS:
>
> This Indian National Trust for Art and Cultural Heritage (INTACH) invites you as an Indian to join the fight for conserving India's Heritage. You don't have to be an archaeologist or a historian to join INTACH. You just have to care enough for India. Today more than ever, there is an urgent need for action—to pool our resources, to voice our concern and if necessary, to fight to preserve India's heritage.
>
> A HERITAGE ONCE LOST IS LOST FOREVER
>
> In the past one hundred years, more historic monuments have been destroyed, more artefacts stolen, more oral traditions lost forever than in all the years our civilization has been in existence.
>
> Somehow, we seem to have lost the reverence our ancestors had for all that nature and man have created. We seem no longer to care and our indifference has already begun to take its toll.
>
> Every day, somewhere in the country a historic building is pulled down in the name of progress. Others are damaged in flagrant vandalism or allowed to decay and fall.

2. INTACH's mission is defined as follows: Sensitize the public about the pluralistic cultural legacy of India. Instill a sense of social responsibility towards preserving India's common heritage. Protect and preserve India's living, built, and natural heritage by undertaking necessary actions and measures. Document unprotected buildings of archaeological, architectural, historic and aesthetic significance, as well as the cultural resources, as this is the first step towards formulating conservation plans. Develop heritage policies and regulations, and make legal interventions to protect India's heritage when necessary. Provide expertise in the field of conservation, restoration and preservation of specific works of art; and encourage capacity-building by developing skills through training programmes. Undertake emergency response measures during natural or man-made disasters and support the local administration whenever heritage is threatened. Foster collaborations, Memoranda of Understanding (MoU) and partnerships with government and other national and international agencies. Generate sponsorships for conservation and educational projects. See www.intach.org/about-mission.php

Invaluable works of art and manuscripts are dumped in godowns, without documentation or record. No one even knows how many are lost, stolen or damaged beyond repair. Priceless manuscripts are sold, unknowingly to *kabaddi wallas*, ancient wooden carvings are broken down and burnt as firewood.

Commercialization and mass production have begun to erode the oral tradition and craft skills.

At this rate our children may never be able to experience the richness and wonder of our heritage.

You as citizen of India have a right to put a stop to this senseless destruction. You have right to voice your concern. And a responsibility to protect your environment—and your heritage—whether it is preserving the character, beauty and greenery of your locality or conveying the glory of the Taj Mahal.

INTACH: FIGHTING TO PRESERVE WHAT IS RIGHTFULLY OURS

INTACH is committed to the cause of preserving India's heritage.

By creating a greater awareness of the growing threat to our heritage, we hope to awaken a sense of responsibility to arouse public opinion against destruction, to pressurize the government to take action.

India currently prides itself in being one of the fastest growing economies in the world which is the result of the path of liberalization and globalization which the country is following in the footsteps of the rest of the world. It is not my intention to debate these policies even when these cause grave anxieties . It is however, legitimate to note with concern the impact of the above two trends on heritage and environmental policies and regulations.

This has been our contribution to involve citizens to be volunteers for the protection and preservation of the country's heritage. We have made a difference by bringing heritage issues to the forefront all over the country but we need to have many more organizations to participate in this endeavor.

INTACH is a voluntary organization which currently has over two hundred chapters across the country and approximately ten thousand members. The central office in New Delhi is managed by an elected board of governors, which includes some ex-officio government officials. The day-to-day running is in the hands of the member secretary and the heads of the various departments for Architectural Heritage, Material Heritage, Natural Heritage, and Intangible Cultural Heritage as well as a Heritage Education and Communication Service to guide the chapters and members. Essentially, it is a membership organization driven by the enthusiasm and passion of the members.

CALCUTTA, A CASE STUDY

In 1690, Job Charnock, agent of the East India Company, set foot on the "insalubrious mud flats" on the banks of the Hooghly river. Calcutta (nowadays Kolkata) grew to become the "second city in the British empire." The British demonstrated their power and might through the grandeur of their edifices. Indians who amassed fortunes in trade followed suit. This led to a vast inventory of palatial mansions and commercial buildings giving the city another epithet, the City of Palaces. Philip Davies, author of several books on architecture and architectural history, including *Splendours of the Raj: British Architecture in India, 1660–1947*, argued that the city's extraordinary architectural heritage was a priceless economic, social, cultural, and environmental asset, which rival cities had lost. However, Davies continued, this heritage is a neglected asset, which is crumbling; much has been lost or blighted by poor planning a strategic conservation plan is urgently needed. Unless the city capitalizes on its unique assets, it faces losing out to other cities in India and Asia in the race for prosperity.

However, the city suffered decay and decrepitude due to various reasons, mainly political, including the shifting of the capital to New Delhi in 1911, the partition of the country, and war with Pakistan. When the state of West Bengal, in which Kolkata lies, came under Leftist rule from 1967 onwards, the resulting flight of capital from the city was a saving grace as far as the built heritage of the city was concerned. There was less pressure to redevelop the city center, unlike Mumbai and Bangalore which exploded with high rise construction and chaotic traffic. At the same time, however, West Bengal's weak economy meant lower incomes and fewer resources for maintenance.

Mumbai took the lead in protection of built heritage by integrating laws in its Development Control rules in 1995. This was followed by Kolkata which, under the Outline Development Plan of the Kolkata Metropolitan Development Authority, listed seventy-two buildings as having heritage value. Some of the buildings listed showing the variety and grandeur of the built heritage in the city were: Sovabazar Rajbari, one of the oldest mansions of North Kolkata; Belvedere House, which was at one time the Viceroy's residence and now houses the National Library; Jorasanko Thakur Bari; the Nizam's Palace; Old Silver Mint; Military Secretariat; Currency Building; Metropolitan Building; Grand Hotel; and Calcutta Club. This was an arbitrary list and many buildings worthy of listing were not included. This was by a notification on October 6, 1996 by the Calcutta Municipal Corporation.

In 1997, the West Bengal Legislature passed the Calcutta Municipal Corporation (Amendment) Act 1997 (CMC Amendment Act), which included among its aims: "Preservation and conservation of buildings of historical and architectural importance in Calcutta" and contained a separate chapter (XIIIa) on "Preservation and Conservation of Heritage Buildings." Some of the Act's key points are as follows:

> As indicated by its title, instead of the narrow concept of 'historical buildings' it adopted the wider, current concepts of 'Heritage Building" which was defined as being "one or more premises" requiring "preservation and conservation for historical architectural, environmental or ecological purpose."
>
> It provided for the appointment of a Heritage Conservation Committee (HCC), to be appointed by the Mayor-in-Council, which would include as members an eminent architect, an artist, an environmentalist and a historian. The composition of the committee is laid down in the Act whereas in many other states it has been laid down in the regulations framed under the Act, allowing some flexibility in the composition, which is absent in the case of the Calcutta Act.
>
> Section 425A places a duty on the owner or occupier of any heritage building to "maintain, preserve and conserve it," and also imposes restrictions on change in use of heritage buildings. But is does not mention anything about who will pay for the upkeep. This aroused a great deal of opposition from property owners and is a great disincentive to include buildings on the heritage list.
>
> Another clause which caused distress was Section 425B which stipulated that during the period that a building is being considered for declaration as a heritage building, no transfer of the building by way of sale, lease or mortgage will be permitted without the prior approval of the Municipal Commissioner.

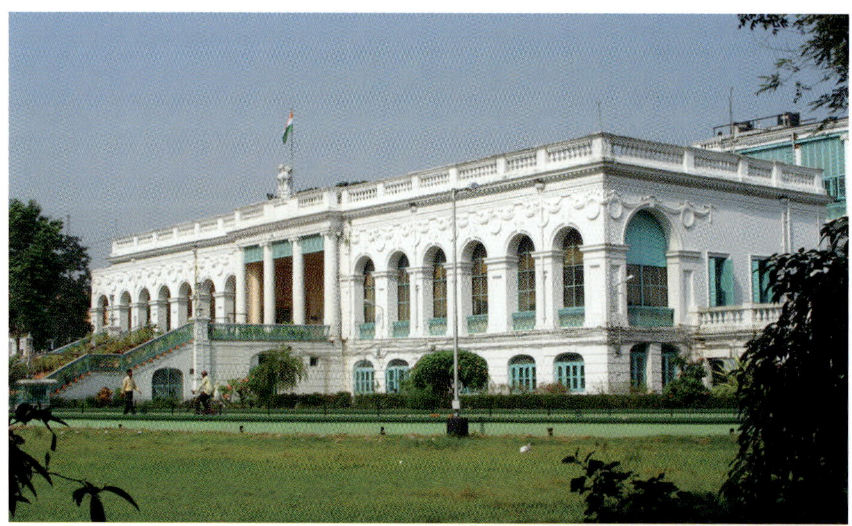

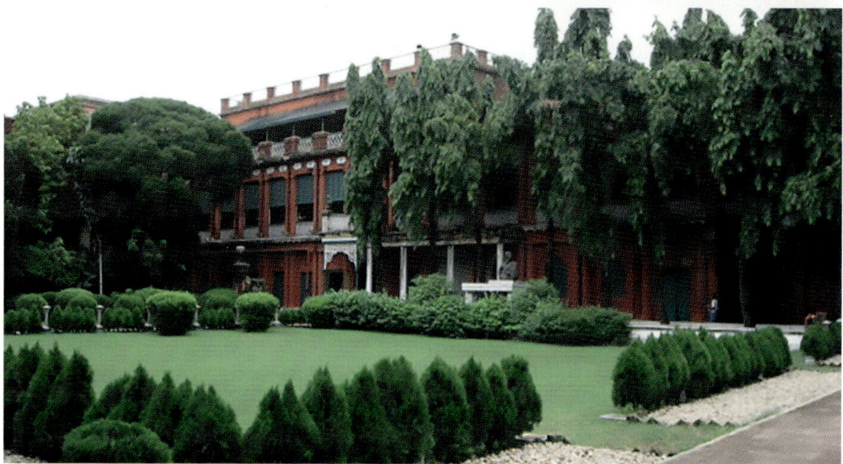

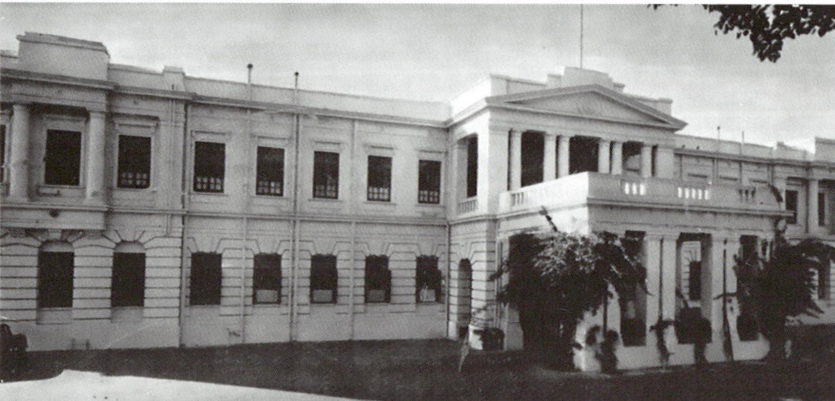

Figure 2. A sample of Kolkata's heritage. (left from top) Belvedere House; Jorasanko Thakur Bari; Calcutta Club; (right from top); Old Silver Mint; Metropolitan Building; Sovabazar Rajbari.

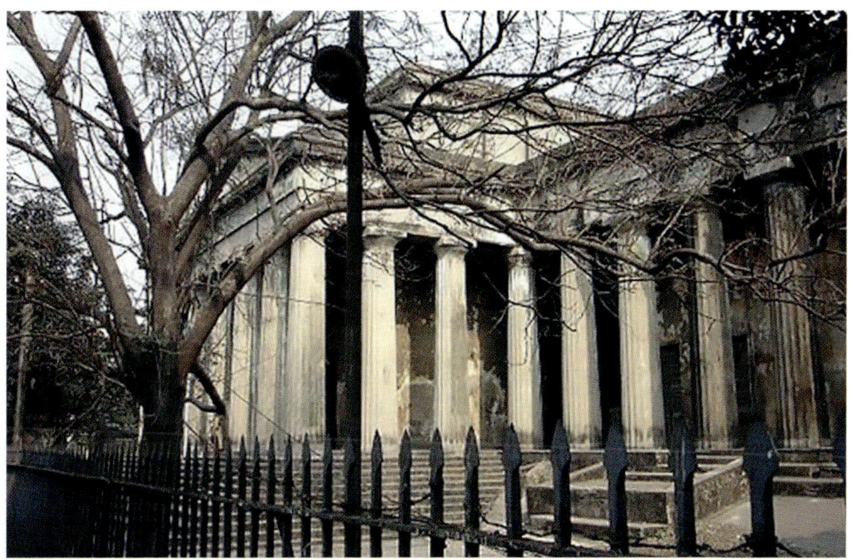

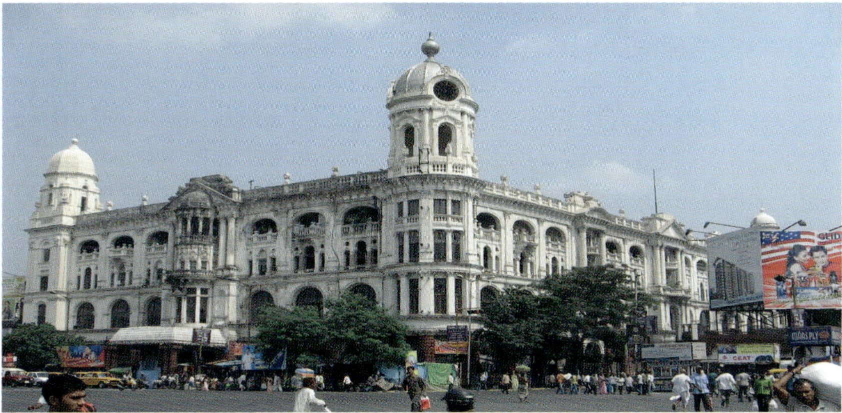

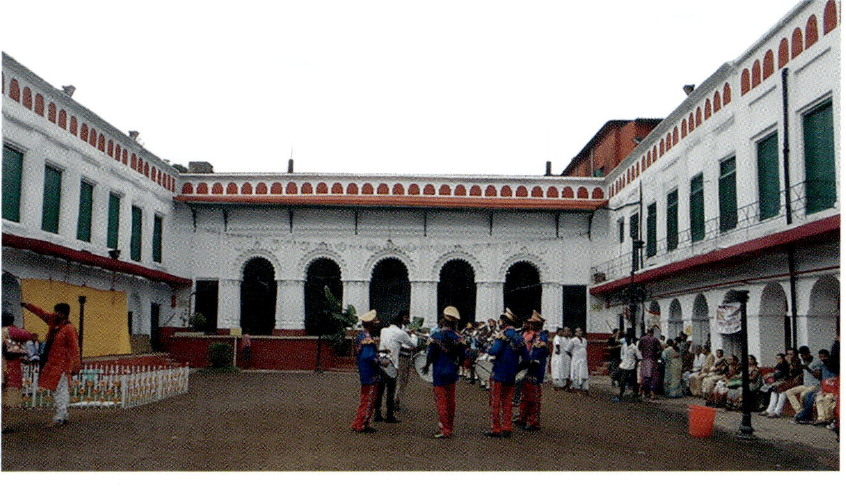

Incentives such as waiver of property taxes under certain terms and conditions, provision of Transfer of Development Rights (TDR), a heritable and transferable right are also part of the provisions of the Act but have been granted very sparingly or not at all.

Section 425 O runs: "If the Corporation decides that any heritage building has ceased to be of public interest or has lost its importance for any reason whatsoever, it may, with the approval of the State Government, declare that such heritage building has ceased to be a heritage building for the purposes of this act." This clause is the most damaging as far as heritage protection is concerned as it gives the municipality unbridled powers to delist heritage buildings and allow their demolition.

Barun De Committee:

In 1997 an Expert Committee on Heritage Buildings was constituted by the West Bengal Government under the chairmanship of Professor Barun De, a well-known historian, and tasked to review the various lists of heritage buildings available with the KMC. The committee included various eminent experts as well as representatives from INTACH. The Committee had several broad propositions which were part of the principles that guided their initial work, including the following:

> The heritage embraced by the people of West Bengal is a composite of diversities of various secular, religious, political and public institutional traditions going back in Calcutta's case for more than 300 years. It is necessary to retain this variety in a metropolis of national importance, which was the capital of British India from 1772 to 1911 and which today is no less important than New Delhi.
>
> Onslaughts of time and nature have affected a certain decay in the maintenance of the architectural remains of the older traditions. Ravages of a damp climate, sheer neglect of historical monuments, lack of incentives by relaxation of taxation and municipal rates for old buildings, particularly those built before the 20th century, and also a certain vulgarization of building styles planted among the older milieu and in historical precincts have all contributed to a desolation of Calcutta's architectural environments. (*Expert Committee*)

One of the Committee's recommendations was that "to maintain the character of Calcutta as a heritage city and as the capital of British India for more than 100 years, in its pristine historical and aesthetic appearance it will be necessary also to identify the heritage of architectural styles, old colonial Bungalow style, Classic, Romanesque, Neo Gothic and even Indian Baroque and Rococo and New-Classic etc."

The committee paid a special tribute to INTACH by saying that "A very rich and painstaking enlistment by INTACH in four volumes has been submitted to the committee and shows extensive documentation and field work. The committee, drawing heavily from INTACH's list, published a list of about 1300 heritage sites."

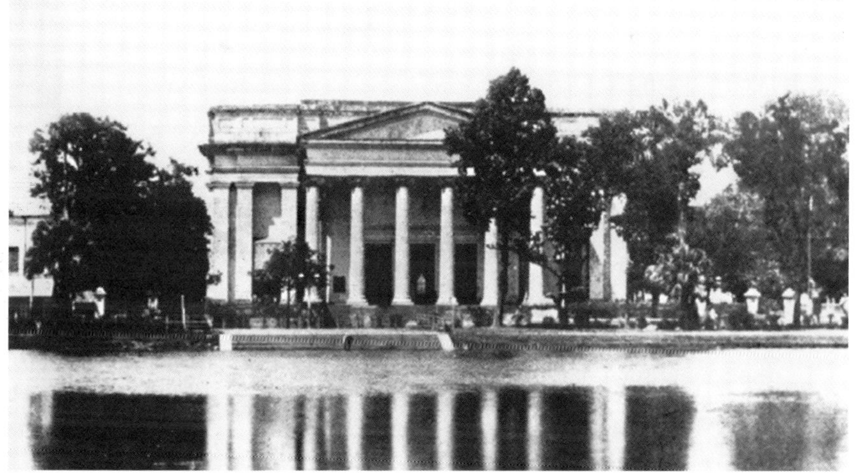

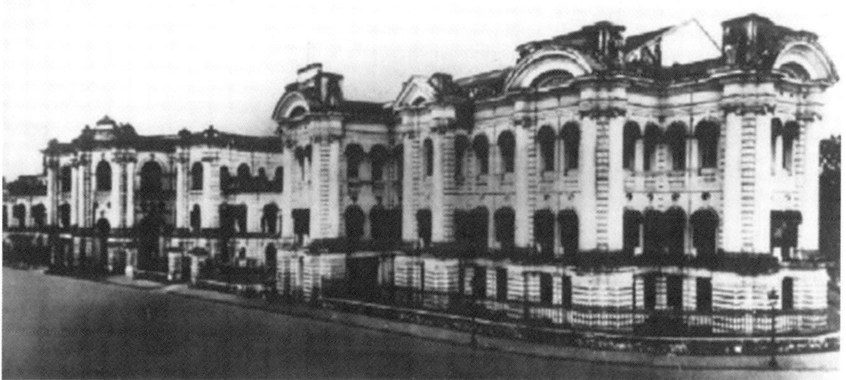

Figure 3. Demolished examples: (top) Senate Hall of Calcutta University; (bottom) State Bank of India.

Prior to the legislation some of Kolkata's built heritage had already been demolished, including the Senate Hall of Calcutta University, State Bank of India, and Bengal Club.

Even with legislation in force, there has been considerable breach of the law for conservation of built heritage, due mainly to:

> Lack of rules for providing incentives for listed heritage building owners though the law provides for the same. Many owners are unable to maintain their buildings because they lack finances and are lured by real estate developers who "manage the environment" and get the listed buildings delisted.
>
> If incentives such as waiver of property taxes, transfer of development rights, relaxation of tenancy laws for heritage buildings and permitting change of use, it would help to sustain such buildings.
>
> Political pressures, where a blind eye is turned towards demolition for political gains.
>
> Pressures of the real estate lobby.
>
> Rigid rent control laws which make it uneconomic for owners to maintain their buildings as they continue to get rents which are much lower than the market value leaving them with no surplus to even pay their property taxes leave alone maintain their buildings.

INTACH facilitated the legislation by providing the legislators with a draft of the legislation based on the Mumbai model, and a partial inventory of some 1,300 heritage sites in four volumes, compiled mainly by students and faculty from a local university.

The enforcement of the law will always be difficult, because of economic and political pressures, as illustrated by the case of the Episcopal Palace.

5B Russel Street was the residence of the first bishop of Calcutta. It was declared a heritage building by the Kolkata Municipal Corporation in February 2009, but was delisted in the following October without assigning any reason. INTACH filed a Public Interest Litigation to have the building relisted as the historicity or the architectural merit could not have changed in these six months. The High Court of Calcutta agreed with our view and directed the KMC to relist the building.

The variety of architectural styles to be seen in the city is fascinating. Calcutta has been the crucible of culture of the nation, both tangible and intangible. Theater, music, dance and other performing arts as well as literature, fine arts, poetry, and filmmaking have flourished in the city. With the weak economy, there was a considerable loss of this cultural tradition but the city has proved capable of resurrecting itself and reclaiming its former glory. This intangible culture is hence alive and kicking. The non-colonial built heritage has also been looked after, especially religious heritage such as temples and mosques as well as educational institutions. Overall, the spirit of heritage conservation has been revived over the years.

CONCLUSION

The Indian laws for the conservation and protection of tangible and intangible heritage, though founded on Western conservation philosophy, have over the years been adapted through local ideas to render them amply suitable for taking care of heritage.

It is implementation which is lacking for many reasons: lack of political will, insensitive bureaucracy, development pressures, real estate lobbying, lack of sufficient knowledge of value of cultural assets, lack of awareness among a large section of the population, and sheer apathy among others. The size of the country, the large number of heritage sites and their remote locations, and the conflict between development and conservation remain a challenge with respect to tangible heritage.

Intangible heritage has unfortunately remained outside the purview of most legislation which is a cause for concern. Legislation has failed to appreciate value systems that should form the basis of legislation. Also, most heritage legislation is concerned with monumental heritage and neglects vernacular architecture as well as intangible heritage.

Civil society has acted as a watchdog and played an important role in filling gaps in legal enforcement by inviting judicial intervention. Pressure from this group of concerned citizens has brought about many of the changes to improve enforcement.

Creating awareness at the grassroots level and empowering of local communities is very important for the protection of heritage. Not only creating community involvement, but also recognizing and respecting the living nature of the heritage is also important for its protection and survival.

Policing of a country as vast as India with heritage at every remote corner, is not possible by the government alone. It has to be a citizens' movement without which conservation and protection will be difficult. Here again, while the government has a role to play, it is organizations such as INTACH which can make a difference. The law can be made to work for heritage if it becomes a people's movement which will ensure that the government acts on the laws which are in place.

The Law can be made to work for heritage, if: suitable legislation is passed, taking into account the value systems of society at large; if there exists political and bureaucratic will to implement the law; and if awareness of the importance of heritage conservation and protection is conveyed to the masses.

This is where organizations such as INTACH can create awareness of the importance of heritage to the general population and convey to them that heritage belongs to them and its protection requires their help, including putting pressure on authorities to pass suitable legislation and ensure its enforcement. Due to various other priorities in people's lives, heritage tends to take a back seat and some top-down pressure is required.

Community concerns must be addressed and the community must become involved in the conservation and protection process. Suitable incentives and economic benefits are needed for the owners and protectors of the heritage. Pride in their heritage needs to be aroused in the community by rewarding people's efforts in conservation of tangible as well as intangible heritage.

References

Davies, Philip. 1985. *Splendours of the Raj: British Architecture in India, 1660–1947*. London: John Murray.

Expert Committee on Heritage Buildings, established by Government of West Bengal resolution No. 5584-UD/O/M?SB/S-22/96 dated 6 October 1997, final report submitted on 2 November 1998 (Barun De Committee).

INTACH. 2018. *State of Built Heritage in India*.

INTACH website: www.intach.org/

Khanna, Hans Raj. 1981. *Making of India's Constitution*. Lucknow: Eastern Book Co.

Preserving Cultural Heritage as a Private Enterprise: Lao Textiles

Veomanee Douangdala and Joanna Smith

This chapter describes how Ock Pop Tok, a social enterprise based in Luang Prabang, Lao People's Democratic Republic (Lao PDR), is preserving traditional Lao textile production methods through women-led entrepreneurship and fair-trade principles. It explores the role ethical business practices can play to promote cultural industries and suggests how government and civil society can facilitate mutually beneficial engagement between artisans and entrepreneurs to support positive outcomes for heritage preservation.

Ock Pop Tok (meaning "east meets west") was established in 2000 by the two of us: a Laotian, Veomanee (Veo) Douangdala; and an English woman, Joanna (Jo) Smith. Our mission was to elevate the profile of Lao textiles and artisans, increase producers' income, and facilitate creative and educational collaboration among Lao people and the international community. The idea was "to bring people together through textiles to share knowledge and ideas." This commitment to collaboration bridges geographic and cultural boundaries, creating textile designs that combine Lao traditions and innovation.

Ock Pop Tok has grown from a small shop selling only a few designs to becoming one of the most important textile and artisanal institutions in Laos and Southeast Asia. On the principles of fair trade and sustainable business practices, Ock Pop Tok was a pioneering social business and ethical fashion in Laos well before these concepts were globally widespread. Ock Pop Tok is committed to preserving and promoting Lao textiles and their weavers' creative energy.

The partnership between the two of us dates from 1999 when Jo Smith was on an EU-funded assignment to photograph development projects in North Laos, and Veo Douangdala was carving out her own unique niche and making a name for herself among the Lao artisan community. Coming from a family rich in textile and artisanal roots, Veo was constantly challenging old ways and methods. She was designing unique *sinh* (traditional Lao skirts) and patterns that differentiated her from her peers.

While Veo Douangdala was busy trailblazing a new path for Lao textiles, Jo Smith was becoming increasingly enamored with the intricate woven textiles and the women who produced them. Veo Douangdala's creativity attracted Smith like a magnet as she was looking for like-minded artists with whom to collaborate. We had a shared commitment to preserving and promoting these textiles and a similar creative energy. Seizing the opportunity when Veo Douangdala asked Jo Smith if she wanted to work together on a permanent basis, it turned out that was her dream too!

Based on the philosophy "one can discover Lao through its textiles," Ock Pop Tok runs several initiatives to promote greater appreciation of weaving traditions. First, its Living Crafts Centre operates principally as a place to learn about Lao textiles, such as their function, traditions, fabrication, and place in society. Second, the Village Weaver Projects help to reinvigorate declining traditional textile production in remote areas by providing artisans with a reliable market for their crafts. Third, the non-profit foundation Fibre2Fabric preserves hundreds of rare and unique textiles from the various regions and ethnicities of Laos. Pieces in Fibre2Fabric's Lao Heritage Textile Collection are professionally exhibited free of charge at the Living Crafts Centre and frequently at national and international exhibitions.

In eighteen years, Ock Pop Tok has grown from a small workshop with a few weavers to three boutiques and the Living Crafts Centre that consists of a weaving and dyeing studio offering workshops to visitors, textile and craft exhibitions, two cafés, and a small guest house. In a typical month about three thousand pieces are sold, ranging from intricate wall hangings to simpler silk and cotton scarves, clothing, accessories, jewelry, gifts, toys, and home décor. This generates employment for nearly eighty people, including fifty weavers with average earnings up to three times the national minimum wage, and others working in production, finance, visitor interaction, and retail. Another five hundred are based in rural locations. Our future plan is to take this model full circle and create a center in the West. Here in Laos we have seen a resurgence in both civil society and government interest in cultural preservation. By creating an attractive workplace both in terms of re-numeration, skills development, and a fulfilling mission, we have helped Lao youth to become more engaged in cultural heritage protection.

Ock Pop Tok regularly works with government and civil society organizations to preserve Lao cultural heritage and generate much-needed income for local artisans. However, the government and other civil society groups can make additional steps to further facilitate the preservation of Lao textiles, to be discussed below.

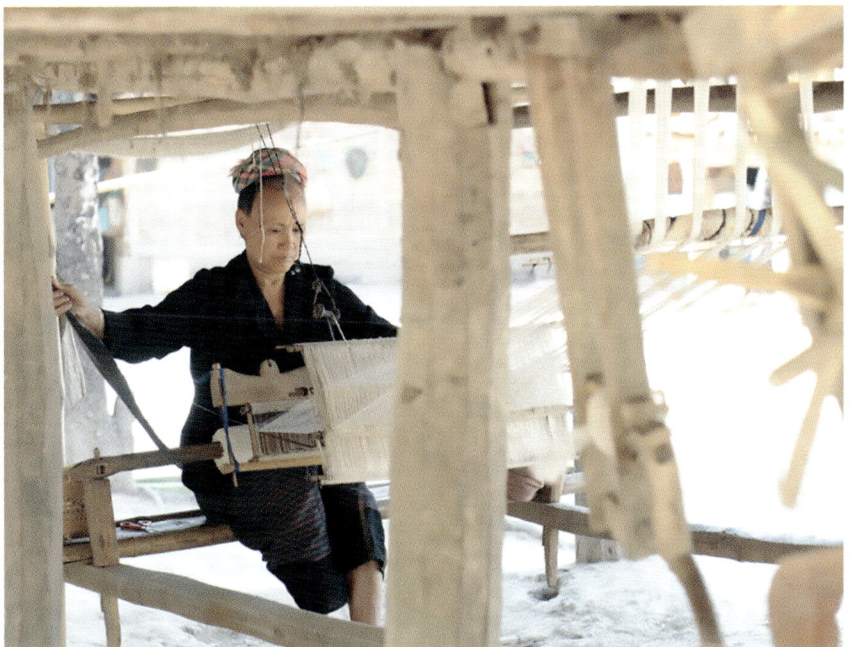

Figure 1. A Tai Lue woman weaving on a traditional standing floor loom at a Village Weaver Project community.

HOW CAN ENTREPRENEURSHIP BE HARNESSED TO FURTHER CULTURAL PROTECTION?

The mission of entrepreneurism is to generate money. As social entrepreneurs, we are looking to make profit whilst solving social problems and affecting social change for the better. As a fair-trade business, Ock Pop Tok aims to improve the social and economic wellbeing of its employees, artisans associated with Ock Pop Tok and their communities through our business practices. Women of Laos, as the primary producers of cloth, are empowered by being able to earn a fair wage through their cultural traditions. In the case of Ock Pop Tok we don't just design, make, and sell traditional textiles, we are adding value by working with local stakeholders in every step of production through to sales and marketing. Sustainability is increased when improvements in the value chain are implemented. The raw materials—thread and dyes—are natural so we conserve the environment through responsible management of resources. The textiles produced by Ock Pop Tok are embedded in cultural heritage, but value is added through innovation. Ock Pop Tok's products attract a wide range of customers throughout the world, increasing sales and returns to the producers. The social entrepreneurial approach that we have embraced adds value and thus fosters cultural heritage protection.

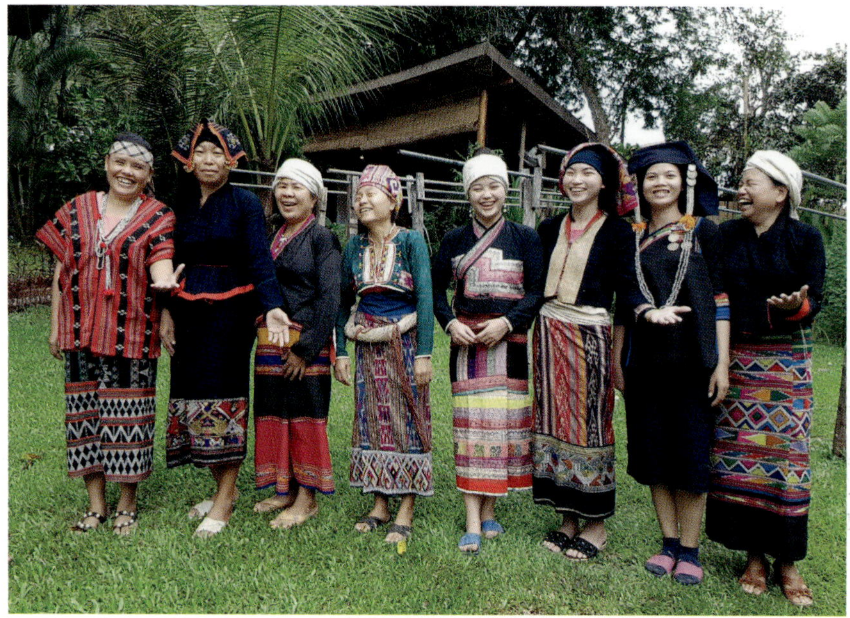

Figure 2. Textile diversity in Laos; members of Ock Pop Tok in the traditional outfits of various ethnic groups.

In a small population of less than 7 million, Laos has fifty officially recognized ethnic groups and each group has its own textile traditions, techniques, materials, and style. Weaving is part of these groups' identity and reflects their rich cultural tradition. This is one reason we started the Village Weaver Projects. This program creates economic opportunities for artisans in rural locations. We help develop ranges of handicrafts that combine craftsmanship and tradition with artistic creativity, market knowledge, and basic business practices. Our team of weavers, dyers, designers, and tailors transfer their skills to aid artisans to make a better living from handicrafts. Currently we work with more than five hundred women from fourteen ethnic groups in fourteen out of the seventeen provinces in the country. Primary products are silk, cotton, hemp, *piek* (jungle vine), and other natural fibers, using techniques including weaving, batik, embroidery, and applique. Combining a passion for these deep-rooted cultures and their handmade traditions with our business savvy, we can create thriving village enterprises that help to keep cultural traditions alive.

Most textile artisans are women for whom textile production is only one aspect of their daily life and income. Supporting the businesses of women has been found to have significant benefits for their families, thus effectively reducing poverty. There are limited income-generating opportunities in rural areas. Strengthening the textile production businesses provides rural people with the opportunity to remain in their community while increasing their income and preserving their cultural traditions. It also keeps the income in the villages, which further contributes to sustaining cultural heritage in the village.

One of the key elements of an Ock Pop Tok created handicraft is that it is, as far as possible, an authentic Lao handicraft. This means that the raw material is made in Laos, that the design is traditionally Lao or designed by a Lao person or has a obvious visual connection to traditional Lao culture, and that the handicraft has been made in a traditional Lao way, such as on a traditional loom, using a traditional skill.

Textile production is a "value added" activity that provides a much better financial return than selling the raw fibers as commodities. Keeping this added value within the villages strengthens their industry and income. Production in Laos has strong cultural significance. Much of the technical and esoteric knowledge is passed from generation to generation within the village and often has a distinct character from group to group. This means that there is a strong geographical link to preserving the cultural integrity of Lao textiles.

For us the key to furthering cultural protection through our business endeavors is through education, by creating a greater sense of appreciation about the very culture that the textiles represent. This is why we created the Living Crafts Centre to demonstrate that textiles and the culture behind them are from a living, breathing culture and that by learning about these cultural traditions, whether you are a young Lao student or a tourist from France, will help to sustain these traditions for future generations.

One great story of Ock Pop Tok is about its first connection with a remote Tai Daeng group, based three-days travel from Luang Prabang. The Tai Daeng ethnic group is well-known for its exquisite and unique textiles based on a long history in sericulture and weaving tradition. One day, a local textile trader popped into the gallery with a bag of textiles from Houaphan Province. In the bag was a 5-meter long cloth of *ikat* and supplementary weft design. Veo Douangdala, a textile connoisseur, was rendered speechless. Ethnologists write that Lao textiles can be traced back to specific villages because each design is representative of a unique culture or family. We decided to put that theory to test. Five of the Ock Pop Tok team set off for Houaphan, textile in hand, looking for the woman that had made this cloth. To cut a long story short we did indeed find that artisan, made the connection with a remote community, and together started working on reproducing textiles that took, in some cases, six months to produce. This was how the Village Weaver Projects started.

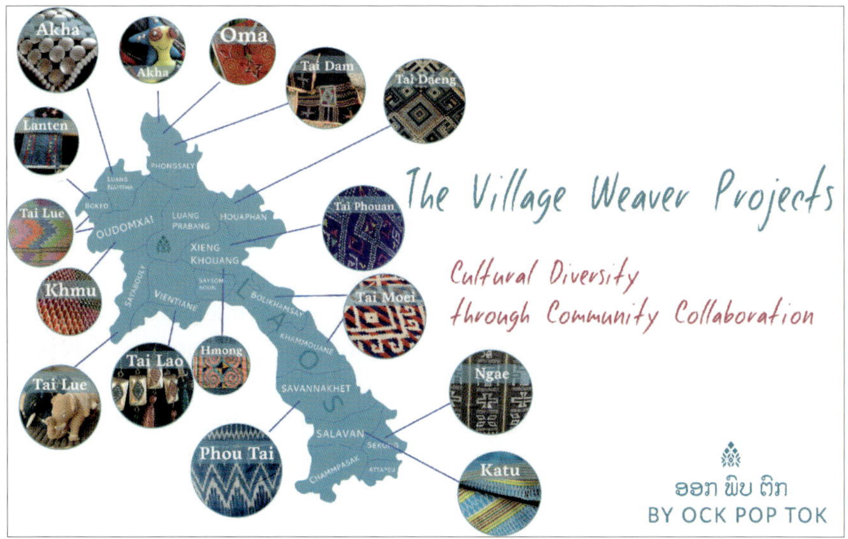

Figure 3. The ethnic groups and provinces where Ock Pop Tok works with its Village Weaver Projects.

Through the long-term relations with our village partners and artisans, we have seen many villages improve their business skills and open their minds to developing new designs while they carry on their cultural traditions. Our master weavers competition was a big success. We provided raw materials and an open canvas for weavers to create any handicraft they liked. With the freedom to use any technique, they applied their skills to create masterpieces to showcase their art for recognition from the public. In 2014, in order to encourage more weavers, especially younger ones, to create the masterpieces that reflect their culture, we created a space called the Master Weaver's Room at our Heritage Shop in the old quarter of Luang Prabang. In this space visitors can learn more about the stories behind each piece.

Another program we run is the Village Weaver intern program. These internships give younger handicraft producers the opportunity to live and work in the urban environment of Luang Prabang. Here, youths who would otherwise have very little opportunity to live outside their village have the chance to study and work in our dynamic environment. They are supported to study everything from languages to computer skills and have exposure to business as a driving force for positive change. Whilst in Luang Prabang they continue to produce handicrafts using the traditional skills they have learnt in the village, and their creations are sold by Ock Pop Tok. They have first-hand experience that their traditional skills are both valuable and valued by others. These youths have the opportunity to travel abroad as cultural ambassadors sharing their skills and crafts with a global audience. These opportunities and experiences demonstrate that their unique cultural heritage has a valued place in this modern world. Their cultural survival can support them and their family members and their communities.

In December 1995 Luang Prabang was declared a UNESCO Heritage Site. The royal capital of the former kingdom of Lane Xang is a unique blend of Buddhist and French colonial architecture, one of the truly special sites of Asia. Suddenly Luang Prabang was thrown into the tourism spotlight and the number of visitors increased (UNESCO 2004). Tourists were intrigued by the traditions, natural beauty, and heritage they discovered in Luang Prabang. Tourism has helped sustain cultural heritage in Laos, and this has spurred renewed efforts to preserve and sustain many cultural traditions. The Lao people in general and Luang Prabang residents in particular participate in the traditional festivals such as Lao New Year, the ceremonies for the beginning and end of Buddhist lent, and daily ceremonies such as alms giving and *BACI* (a local ceremony). Entrepreneurs have benefited from these traditional practices. This is both a risk and a benefit, as the commercialization of traditional cultural practices can dilute its relevant place in society. We can call this the double-edged sword of tourism—it brings both benefits and risks.

WHAT ARE THE BENEFITS AND RISKS OF ENTREPRENEURS PLAYING A MAJOR ROLE IN CULTURAL HERITAGE PROTECTION?

The primary risk that we encounter is that entrepreneurs are involved in change. Change is not always welcome in cultural heritage preservation, however it can be necessary to help keep culture alive. We believe that culture is dynamic and evolving and as traditions naturally represent culture they naturally change and evolve. This can be the difference between a surviving culture and a dead culture. At Ock Pop Tok we are aware that we are perceived as a cultural authority on Lao textiles, craft, and culture and we must be careful that we disseminate the correct information. We are a social enterprise and not an academic research center. It can be all too easy for a business to portray traditional culture in ways that suits the business best and not the communities. Misrepresentation can lead to changes in traditional cultures. There is a theory that, "if you tell a lie big enough and frequently enough it will come to be believed." For businesses operating in the field of traditional culture it is imperative that thorough and accurate research is carried out, and that this information is then correctly distributed throughout the team.

We have approached our role as information giver very seriously and Ock Pop Tok's team members are involved in research, documentation, and training to ensure that we deliver the correct information to our audience. To give an example, we offer a free tour of our Living Crafts Centre to everyone that visits. The tour attempts to create a greater sense of appreciation of all the different steps, skills, and hard work that is required to make an authentic Lao textile. On the tour the guides tell stories about the weaving traditions, about certain cultural beliefs connected to natural dye processes, and how these beliefs vary from ethnic group to ethnic group. We talk about the symbolism of motifs and the relevance of certain motifs to different ethnic groups and villages. If the guides get the delivery of information wrong, we run the risk of misrepresenting true artisan culture. This is cultural heritage protection at its worst. There is no authority or regulation on what information we deliver to our audience. This freedom must be carefully self-monitored.

A benefit of being an entrepreneur is that we are good at raising funds to support research. We often make trips to communities both near and far from Luang Prabang to meet the artisans that we represent in our shops, galleries, exhibits, at conferences, and on our tour at the Living Crafts Centre. Often in the academic world you hear complaints of lack of funding for research. At Ock Pop Tok we both realize the importance of spending money on research and are in a position where we can spend money on research. Its our company policy to send everyone out into the field to meet artisan groups and have the opportunity to make personal connections with the people that they represent. Through our business connections we have met with organizations and individuals that are driven by a similar social mission. Two examples of these relationships have led to funding for certain projects. The Treadright Foundation has given us two grants to develop strategic tools that can help our team make decisions, foreign language training for the team, and marketing support. Dr William Klausner has supported Ock Pop Tok and Fibre2Fabric (its non-profit foundation) with funds for field trips and creating exhibitions that showcase important ethnographic research related to textiles.

Entrepreneurs are perceived as a dynamic force in achieving their goals. If the goals have a crossover with other organizations working in the field of traditional culture, either as social or economic development agencies or storytellers of traditional culture such as museums, then the entrepreneurs can be used as collaborators and agents for change or development. It is imperative that, as a market-driven business, we don't compromise our commitment to traditional cultural heritage whilst seeking to make profit. Finding the balance between making profit and protecting cultural heritage is at the core of our training programs in villages. All our village weaver training programs start with a value chain analysis. We are looking to identify why the value chain is not working, essentially why producing traditional crafts is not a viable source of income for the artisans. Once we have identified the problems in the chain, we can propose training and solutions. If there is a product design training element to the program we ensure that the proposed handicraft to be produced for a commercial market is either a traditional handicraft from the village featuring exquisite workmanship or a handicraft that has a direct link to the traditional culture of the people that made it. This way the village is participating in cultural heritage protection whilst also making a viable living.

A major risk to cultural heritage protection occurs when an entrepreneur does not value the heritage or has not found markets that value traditional heritage culture. There are still many artisans and small enterprises that are struggling to find local materials and sustainable markets for their works. External trade opportunities with countries producing man-made fibers and dyes has affected the production and quality of handicrafts in Laos. New materials such as nylon and polyester, factory-made cotton and silk, chemical dyes, and automated weaving equipment have found their way to Laos. Demand from both Lao and international markets has grown rapidly since the end of the 20th century, putting pressure on producers to make things cheaper and faster.

Part of the success of Ock Pop Tok is that, as a socially motivated entrepreneurial entity, we want to communicate with our market and increase the appreciation and value for traditional heritage culture. By telling the story of authentic traditional Lao textiles we add value to the textile and thus can continue using the natural materials and dyes even though they are more costly.

Something that is both a benefit and a risk is that entrepreneurs have the ability to purchase cultural heritage. In many cases an entrepreneur will see the potential to make profit by trading cultural heritage. For example, in Luang Prabang there has been an illegal trade of antique Buddha images. There are also many entrepreneurs buying and selling antique textiles. These textiles may be bought in villages for not very much money and then sold to foreigners for profit. Here is a story below that illustrates this movement of cultural heritage.

> In late 1980s, The Lao government implemented the new economic mechanism (1988) which included opening doors to both neighbouring and distant countries, which had similar and different government systems. The result was an increased traffic of visitors in and out of the country.
>
> The opening up of the country and economy had both negative and positive impact upon traditional textiles as well. The traditional textiles from many remote regions become popular and highly visible both in every day use and with collectors both in the country and oversea. Lao Traditional textile were suddenly in high demand. Old patterns from various regions, both for skirts and shawls were revived and reproduced. Due to this free market, traders could seek out the traditional textiles in remote areas and market them to international consumers with no control or records of the exports. For example, a foreigner who had lived in Laos for many years had acquired a collection of ancient Lao textiles during many travels in Laos, when she returned to her country with ten cases of Lao textiles. The author had opportunity to meet her and see the textiles, saying that: "These textiles are heritage of our people which we inherit from our ancestors and are the treasure of the Lao people. Thus, they are very valuable to us." As the result of this conversation, the foreigner contributed thirty pieces to the author and promised that the remaining textiles, almost ten cases, would one day be returned to Lao people and the homeland. (Douangdeuane Bounyavong et al. 2001: 4–6)

At Ock Pop Tok we have been fortunate enough to be in a position to buy antique textiles since 2000 and have amassed a large collection. There are many collections containing Lao textiles, particularly in Thailand, that remain unavailable to the greater Lao community. Ock Pop Tok founded Fibre2Fabric in 2006, a non-profit foundation that buys, conserves, archives, and exhibits handcrafted textiles. The foundation is dedicated to upholding the social role of traditional textiles in Laos and has become a major archive for Lao textile heritage. Our Lao Heritage Textile Collection is a significant cultural resource comprising over a thousand traditional textiles, with examples from almost half of the fifty officially recognized ethnic groups. We saw the urgency to create a collection when it was apparent that collectable older Lao textiles were rapidly leaving the country. This collection helps to preserve textile traditions, document the history, and is an important inspiration for our designs.

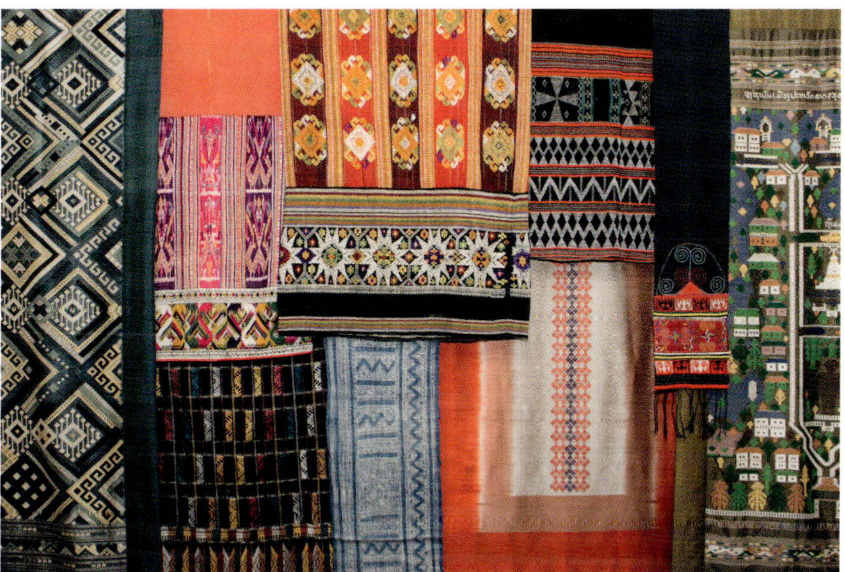

Figure 4. Lao Textile Heritage Collection.

Ock Pop Tok's Lao Heritage Textile Collection is one of the few collections accessible to the public, and it complements the efforts of the private collection such as the Traditional Arts and Ethnology Center, Madame Bangon Douangdala's collection in Luang Prabang, The Ho Moun Thaentaeng Museum (Madame Bounyavong's collection), and the Textile Museum in Vientiane, the national capital. It is hoped that the profile of Lao textiles as an important and threatened cultural resource, a valuable heritage resource and art form, is increased, and that the profile of weavers as artisans is raised. An increased interest in Lao textiles will support the demand for Lao textiles and stimulate interest in weaving as a viable and attractive source of income. The collections mentioned above ensure that the Lao younger generation has access to these valuable textiles.

With great diversity in ethnicity, design, fabric, and technique, all of the collections mentioned above consist of examples which are now rarely found in Laos. Our archive is a primary resource for textile techniques and design, primarily to sustain and promote the weaving culture for Lao weavers, as well as a general repository of Lao iconography for design. Further, it will provide a base for community engagement initiatives in conservation and heritage and exploration of Lao cultural identity to support an increase in capacity for the Lao people to continue to interpret and conserve their own cultural heritage.

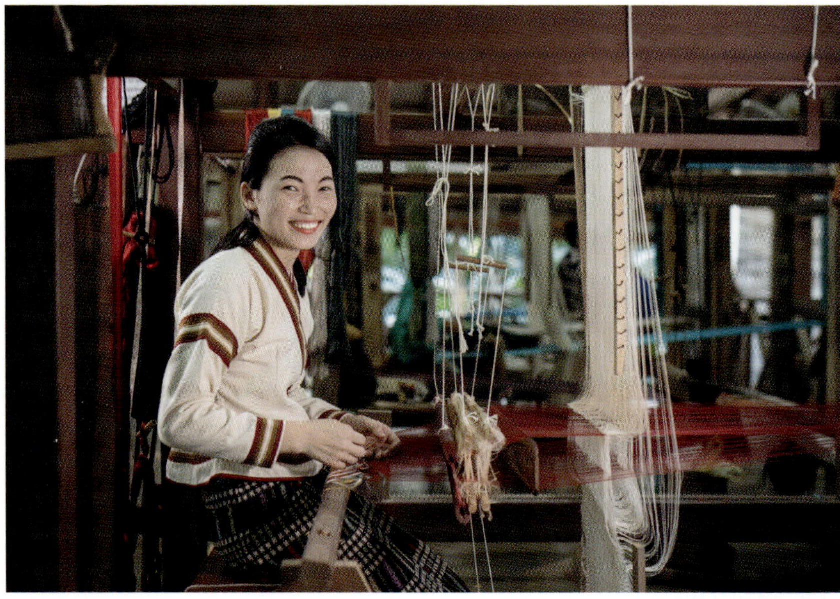

Figure 5. A master weaver working on modern designs using traditional techniques at the Living Crafts Centre.

Ock Pop Tok, as custodians of the collection, is striving to perpetuate a very significant cultural resource at its origin, by engaging with a cultural material conservator, a long-term foreign resident of Luang Prabang, to create a sustainable archive within the local environment and community. The Lao Heritage Textile Collection archive is an example of combining ingenuity with creativity and best practices to develop correct long-term storage suitable for the local weather conditions, along with documentation, cataloguing, and conservation treatment for the collection, to satisfy the need for greater accessibility and long-term preservation goals. The aim is to develop the collection and archive into a center which will support exhibition and further textile conservation work.

One of our proudest achievements in cultural heritage protection has been the creation of the Living Crafts Centre, established in 2005, where people can learn and experience Lao weaving culture. This center is for both tourists and students from primary school up to university who come to study about sericulture, natural dyes, and weaving cultures. We offer different classes such as natural dyes, weaving, Hmong batik drawing, and bamboo weaving. Our goal is to offer a unique experience with Lao handicrafts, where guests can attain a hands-on experience and gain insight into Lao weaving culture. Also, guests can meet our artisans in person. In 2014 this center won an award as Wild Asia Responsible Tourism Initiative for Best in Cultural Preservation category.

Most of our weavers have been with us since we started operations. We can see their quality of life improve every year. Our weavers send their kids to school and many have graduated from university. This younger generation now understands the value of Lao textile traditions and many of them continue weaving in their free time after school or after their regular job because it allows them to earn extra income while carrying on their cultural heritage.

We recently added a trained lawyer and accountant to our weaving team. Many Ock Pop Tok artisans, including village weavers and other team members, have had the opportunity to travel domestically and internationally. This is important for them, for the company, and for Laos. One of our first major international trips was to Santa Fe, New Mexico, USA, to participate in the International Folk Art Market. This market brings together artists from over fifty different countries to sell their artwork and interact as a community. Ms Kieng was our first weaver to travel to America for this market. When she returned, she told everyone about her trip. The event helped her understand her value as an artist and cultural ambassador for Laos. She saw that Lao weaving is respected around the world. Participating in this market had a big impact on our business and our artisans. It helped Lao textiles become better known and valued in the international marketplace. We met contacts that helped us increase our export market and helped the world to discover Laos through textiles.

HOW CAN GOVERNMENTS AND CIVIL SOCIETIES FACILITATE THIS ROLE?

There are many ways that governments and civil societies can facilitate the role of entrepreneurs in the protection of cultural heritage. In Laos there are many policies and initiatives that do so already. Both civil societies and government have recognized that protecting cultural heritage in Laos will strengthen the country's potential as a tourism destination and will expand export markets for Lao-produced handicrafts. Government policies range from zero export tax on handicrafts to mandatory national dress requirements for women in government buildings, to the use of the Lao alphabet in all branding of private sector businesses. The government also generates reports on economic sectors, and sponsors campaigns, competitions, and awards. These are some examples of cooperation between government and the private sector in 2018:

> The project is a special collaboration between Lao Young Designers Project under Lao Fashion Week and the Tourism Infrastructure for Inclusive Growth Project, the Ministry of Information, Culture and Tourism.
>
> "The special collaboration aims to give opportunities for leading Lao young designers to turn local textiles from each province in Laos into modern fashion wear," Ms Pany Saignavong, Founder and CEO of the Lao Fashion Week told a press conference in Vientiane on May 22, 2018.
>
> "The objective is to add value to local fabrics and showcase to international fashion industry that Lao textiles can be worn in various ways not just the traditional ones and can be used in modern fashion wear," said Ms Saignavong.
>
> Textiles from seventeen provinces across the country will be given to fifteen leading young designers to design and produce modern fashion wear which will be showcased at the Lao Fashion Week 2018 in September and at the Laos booth at various international tourism fairs.

> "I hope that modern wear made from local textiles will make foreigners interested in Lao textile and want to visit Laos," said Mr Thaviphet Oula, Deputy Director of Tourism Promotion Department, Ministry of Information, Culture and Tourism, who is the Director of the Tourism Infrastructure for Inclusive Growth Project.

> "I am happy and very proud to have the opportunity to join the program to promote culture and customs of Oudomxay," said Mr Viseth Sithilath, the winner of Young Designers Project 2016, who has chosen textile from Oudomxay for his fashion design.

Handicraft business is a priority sector for the Lao government to support. The government wants to maintain handicraft practices as an art and as an expression of heritage, and it needs to find ways to generate revenue for the artisans and small and medium enterprises (SME). A recent policy aims to promote industrialization through SME development, especially SMEs run by women, by such measures as giving SMEs better access to affordable credit and other financial services, supporting SME integration into value chains and markets, making SMEs more competitive, resolving the bottlenecks constraining the expansion of SMEs, and helping women entrepreneurs to start small businesses (UNDP Lao PDR 2015). There are many NGOs and government partner projects that support cultural heritage protection, such as opening of ethnic museums and the creation of "Help Desks" for entrepreneurs that need advice on writing business plans. There are funding opportunities through projects like the World Bank partnerships with local banks that support SMEs with low interest rates and long-term loans. There is assistance for attending trade fairs, mostly in the ASEAN region. The government believes that promoting SMEs will achieve a more balanced, inclusive growth.

In 1989 citizens interested in preserving Lao culture heritage founded a group called "Promotion of art and traditional textiles." The group produced a video about silk production, entitled "*From the Mulberry Leaves to Finished Silk Textiles*," and organized an exhibition of antique textiles to premier the video. The local and international community living in Lao PDR gave support. The profits from this exhibition went towards a first Textile Festival in 1996. Over the years the group has expanded. In 2001 it organized both the annual handicraft festival and the first contest for Lao handmade products in Vientiane—a big success that attracted more artisans and entrepreneurs to join the association. Later, the group evolved into the Lao Handicraft Association. From 2005, the Lao handmade products contest was opened to youth and artisans from anywhere in the country. The Lao Handicraft Association partnered with other business associations, NGOs, and Tourism Infrastructure in an inclusive growth project headed by the Lao National Chamber of Commerce and Industry under the Ministry of Trade and Commerce. The association distributes awards to master weavers as a strategy to raise the profile of artisans and increase communities' support for handicrafts as a viable and respected career. For example, in 1991, after Ms Khongthong Nantha-vongdouagsy won second place of UNESCO prize on Traditional Textiles in Southeast Asia in a weaving competition in Chiang Mai, Thailand organized by UNESCO, other Lao weavers were encouraged to start replicating antique Lao textiles. Traditional patterns from Bokeo and Oudomxay became popular. Two weaving galleries in Vientiane, Phaeng Mai and Sin Sai Mai, started to preserve and promote Lao weaving traditions. In 1995 the Lao Women's Union published *Infinite Designs*, the first book about Lao textiles written by Lao people, in Lao and English, containing information on weaving techniques, dye recipes, patterns, stories, and many pictures of old textiles (Douangdeuane and Thomas 1995). After this publication, newly woven textiles replicating the old weaving traditions started to appear in the markets of Vientiane. This book succeeded in its mission to promote Lao textiles.

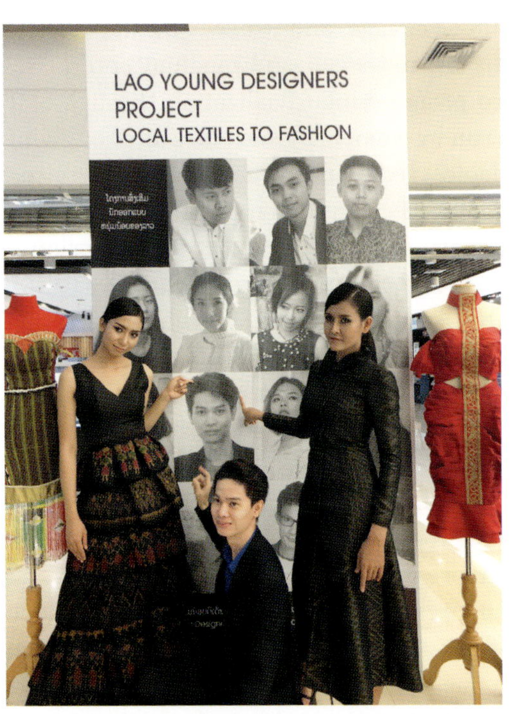

Figure 6. The Lao Young Designer project helps inspire young people to take an interest in their cultural heritage.

The Lao Handicrafts Association has a sub office in Luang Prabang called the Luang Prabang Handicrafts Association, including entrepreneurs and Lao consultants. Under a project launched in December 2012, a regulatory and labelling committee of the Association authorizes "Made in Luang

Prabang" labels for products that qualify as authentic Lao handicrafts made in Luang Prabang. Within a year artisans reported that sales were up 30 percent. In 2018, the Association joined with Heuan Chan Heritage House in the restoration of a century-old Lao traditional house and a week-long event called Laad Bhu Han, the ancient market. With sponsorship from local government and NGOs, artisans came from all over Luang Prabang Province to show their traditional crafts to local and international visitors. It was a celebration of cultural heritage with traditional clothing, music, foods, and crafts being exhibited and consumed.

Any visitor to Laos will not fail to notice many local women wearing the traditional *sinh* (skirt), a long tubular fabric woven with various colors, patterns, and motifs. Handmade textiles often struggle to remain relevant in the globally changing economic environment, but in Laos the *sinh* is still everyday attire for women from market sellers to high society brides. Government requires all women to wear *sinh* in the workplace, even at bars or entertainment places. Possibly this rule has created a sense of cultural pride and Lao skirts have their own fashion and trends.

Since 2016, the ASEAN Business Advisory Council Laos presents awards to businesses and entrepreneurs that have made a positive impact on the growth of the Lao economy and helped elevate the country's image. The aim of the awards is to recognize outstanding Lao enterprises and use them as a means to spread knowledge about the ASEAN Economic Community; to inspire and rally Lao businesses to participate and become key players in the broader market; and to strengthen overall competitiveness of Laos in the ASEAN Economic Community. In September 2018 Ock Pop Tok was honored to be given two awards, the SME Excellence Award for Corporate Social Responsible and the Promising Women Entrepreneurs Award. These awards have raised the profile of our company and artisans. This is in line with government policy to develop entrepreneurs and encourage young people throughout the country.

THE WAY FORWARD

The government is supportive of entrepreneurship that contributes to the preservation of cultural heritage, but more could be done, such as improving sources of funding for private enterprises, opening a Lao textile museum and ethnology museum, hosting textile conferences and expos, and providing incentives to businesses that make an effort to preserve traditions and to young entrepreneurs. Civil societies can help with funding and with programs to spread awareness and appreciation of Lao textiles through exhibitions and events. The Lao Heritage Textile Collection would like to move faster with the conservation and digital cataloguing of the textiles.

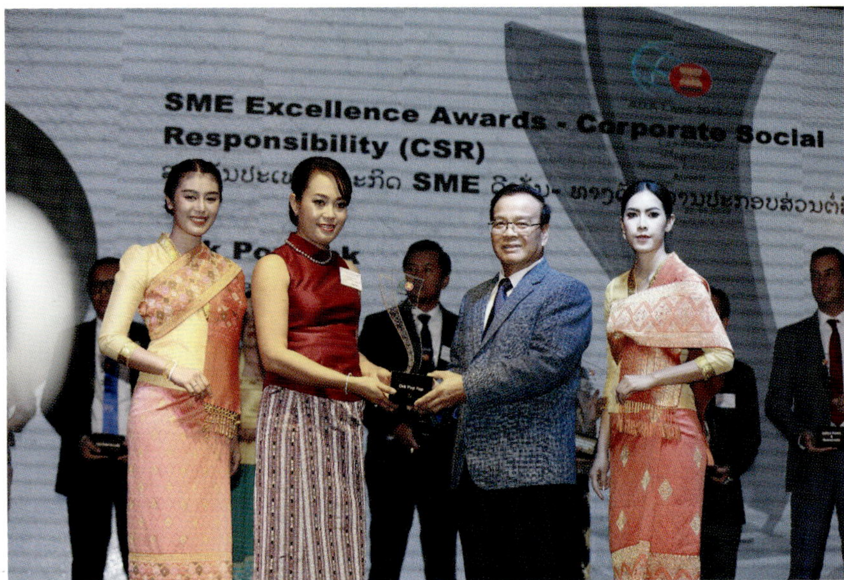

Figure 7. ASEAN Business Awards 2018.

References

Douangdeuane Bounyavong et al. *Legends in the Weaving*, Vientiane 2001.

Douangdeuane Bounyavong et al. *Infinite Designs: The Art of Silk*. Vientiane: Lao Women's Union.

UNDP Lao PDR. 2015. *Lao PDR Country Analysis Report: Analysis to inform the Lao People's Democratic Republic–United Nations Partnership Framework (2017–2021)*. November 13. www.la.undp.org/content/lao_pdr/en/home/library/mdg/country-analysis-report/

UNESCO. 2004. *Impact: The effects of tourism on culture and the environment in Asia and the Pacific: Tourism and heritage site management in the World Heritage Town of Louang Prabang Lao PDR*. Bangkok, UNESCO.

Ah-Mwe, Inheritance, Heritage: Family and Enterprise at Inle Lake

Yin Myo Su

CHILDHOOD MEMORIES

We have a saying in Myanmar tradition: "there are two kinds of *Ahmwe*, or inheritance—*PyinNyar* and *OakSar*." *PyinNyar* means education or knowledge (intangible) and *OakSar* means material (tangible). Today, we know this as tangible and intangible heritage.

I was born and raised in a small town called Nyaungshwe (Nyaung Shwe), located by Inle Lake in Shan State, Myanmar. I grew up in a big family home where three generations lived together, grandparents from my mother's side, my parents, myself, and my brother. My entire childhood was busy and joyful with the daily activities of grandparents, parents, neighbors, school time. and friends. My grandparents and parents used to say that the "intangible heritage" is the one everyone should pursue as it cannot be stolen, while "tangible heritage" can be destroyed by five means: water; fire; theft; bad inheritance, or bad children of your own; and bad government. At this point intangible means "knowledge or education or wisdom," whereas tangible stands for "material or worldly things." The instruction from grandparents simply means that as long as the intangible heritage is possessed, all tangible heritage can easily be created.

My grandfather was a trader who also owned and ran a few different businesses, including making *cheroots* (mild cigars), a printing house, and a rice mill. My grandmother was what people called a "housewife," or "dependent." However, I see that she was the busiest and most responsible person in our household and everyone seemed to depend on her! I spent most of my early childhood with my grandmother (or I should say she raised me by many ways). I accompanied her from dawn in the morning until night. I shared her bed. I felt very safe and secure when I slept with her. She was not only my grandmother but my friend, my babysitter, my teacher, my mentor . . . my guardian angel. She played a very important role in my life and I owe her a lot for whatever she had done for me without always knowing about it.

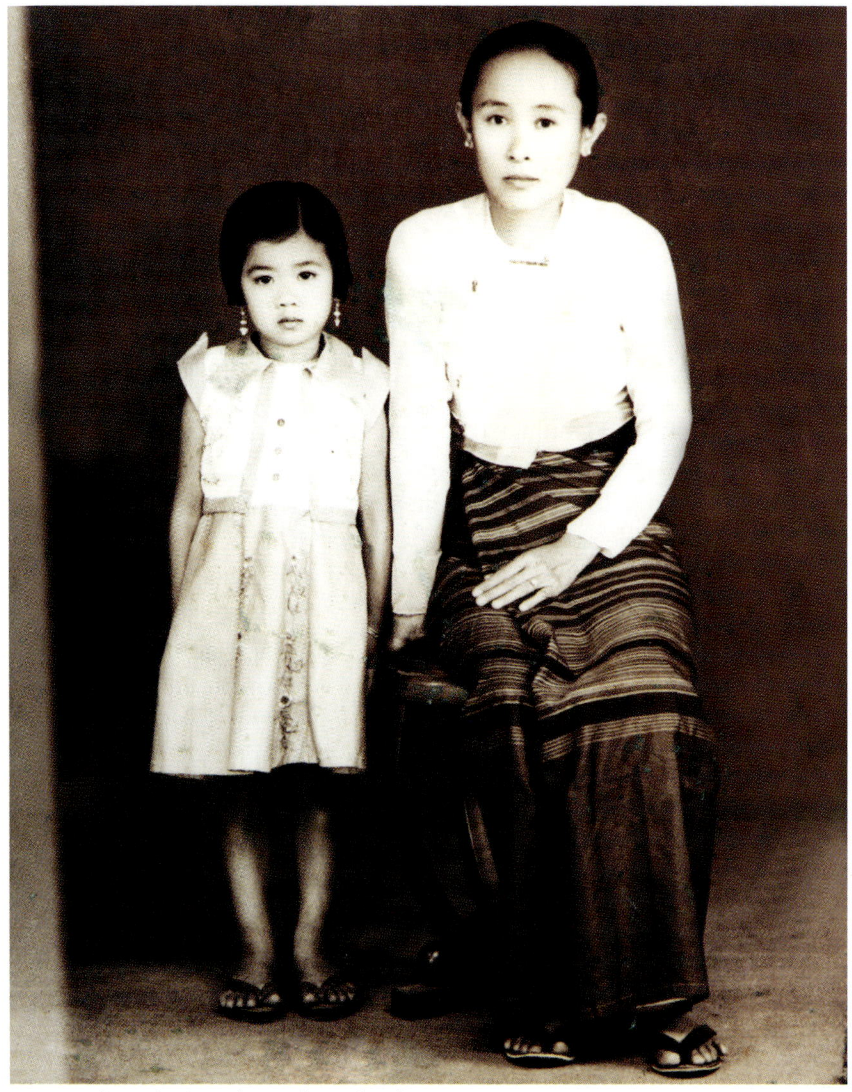

Figure 1. The author's mother and grandmother.

My grandmother was not only a soft speaker but also a good listener. I always knew and remembered that. She was one of the most gentle, gracious, and humble ladies, full of compassion, empathy, and wisdom, among the ladies of her age I knew. In the Buddhist way of life, making a donation of rice and curries in the morning to the Buddha and the monks is essential, and her life was devoted to such duties. She got up every day very early to cook rice for monks who came in front of our house in the morning to receive the rice donation. Then she would start preparing menus for the day for the entire family. On market days (which happen

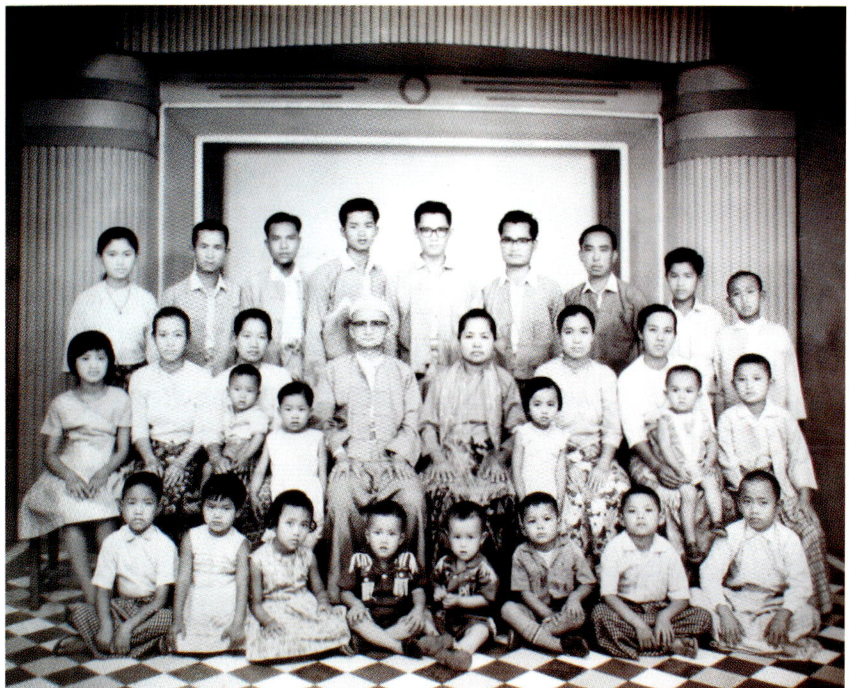

Figure 2. The author's grandparents from her father's side with their twelve children and some grandchildren.

every five days in the Inle region), she would go to the market early. My grandfather was the one who sent her to the market and waited for her in the barber or tea shop nearby. There he would do his business deals and listen to what was going on in the market. My grandmother would need to bring one or two helpers as she shopped not only for the family but also for the monks who were studying Buddhist Studies in the six different monasteries in the town. She always prepared and cooked lunches for the monks on two of every five days. The number of the monks could be from four to five hundred. Being a very devoted Buddhist and having time and money, she never missed doing so until the end of her life. She definitely was a great cook!

This was her ritual before I was born; twelve days of real cooking and twelve days of preparing beforehand, so she spent twenty-four days cooking for the monks, as well as managing to spend a day of meditation at the nunnery on most full-moon days. She even managed to instruct or organize her team and friends when she was on her death bed. She was also a very socially engaged person. She would not give any excuse to miss a social or religious event in the community. What she always said was: "You could give any excuse to miss something, but never miss the funerals." On very busy days, my grandfather or my parents had to help. She took it as honoring the host or community by being present. The sense of community was what my family breathed for every single day of their lives. They transmitted this to me since my childhood and I am thankfully embracing it in my own way nowadays.

When my father married my mother, he started working for my grandfather in the rice mill alongside a canal to Inle Lake. Later my father built and ran an ice factory where he sold big ice blocks which the fishermen from the lake used to freeze their everyday catch for sending to other places. In the 1970s we started to see some foreign visitors to Inle Lake. There was only one government-run hotel in Taunggyi, the capital of Shan State, which in those days was about 75 minutes' drive from Nyaung Shwe. From time to time, tourists would miss the last bus and would end up trying to find a place to stay for the night around town.

My father was one of very few people in town who could speak English because he went to the American Methodist School for high school. As his rice mills were set on the canal, he would normally give a helping hand to the tourists who needed help or information. The tourists would often end up at our home for dinner, and I still recall many backpackers in our living room. The tourists and my father enjoyed themselves talking in English, but at some point however it became not very convenient as our home was already crowded with three generations of family members with our own ways of life and rituals. Finally, my parents invested in a small guesthouse with five bedrooms where tourists could stay. Everyone in our family had a role to play: my father welcomed and hosted the guests after his work at the ice and rice mills; my mother cooked dinner; and I had to dance to entertain the guests as there was nothing for tourists to enjoy after the sunset in those days. I did not know that my dancing for the tourists would lead to my future career in this industry.

Back in the 1970s, the daily routine of our family was quite simple though nothing was predictable at my parents' guesthouse. I recall the fascination of seeing outside visitors and their strange manners, unusual clothing, different smell, the languages I did not understand, and sometimes their weird actions. The tourists often teased me and my friends and made us laugh. We found they were scary but funny at the same time, and they made my curiosity grow about how they lived and what they ate in their home countries. I felt my childhood was different from that of many of my friends as I was raised and grew up in two different environments—a very simple and humble traditional Asian family-style environment, and something opposite through the interaction with Westerners and the sense of curiosity they aroused.

Despite having a simple and stable life at home, I was always so thrilled to be with my grandmother, copying her actions as other children do. I got up early like her, helped her with jobs, and was happy to have her recognition which made me feel as if I was becoming a grown-up lady like her. She always had a quiet manner with a soft tone when speaking, which made me happy and secure to be around her. She taught me many things in a very grandma way, from planting and watering seasonal vegetables to preparing and cooking for the family or monks. She normally drew from the Buddhist Jataka stories whenever she was teaching me something, and I still have my memories of these lessons:

- "Patience and Listening" while gardening, when she talked about the importance and value of patience for seasonal produce because unlike instant foods, the freshness is subject to time and seasonality. That needs patience.
- "Balance and Harmony" (the middle way) while preparing a healthy meal.
- "Empathy and Compassion" while listening to me or anyone else and giving feedback to those who needed.
- "Adaptability and Flexibility" when things are not as expected and we need to plan to adjust ourselves and move forward.
- "Courage and Resilience" when I needed confidence and she wanted to boost my energy through inspiring stories of "Maha Zacnakka."
- And last but not the least, "Dignity and Integrity" when she had to take a decision that was inclusive and collective.

I should not forget to describe my grandfather. He was in fact another hand who shaped me together with his wife. He was someone that we can call *un bon vivant* and a self-made man. He is a hero of his generation and I took inspiration from him in a big way. My grandfather also taught me many small lessons about "seeing is believing"; "your life is in your hands and you can shape it the way you want"; and "if you want to get something done the way you want, do it yourself." He always told me not to lean on someone, and encouraged me to be independent—financially, intellectually, emotionally, physically, and spiritually. He often mentioned how he started his life with two buckets filled with containers of potable water that he used to sell door to door; how they had survived, adapted, and worked smartly during the post-World War II era; and how these were the qualities underlying what he had achieved in his life. He was a practical and realistic man, and knew exactly how to get things done the way he wished. No wonder that I was very impressed by him and I looked up to him a lot.

JOURNEY OF A TROUBLEMAKER

In 1988, during and after the students' movement in my country, life was not as planned before for all of us. I joined the student movement, as I particularly liked to point a finger at those who made decisions, about the bad choices they had made for our country, and to give speeches about how terrible their mistakes were. And the mistakes had been many. Many young people, including some of my friends, "young troublemakers" who asked too many questions in 1988, paid for other people's mistakes with their lives.

Well, our country has come a long way over the past few decades. Much has changed, much has been gained, but much has been lost. In all that time whoever was running our country, no matter how "good" they thought their intentions were, repeatedly failed. International organizations, again, no matter their good will, rarely had a lasting impact. So what does a troublemaker do when governments cannot help and no one else is able to intervene?

It's taken me twenty years and a lot of trying and failing to work it out, but I hope that I and the people I work with are getting there. What we've found is that often our best hope for change lies not only with governments, NGOs, or big international agencies but also with business and entrepreneurs, especially young entrepreneurs.

Put simply, I believe that the private sector, with all its strengths and weaknesses, is often the best hope for providing positive, ethical, and equitable change for those who need it most. Business that recognizes all forms of profit are connected to more than just a transaction but a web of relationships and trust, of shared history and a shared future.

As my grandmother would say, we all eat from the same rice pot and if someone breaks the pot, we all will starve. Why do I believe this? Because this is how we have built our hotels and how our family businesses have survived through financial crises, political instability, and natural disasters. Not out of some vague desire to do good, but because it was the only way that my business could survive.

So how does a troublemaker in the 1990s start to understand this and start to make this happen? The first thing I want to say is that I was lucky. Not just in my business but in the chances I had. Lucky during one of our darkest times to be able get out of the country while members of my family and friends went to prison, or worse. Lucky to be able to study in Europe in a small vocational school to learn about basic hospitality skills when all the schools were closed for many years in my country. Lucky to eventually be able to return home. I guess that's why I'm still trying to look for radical answers, but now through business not through politics, and not only by pointing fingers.

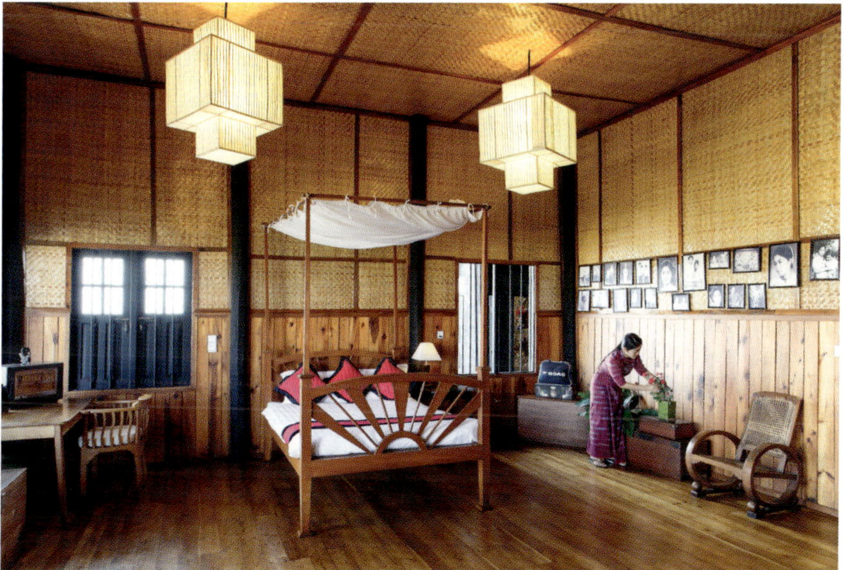

Figure 3. The author's grandfather's bed at Inle Heritage in a room dedicated to grandparents and family.

I returned to Myanmar in 1995 and helped my parents to renovate their first guest house and build a couple more in the Inle region. In our hotel and resorts, we had to produce almost everything we needed for our guests. In a country cut off from the rest of the world's business supply chains, designing, building, creating, growing and maintaining the things you need is not a lifestyle choice, it's an operational necessity. But the challenges we faced forced us to learn to survive with what we had in our hands, and pushed us to be more creative. So, in our hotel we have a village of artisans who design and create everything, from the lampshades in guest rooms, to the clocks around the hotel, to the menus on the table. We grow most of the food in the property compound, while educating and looking after the children of our team and trying to protect the environment within which all of this exists. Again, we do not do this just out of "goodness" but because it makes business sense.

Although there were economic sanctions and few visitors were coming to visit Myanmar, some European visitors were curious and read up before their visit as they wanted to know the people better and see the country with their own eyes. The supply of transport, accommodation and communication was lacking, but because the demand was not too high, our family business was fruitful. More than profit, what I also appreciate in my line of work is that the visitors were like a window onto the outside world. I have had opportunities to meet many interesting visitors and I have learned a lot from their questions, comments, feedback, and suggestions. I also have learned to explain better about our community, our culture, and our nature, something I really appreciate in the tourism and hospitality industry. As I always said, I felt like "a blind chicken falling into rice basket" because I did not know everything, and I was not an expert on anything. However it was the right time, the right place, and the right conditions for me to learn better about what visitors wanted and what were our strengths.

THE MAKING OF "INLE HERITAGE"

Among all those interesting visitors to our resort, in 2006 I hosted an explorer who is based in Hong Kong. His name is Wong How Man and he is also the founder of the China Exploration and Research Society. During one dinner with my family, How Man asked us if we still had any Burmese cats available to see in Myanmar nowadays? To be honest, I had no idea what he was talking about. I used to hear about Burmese cats when I was abroad. Whenever I introduced myself that I came from Burma/Myanmar, someone would say: "Oh, I used to have a Burmese cat" or "I have a Burmese cat." I don't know why people are so fussy about it and I didn't really pay attention to it. To make the story short, How Man proposed to bring some pedigree Burmese cats to reintroduce into the country as the animal could be considered as part of our national heritage. So, we agreed to take part in this "unusual project." Two years later in 2008, we welcomed seven Burmese cats at Inle Lake.

If a friend dares you to save a native species of cat, it's always good to think it through. Initially I thought we could just put all the girl cats in one house, and all the boy cats in another and control it from there. However, it turns out that the boy cats will swim for love. This was great for more Burmese kittens, but not for a controlled breeding program! So I had to find another solution to help the cats control their love life. I decided to build a "cat sanctuary" so they would be more comfortable with a playground, dormitory, day room, sick leave corner, and even with a matchmaker and a honeymoon suite!

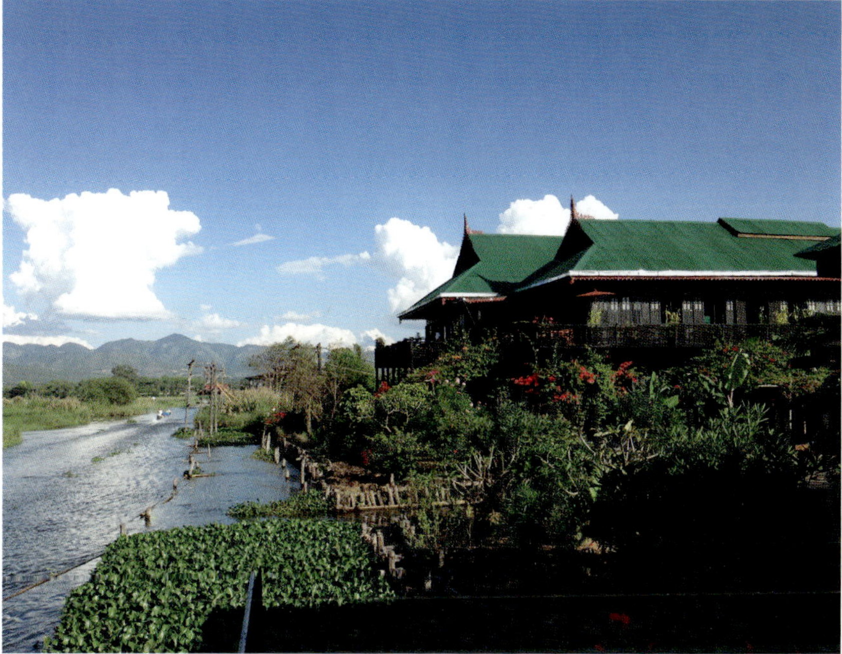

Figure 4. The entrance to Inle Heritage.

In Inle, nearly all the houses are traditionally built on stilts. So I decided to house the cats in a traditional Inthar house, like the home of my grandparents and generations of my family before. But once the house was finished, the size was a bit astonishing! I live in an area where many people lack a solid roof over their heads. And here I was building a big wooden house just for a bunch of cats! It sounds politically incorrect and I felt so guilty that I needed to find a solution to make good use of this project.

Now, you must also know that preserving the Burmese cat for our national heritage is costing me a lot of money. So I decided to attach a restaurant, which would help us pay for the cats, maintain the house, and also forgive myself for building such a house. I also remembered that my grandmother's home was always filled with the smell of cooking. We created a menu for the restaurant based on the recipes that our

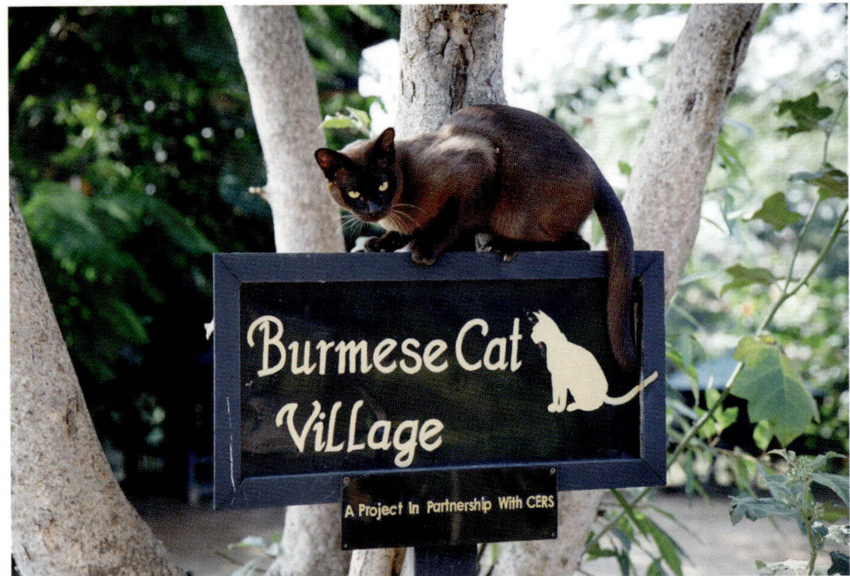

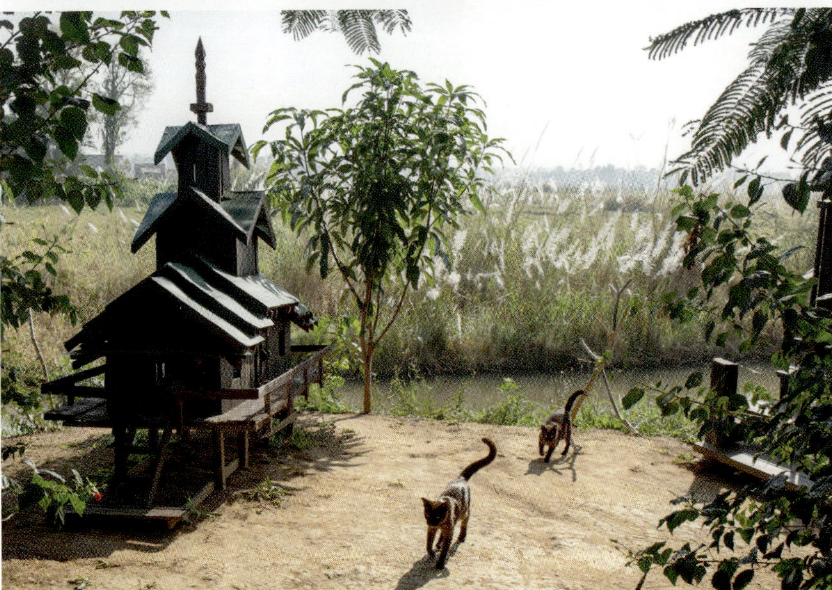

Figure 5. Inle Heritage's Burmese Cats Sanctuary.

grandmothers used to cook for us. Another piece of our shared history preserved.

Fortunately for us we don't have 24/7 shopping or supermarkets in Inle yet. So we have to grow our own seasonal vegetables at the back of the house, just as our grandmothers did in their time. Now tourists being tourists, we got asked if our food was organic? That was when we found

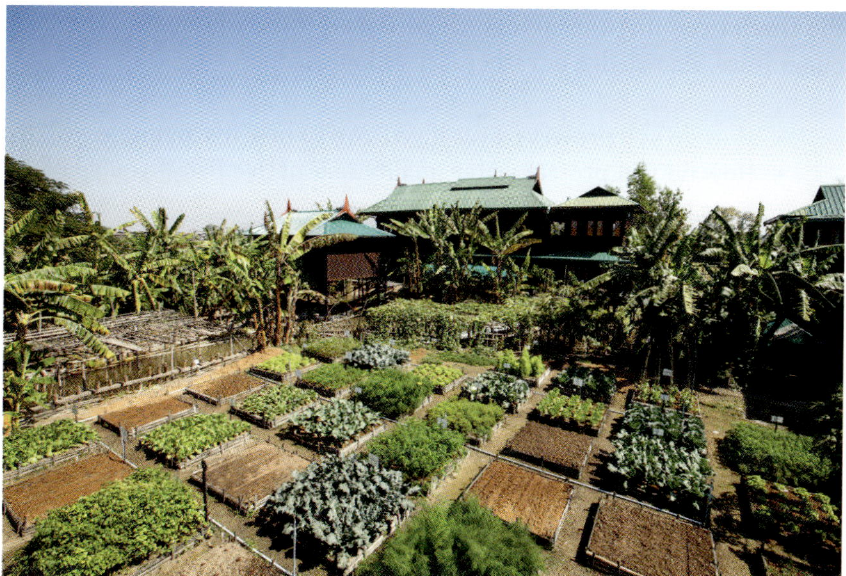

Figure 6. Inle Heritage main house and kitchen garden.

out that though we work hard to use good agricultural practices, no one would certify our produce as organic because the water quality in our lake is not good enough. So we decided to start a water testing and monitoring program to see how pesticides, sedimentation, waste management, and intensive farming were affecting and changing the lake. Of course, the water quality also has a huge impact upon the fish and other organisms that live in the lake. That is how we found out that our lake, home to many rare species, is being invaded by fish like Tilapia from other parts of the world, put there by human thoughtlessness and damaging the ecosystem. Guess what? I ended up building an aquarium where we have a collection of fishes from Inle Lake! By doing so I learned so much about the fragility, as well as the importance, of natural heritage.

So, from cats to fish. In just a couple of years I had gone from a hotelier, supporting and promoting local culture and tradition, to trying to preserve Burmese cats—cats with neverending consequences. I took a step back and looked at how these cats had got me, the troublemaker, into a lot more trouble . . . .

To be honest, I was exhausted and did not need another project. Yet I started to understand that this preservation work for our culture and natural heritage was not a one-woman job. Not a one-person job. Not a one organization, or one business, or one government, or even one country's job. Looking back on all I had been doing on the lake with my people, I saw the thread running through all these issues—cats, water, fish, the lake, our culture. Knowledge or rather lack of knowledge:

- How do you preserve a cat if you don't know it's almost gone?
- How do you protect water quality and native fish if you've never been told how?
- How do you conserve and protect a culture if no one is telling you the stories and history of where you are from?
- How do you care about any of these things if you can't put food on your table or pay for your kids to go to school?

It was then that I decided to do something about all this and the only way I knew was through education. And if you're looking to help people learn, the best thing is to start a school.

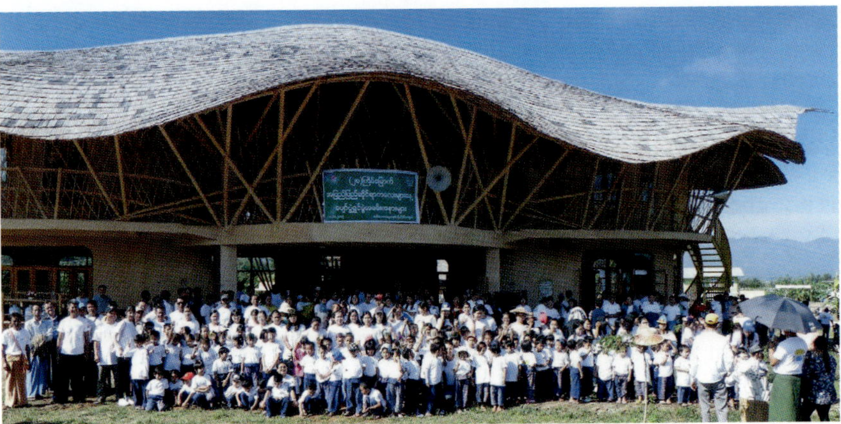

Figure 7. Students and teachers at Inle Heritage Private School.

So, we did—a vocational school to give young people, who are like me and did not get a chance to finish their formal education in our country, a second chance to learn not just about a trade, but also about why the lake they live on is so important and why we all need to make sure it's still there for the next generation. Two hundred young people have graduated over the past five years and gone into a job, with another forty students training this year. But with the population of Inle growing fast we need to do much more. We need more than just one school and one way to learn, so that people don't have to leave the lake to get better jobs or improve the chances for their families.

By giving something to them I felt like I am receiving more. By listening and exchanging with all these young students, I finally realized how lucky I was to have my grandparents who raised me with wisdom based on our culture and tradition, how grateful I am of having parents who gave me many chances to meet people from around the globe in their tiny guesthouse where I was applauded whenever I danced or entertained them. They made me feel like the center of the world with their kindness, attention, consideration, recognition, unconditional love .... Those were the roots of my early childhood development.

Some of my team have been working with me for two decades now. Their lives have grown along with our businesses and projects. We have already celebrated about 150 weddings and more than 160 children born over the past twenty-two years. Seeing the children of my team running around the resort compound made me think about their future, which is also the future of the Inle Lake community, I felt the need to build a real center for learning, a school where children could receive kindness, attention, and recognition the way I had when I was little. I also realize that I had learned more when I was having fun. So I decided to build a fun learning center where children are encouraged to ask as many questions as they wish. Because I believe that you stop learning the day you stop questioning. So Inle Heritage Private School was born as a result of the needs of my community, as well as reassuring me that I one day can be lying on my death bed with full satisfaction.

Today the private elementary school is hosting 130 children aged from three to nine years, and I plan to keep expanding it through to a high school that can also serve as an example and inspiration for others who can chose to make a difference.

THE GUARDIAN ANGELS

But let me tell you something else. I used to hate cats. I was just trying to be polite to a family friend who wanted to bring a bunch of Burmese cats! Again, here I have to share a bit more about what my grandmother taught me. Each time I said I hated cats, she told me not to express my feelings so strongly, because everything is like a coin, there are always two sides. If you say you hate something so much, life will teach you until you learn to appreciate the good side of the thing that you hate. If you say you love something so much, life will teach you until you know how to let it go graciously because nothing lasts forever.

I sometimes used to think that my grandmother was just old and what she said went in one ear and out the other. Now, through these cats, I learned a very important lesson that she was trying to teach me when

I was little. I observed that those Burmese cats are very independent creatures, they come and go as they wish with their own desire. I realize that acceptance and respect for other people or other creatures' freedom, and facilitating them to find their own way, seems to be the best way to help. I finally understood that if I truly want to help others, I have to support their independence and let them go their own way.

Actually, I have to admit that those cats taught me "loving kindness" or "true love" and they have guided me so much that I would say they have become my "guardian angels" today.

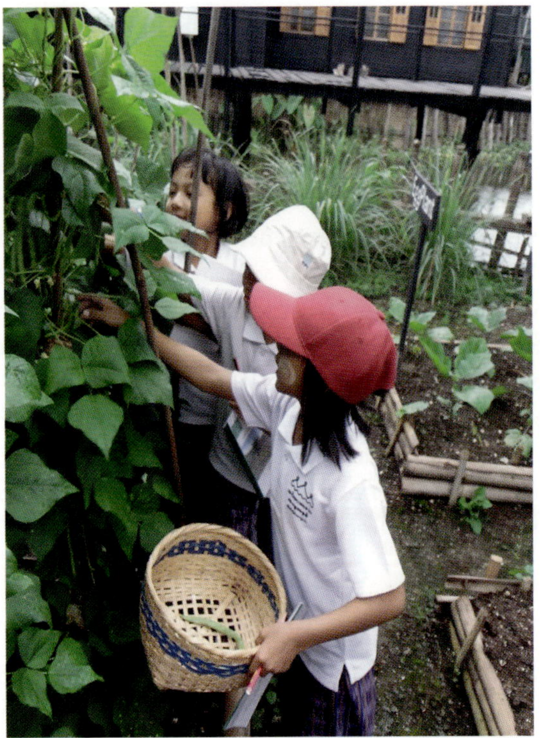

Figure 8. Inle Heritage Private School students pick beans in Inle Heritage's Garden.

CREATING A "WIN-WIN-WIN" AND THE WHY?

When I was a teenager, there was a strong moment when I wanted to become a lawyer. One of my smart cousins was a lawyer and she was so inspiring to me. Also, I was pretty much a troublemaker already and liked to be at the service of those who could not defend themselves. Like a true teenager who likes to say "no" a lot and complain a lot, I thought it was a good choice of profession for me. One of the most important lessons my grandfather taught me, through many little stories, was about how to choose a life skill (a living or a business). In brief, this is what I understood from him and what has guided me throughout my adulthood. A living (business) is like a rice pot. A traditional stove has three legs (or more for stability but three as a minimum). Those legs need to be the same in order to hold the rice pot stably while cooking:

- The first leg represents the "People" with whom you work (your customer, supplier, team, and the community, nature, culture that surrounds your business).
- The second leg represents "Passion" that makes you wake up happily every morning with excitement for the day, and close your eyes every night with great satisfaction.
- The third leg represents "Profit" without which you cannot be self-sustaining! Money is not everything, but it is still a tool (or fuel) to drive your "life purpose."

I got into trouble when I was young for asking questions, and I'm always secretly terrified that one day a sixteen-year-old girl is going to stand up somewhere and point her finger at me, saying that I did not make the right choices for her generation. My own voice from 1988 is still haunting me. So, to hopefully avoid this I've kept asking troublesome questions all my life. So here goes again:

- If I can run a business that does all these projects (while making money and trying to do what I believe is the right thing), why can't others?
- If I, as a woman in a developing country cut off from the world for decades and without many resources can make it work, why can't a big corporation?

I believe that businesses need to recognize that they cannot separate themselves from the cultures and communities in which they exist and the long-term problems those cultures and community face. The private sector is dynamic, fast-acting, able to solve many problems and make money. So I believe that my people and the lake we depend upon won't survive if we have to always depend only on the government or NGOs. We can also rely upon responsible business to provide many of the answers to the problems we face.

My hope is that businesses around Inle lake will see what we do and why, and start to do what is necessary. That people will look at what the business community in Inle Lake has done and realize that they also can succeed, making money and satisfying shareholders, while also creating sustainable businesses in which all people have a stake. I believe that our future and our children's future can be protected, with responsible businesses at the heart of meeting many of the challenges we as a community will face.

ROOTS AND WINGS FOR LIFE PURPOSE

The teaching and wisdom from my family, which was based upon our culture and heritage, enveloped my childhood with a feeling of security, safety, recognition, trust, confidence, and loving kindness. That was the backbone that I needed for my adulthood:

- Without the stable ritual and sense of community, I would not have had a chance to put down my own deep roots.
- Without preparing for the unknown by raising awareness about other cultures and peoples, and without always questioning or being curious, I would not have been able to spread my wings.
- Without using challenges as ladders to push me up to see a bigger picture from above, I would not have had a vision for the future and for the next generation.

For me, "preservation of heritage" is to have a deep connection with strong roots; "transmission of heritage" is being allowed to spread the wings to fly high in order to see a bigger and more inclusive picture of humanity and nature; and "promotion of heritage" is to have a vision for the next generation to help them build a better and a more peaceful future.

With all this profound connection into my roots, and with a safe environment that allowed me to develop critical thinking and a love of all of this, I had the privilege of having my life purpose or my "North Star." I know I will remain happy as long as I can hold on to my "North Star," no matter what challenge I will face along the way. I believe that the spirit of my ancestors will accompany me to pass what they had passed on to me on to the next generation.

Preserving Cultural Heritage through Entrepreneurship: Of Possibilities and Possible Pitfalls

J. Sedfrey S. Santiago

GROUNDING THE DISCUSSION

The concept of heritage has evolved and become subjective to an extent that it poses definitional issues (Vecco 2010: 324; Loulanski 2006: 55). Coupled with the word "cultural" which by itself can spark contentious discussion, the issue, we suggest, becomes more complex. In this article, cultural heritage is defined as "an expression of the ways of living developed by a community and passed on from generation to generation, including customs, practices, places, objects, artistic expressions and values" (cultureindevelopment.nl). As articulated by UNESCO, cultural heritage assumes two basic forms: tangible and intangible, with the first being further divided into a. movable, such as paintings, sculptures, manuscripts, and the like; b. immovable, such as monuments and archaeological sites; and c. underwater, referring to ruins and cities submerged under water, among others. The second form is exemplified by oral traditions, performing arts, and rituals.

As expression of how people live in a certain community, cultural heritage therefore reflects how people interact with one another and with their environment and how they cope with developments and changes taking place in the context of their existence. The Ifugaos, for instance, addressed the topographical limitations to farming by painstakingly carving elaborate rice terraces out of the Cordillera mountains in northern Philippines. Today, these centuries-old rice terraces, which also represent "humanity's accomplishments to modify the environment to suit their needs" are "considered one of the symbols of Filipino cultural heritage" (Acabado 2015: 27, 30).[1] Before the advent of machines, clothing was made mainly by weaving textiles out of tree barks and plants that abound in

1. Acabado (2015: 32) writes that the Ifugao terraces are mainly used for rice cultivation as is done in China and other countries in Southeast Asia.

certain areas (Hamilton and Milgram 2007), as the T'bolis have done with their abaca-based *t'nalak* (Paterno 2001). Even something as destructive as World War II unwittingly contributed to the rise of modernism in Philippine art. The intellectuals grew dissatisfied with how visual artists following the conservative style (the academicians) continued to portray society in an idealized and romantic way even in the face of the people's struggle to rebuild their lives amid the loss, poverty and squalor that was the aftermath of the war (Kalaw-Ledesma 1987: 12: Gatbonton et al. 1992: 117; Kalaw-Ledesma and Guerrero 1974: 35). The intellectuals thus favored the moderns who believed that "painting was not an escape from our daily problems; it was an interpretation of life, a mirror of all its beauties and sordidness" (Kalaw-Ledesma and Guerrero 1974: 15).

CHANGES AND CHALLENGES

But customs and traditions evolve inasmuch as culture and lifestyle evolve for many reasons. The "most critical issue" confronting the Ifugao rice terraces, for instance, "is its battle with conservation and development," and there is fear that progress, as manifested by "infrastructure upgrades" such as roads, will "adversely affect the local culture" (UNESCO 2008: 16). The tradition of rice-terrace farming can also be threatened by the decision of the next generation to abandon backbreaking farmwork in favor of office jobs or migration to other countries for higher pay. And this phenomenon occurs in other cultural enterprises where textile weavers in Bangar, La Union, and Baguio City are able to send their children to universities through their craft, with the children deciding not to follow in the footsteps of their mothers but instead practice another profession for better economic rewards. Or the use of certain plants as natural dyes for textiles may be stopped because of environmental laws that prohibit their cutting or because of the need to expedite the manufacturing process by employing artificial colorants that do not easily fade, as the market demands. Armed conflicts can destroy museums as collateral damage, caught in the crossfire between combatants, or as objects of deliberate destruction for political or other reasons. Natural disasters like earthquakes have toppled centuries-old religious structures that form part of Filipino heritage, as experienced in Bohol in 2013.

The Industrial Revolution, a game-changer, was felt most in the textile industry, including weaving and spinning, with cloth being the "first material to be industrialized on a massive scale, probably due to the urgent need to clothe a rapidly expanding population" (Constantine and Reuter 1997: 16). And "this mechanization of textiles had an enormous impact socially, culturally and economically" (Bachmann and Scheuing 1998: 25–6). In connection with technology-based art, Kyung and Cerasi (2017: 100) write thus:

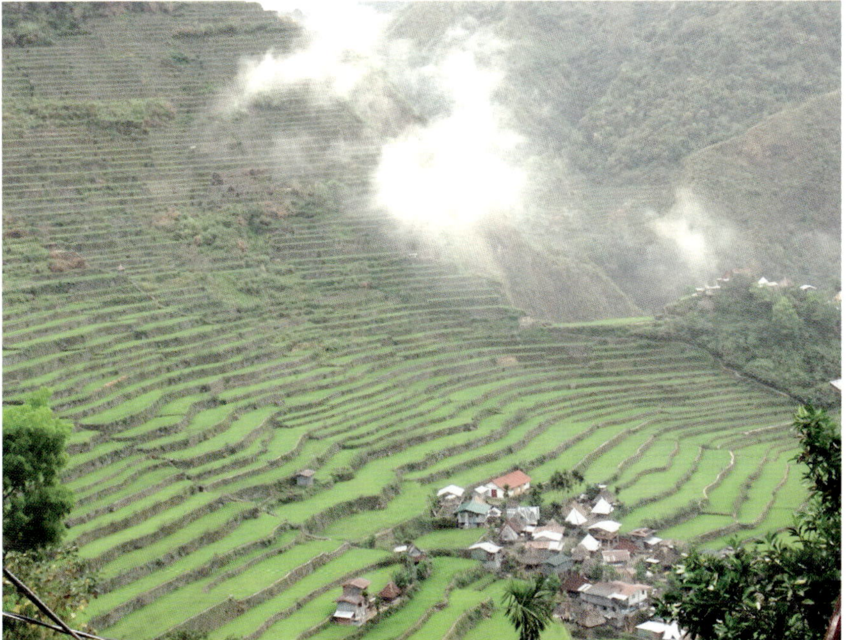

Figure 1. Early morning at Batad rice terraces, Ifugao province. (Photo © J. Sedfrey S. Santiago)

> Suffice it to say that new technologies can bring with them a host of new challenges .... But a growing breed of conservators dedicated to video, film, audio, software and online technologies are now working together to advance the field and build new strategies. As artists adopt new technologies, it is a matter of urgency that skills of preservation keep pace to ensure the afterlife of our cultural heritage.

On the other side of the fence, there are traditions that continue, and even flourish, such as textile weaving in many parts of the Philippines and Southeast Asia (Maxwell 2003; Hamilton 2012) despite the advent of machines and the threat posed by the lack of interest in tradition on the part of the younger generation. Traditions of indigenous peoples can even inspire artists to create contemporary art. Filipino artist Aze Ong, for instance, categorically credits the Talaandig people's influence on her art-making which uses fiber as medium and employs different techniques like crocheting, knitting, and embroidery (azeong.com). The influence may even transcend national borders as illustrated by French fashion designer Christian Louboutin's recent launch of a new line of bags called "Manilacaba" as a result of his introduction to the GREAT brand (Gloria 2018; GREAT stands for Gender Responsive Economic Actions for the Transformation of Women). The bags incorporate different kinds of traditional textiles like Yakan, *binakol*, *t'nalak*, and "bear Filipino design elements such as the iconic jeepney and words like 'Makati'" (news.abs-cbn.com) and are sold at a premium.

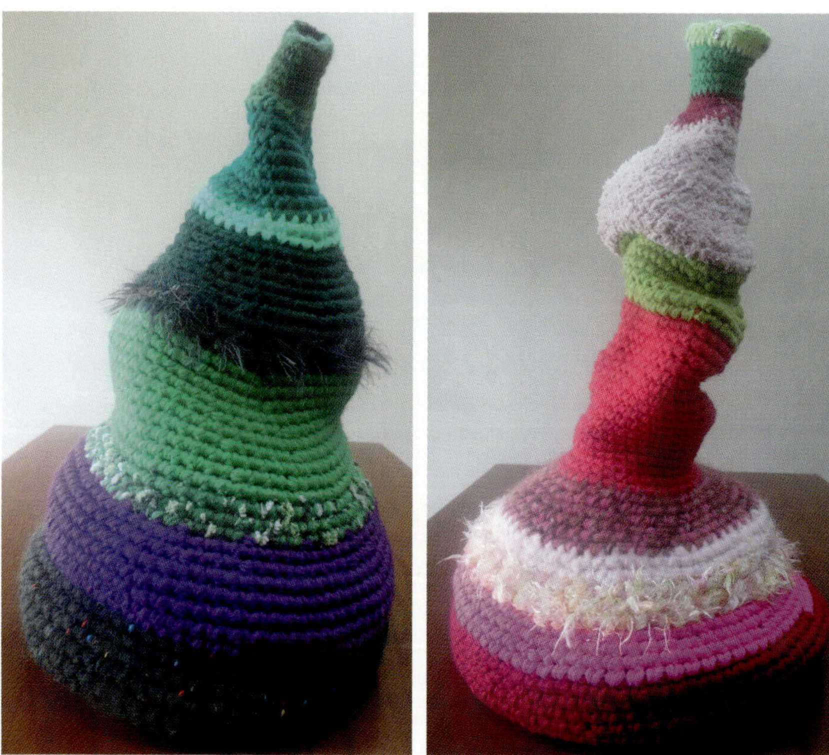

Figure 2. Mini Bathala by Aze Ong. (Photo © J. Sedfrey S. Santiago)

The context within which people live changes, either through natural or human-caused reasons, thus cultural heritage also continually evolves with some customary practices and traditions disappearing, while some undergo innovation due to technological development, and a few remain essentially but not exactly the same. Cultural heritage is not confined to the past, but exists also in the present and the contemporary. And we dare to assert that it includes a glimpse into the future through developments taking place in the present. The acquisition by a museum of an artwork for its collection, for example, is a process of "capturing the visual culture of the present moment . . . effectively predicting what will be historically important for the future" (Kyung and Cerasi 2017: 84). Being expressions of how people live, cultural heritage therefore is a narrative, a colorful one, of a people's story, to paraphrase Hans Ulrich Obrist (2014), a highly regarded art curator.

Entrepreneurship is a way of perpetuating, promoting, and even altering a place's cultural heritage. And by cultural entrepreneurship, we refer to culture-related enterprises leading to a certain objective, whether for profit or not (Santiago and Lopez 2017: 4–5). If the enterprise's objective is mainly to earn profit, and the enterprise's sustainability depends on its profitability, then the enterprise is also called a business. On the other hand, a non-profit cultural enterprise may also, but not necessarily, be a social enterprise where the objective is to benefit a certain community, such as making women safer and economically independent through livelihood programs. Despite the terminology, social enterprises can earn profit, but profit is not the end goal, only a means to attain the main objective.

Here I look at certain facets of Philippine cultural heritage that are not only perpetuated but have been experiencing resurgence through cultural entrepreneurship, specifically: theater, publications, indie films, traditional arts and crafts, and fine arts.

EXPLORING THE POSSIBILITIES

The kinds of entrepreneurial activities differ for every aspect of cultural heritage, although there are also commonalities. One such common activity for traditional arts and crafts, visual arts, and publications is the "fair" that takes place periodically, normally on an annual basis, and "festival" for indie films and theater, which like fairs, is meant to showcase the products and services of participating organizations and entities. Fairs and festivals are fundamentally public activities and they provide a glimpse into the private interface of the act of creating and the act of consuming cultural goods and services.

In whatever form of entrepreneurial activity, there are different stakeholders involved in the process, and these stakeholders are essentially the same as those in the relationship between market forces and the sustainable use of heritage assets to bring about sustainable economic activities in tourism (du Cros et al. 2005: 5). These are: a. the public sector, which provides the regulatory framework; b. the private sector that carries out entrepreneurial activities; c. non-governmental organizations (NGOs) and intergovernmental institutions, such as the UNESCO, that provide support in various forms; and d. the community "which, if permitted to represent its own interests, has the potential to promote greater equity in the distribution of benefits realized from development of heritage assets" (du Cros et al. 2005, citing Hall and McArthur 1998, Page and Hall 2003, and Tosun 2000). Beyond the aspect of sustainability, we can add the market or consumers of cultural products and services, as among the stakeholders, and they may or may not be conscious of the need for sustainability in the use or consumption of heritage assets.

Theater

In 2017, the well-known Repertory Philippines and the Philippine Educational Theater Association celebrated half-a-century of excellent productions, with the former establishing its niche in staging Western plays, "both modern and the classics," "to promote and develop the performing arts for Philippine cultural growth" (repertoryphilippines.ph) and the latter, fearless socio-political plays "using the power of theater as a means of activating the masses to react to their social conditions and demand justice" (Villaraza 2007). Fernandez (2004) writes the following, to wit:

> A special role played by Repertory Philippines has been the training of actors in the modes of the Western theater, training whose effectiveness has been proven by the success with which many of the company's actors (Lea Salonga, Junix Inocian) have found roles in Miss Saigon and other productions in London and New York. For the rest of the country, however, most theater is in Filipino and the other vernaculars, and it is vigorous and daring, even combative when the times call for it.

With their differing philosophies and directions, these two theater icons have inspired and influenced the birth of new theatrical companies. In addition to professional theater, which includes artist-run collectives, there are theatrical groups based in universities such as Dulaang UP of the publicly-funded University of the Philippines (dulaangup.wordpress.com), the Tanghalang Ateneo (founded in 1972) of the Jesuit-run Ateneo de Manila University (ateneo.edu), and the Far Eastern University Theater Guild, one of the oldest drama groups, which celebrated its 80th year in 2014 (feu.edu.ph). Another university-based theater of note is the Sining Kambayoka, founded in 1974, which is "the only Filipino Muslim folk theater company in the country" and housed in Mindanao State University's main campus in Marawi City (msumain.edu.ph), which was substantially devastated during the so-called Marawi Siege in 2017. Much younger is the Tanghalang Pilipino, "the resident drama company of the Cultural Center of the Philippines," established in 1987 (culturalcenter.gov.ph).

Festivals

Adding life to the theater scene are the annual festivals such as the Virgin Labfest and the National Theater Festival, which started in 1992, and claims to be "the country's largest gathering of theater artists, directors, playwrights, designers, critics, and even backstage crew" (spot.ph). The Virgin Labfest on the other hand "has had a major hand in the development of Filipino playwrights and playwriting," and aims "to provide aspiring dramatists a venue where they can present their unpublished, untried and unstaged works" (Tariman 2018). Both are organized by the Cultural Center of the Philippines, with the National Commission for Culture and the Arts as partner for the National Theater Festival.

A third festival, Fringe, is "an open access, non-curated, uncensored arts and community festival that aims to showcase fresh, daring, and groundbreaking material, highlighting the unique point of view of emerging and established artists from the Philippines and all over the world in theater, literature, music, dance, visual art, film, cabaret, performance art, circus and every other artistic genre in between" (fringemanila.com)

Theater is alive!

The theater industry in the Philippines, specifically Metro Manila, may not be as energetic as those in cities with well-developed markets like New York (Broadway) or London (West End). But certainly, it can be asserted that there are more productions compared to the 1970s when prestigious companies like Philippine Educational Theater Association had to cajole if not literally pull in audiences to their old home, the open-air Rajah Sulayman Theater (Samson et al. 2008: 323). The present state of the industry, which can be roughly gauged from the offerings of two big online ticketing companies, Ticketnet and Ticketworld, has given more jobs to stage actors who in the past had to audition for roles in Broadway or West End productions or fly to Hong Kong to perform in Disneyland productions.

A palpable increase in theatrical productions can be reasonably attributed to the building of new luxury hotels that have their respective theatrical spaces, particularly Resorts World Manila with its Newport Performing Arts Theater (rwmanila.com), and Solaire Resorts and Casino's The Theater (solaireresort.com). Both hotels regularly offer franchised productions from Broadway and the West End at higher prices than normal. Through the two hotels alone, local audiences have seen plays like *The Sound of Music*, *Les Miserables*, *The Phantom of the Opera*, *West Side Story*, *Wicked*, *The Lion King*, *The King and I*, and *Cinderella*. Filipino theater lovers need not go out of the country anymore to enjoy plays that in the past were locally inaccessible despite the fact that a good number of them usually include Filipino performers in their cast.

The active theater scene, which is propelled mainly by private entities, that may or may not be subsidized by the National Commission for Culture and the Arts, also means more business for related professions and enterprises like stage design and set construction that not only brings in more money but poses new challenges in execution of design concepts like flying cars in *Chitty Chitty Bang Bang* or buses with revolving tires as was needed in *Priscilla Queen of the Desert*. In all, these could only mean growth and development of theater in the Philippines; as to which direction, no one really knows.

Indie films

In the not so distant past, doomsayers have repeatedly pronounced the impending demise of the Filipino movie industry, especially with the onslaught of Hollywood productions and piracy (Javier et al. 2016: 12). Today, the dire predictions have not come true because Philippine cinema has taken on a new face in indie films, whose ascent in the Philippines is briefly described by Valisno (2011) in this way:

> The advances in digital technology are said to be instrumental in the proliferation of independently produced (or indie) movies. Indie movies have accounted for about 70–80% of the total film output in the country since the beginning of the new millennium.

But how do indie films differ from mainstream movies? In short, mainstream movies are formulaic and made to cater to the market's desires.

Indie films were originally understood as films produced by independent producers, and not by big studios; hence the name. It connoted films with low budget and little if not zero star power but with strengths that lay in their concept. But the foray of big movie studios like Star Cinema into indie films by creating an indie films arm, Skylight Films, makes the original definition of indie films inadequate. In interviews, leading Filipino indie film directors say that indie films are those which are created or "dictated" (as indie film director Sari Dalena puts it) from the director's vision, regardless of what movie audiences want (Oculto et al. 2016: 37–8). A relatively recent category is "maindie," a term for the current influx of films that exude both mainstream and indie qualities which "could be an independent production that casts actors known for roles in mainstream films, a major production company taking on storylines that are edgier than the usual romance formula, or it could be a small budget project earning lots of publicity accompanied by a nationwide release" (Mejia 2013).

Prestige and passion

In any case, Filipino indie films have captured the attention of the international cinema world and arthouse audiences, and triumphed in prestigious international film festivals (Javier et al. 2016: 13). Brillante Mendoza's win as Best Director in the 2009 edition of the Cannes Film Festival for his gory *Kinatay* (Butchered) and Jacklyn Jose being declared as Best Actress in the 2016 edition for her performance in *Ma' Rosa*, also directed by Mendoza, exemplify such critical success. It is essentially prestige that Filipino indie films have brought to the country and not hundreds of millions of dollars or Philippine pesos. Creating indie films is therefore not for making money as investments in productions are hardly recovered, if at all (Valisno 2011). Because of the low prospect of any return on investment, a producer often uses his or her own money, which may come from lifetime savings; or begs from family and friends to lend funds as they may understand if the loan is never repaid; or sometimes may "apply for grants with international film festivals or grant-giving bodies" (Valisno, 2011), like the National Commission for Culture and the Arts. Co-production partnerships with foreign and local producers are another source of financing.

If a film gains a favorable rating of "A" or "B" from the Cinema Evaluation Board, the film's producer earns a rebate from the amusement tax levied on the graded films, 100 percent for A, 65 percent for B (fdcp.ph).

The *Pista ng Pelikulang Pilipino*, which is organized by the Film Development Council of the Philippines, and held for one week in August, is a venue for indie film producers. According to the Council, the event "is envisioned to be the opportunity to discover and showcase films that can transcend the boundaries of international cinema," and these films "are quality-made, well-developed, and produced with a wide local and global audience in mind" (fdcp.ph). But insofar as funding is concerned, the festival most pertinent to indie film producers is the annual Cinemalaya Independent Film Festival and Competition which is administered by the Cinemalaya Foundation in partnership with the Cultural Center of the Philippines. Cinemalaya provides financial grants for the production of, at most, ten full-length feature films which will then compete for the best full-length film award. Cinemalaya also awards financial grants to the production of five full length feature films by veteran directors in the Directors Showcase category (cinemalaya.org).

Films are a significant part of Filipino cultural heritage, which "tell the story and present the identity of a nation and its people" (de Ocampo 2018). Philippine cinema in fact celebrated its centenary in 2018. It is a creative industry that has experienced triumphs and near-death experiences, but has managed to prove sustainable because of the commitment of people whose passion is to create quality and socially-relevant films. Personal funds, whether coming from the producer's own pocket or sourced from the producer's social capital, is still required, however, before government support and incentive can be obtained, whether the incentive is fiscal or financial.

Publications

Every year the Manila International Book Fair takes place, and claims to have "the largest, most varied, and hot off the press collection—from big bookstore chains, indie bookshops, local publishing outfits, academic and religious publications" (manilabokfair.com). Organized by a private entity which charges an entrance fee, the fair attracts tens of thousands of visitors in search of "book sales, book signings, competitions, book launches, meet-and-greets, and other book-related activities catered to bibliophiles" (manilabokfair.com). The "2017 Readership Survey" commissioned by the National Book Development Board shows that a majority of Filipino respondents still read printed books" (booksphilippines.gov.ph).

Republic Act No. 8047, or the Book Publishing Industry Development Act, established the National Book Development Board, "which is tasked primarily to formulate and implement a National Book Policy with a corresponding National Book Development Plan geared towards the development of the book publishing industry" and reflects "the government's attention to the important role of books in nation building" (booksphilippines.gov.ph). Together with the Manila Critics Circle, the Board also bestows the annual National Book Awards in different categories such as literary and non-literary that are further divided into sub-categories. Book publishers and those engaged in related activities are also entitled to fiscal and non-fiscal incentives under Republic Act No. 8047 for so long as they are registered with both the National Book Development Board and the Board of Investments (booksphilippines.gov.ph).

Although the Manila International Book Fair now includes a "comics and pop culture event—POP HUB: Comic Splash X Fandom Fest," there is a more specific fair for comics (komiks) which is called Komikon that started in 2005, and also takes place annually (de Vera 2018). Another public event is Better Living Through Xeroxography. "One of the more established small press expos" that started in Manila in 2010, and has spread to other cities, the "expo feature[s] the brightest emerging stars from the literary underground" (cnn.philippines.com). It is also a venue for budding writers who are still enrolled in the universities to test the market for their works such as chapbooks.

State of the art

In 2014, the chair of National Book Development Board, Neni Sta. Romana-Cruz, reported that "the collective efforts" of "writers, editors, artists, and publishers nationwide produce an average of 6,000 new titles each year" in the Philippines. She adds that "in 2013 alone, a total of 6,860 ISBNs or International Standard Book Numbers were issued to local publishers, among the 26,005 issued since 2009." The figures notwithstanding, Sta. Romana-Cruz is quick to point out that the Philippine publishing industry lags behind its ASEAN neighbors: "Indonesia comes out with at least 2,000 titles per month, which is a total of 24,000 new titles in a year. Vietnam publishes around the same number in a year, but from only 64 publishers. Malaysia, 10,000–15,000 per year. Thailand, 13,000 new titles per year. Singapore, 8,000 to 12,000 a year" (booksphilippines.gov.ph).

Thus, book publication is mainly driven by the private sector, with the government providing support through fiscal and non-fiscal incentives subject to certain conditions.

Traditional arts and crafts

Over the years, the number of fairs that promote traditional arts and crafts has been increasing. These fairs, which cater to distinct markets and are organized by both private and public institutions, serve as one-stop shops for consumers of cultural products ranging from textiles to furniture to food and others that come from the different regions of the country.

The Department of Trade and Industry (DTI) organizes at least two national fairs annually; the first through the Bureau of Domestic Trade Promotion and its Sikat Pinoy fair, one of the DTI's key programs to help micro, small, and medium enterprises in the creative industries to market their products (artplus.ph). Sikat Pinoy is held in a popular mall in Metro Manila and is open to the public for free; thus it is normally well-attended by buyers and enthusiasts as well as kibitzers. It has an education component through lectures and workshops on Filipino heritage, including a fashion show of indigenous peoples' attire and a mini-concert of Original Pilipino Music (thedailyguardian.net).

Exhibitors at the fair report that their sales are good, much more than what they earn from walk-ins at their usual outlets which are not easily accessible, especially those located in the mountains where safety, according to an entrepreneur, may also be a concern. In 2017, Sikat Pinoy attracted 28,500 visitors and generated revenues of Php 26.59 million for its exhibitors (thedailyguardian.net), whose transportation costs (whether by land, air, or water) were supported by public funds, according to two of the exhibitors.

Another event organized by the DTI, this time through its Center for International Trade Expositions and Missions, is the biannual Manila Fame, which is "considered as the country's premier design and lifestyle event" showcasing "craftsmanship, design innovation, and artisanship in Philippine products" especially intended for the international market, with company representatives flying to Manila for the event or buying agents attending on their principals' behalf (manilafame.com). Manila Fame is held at the World Trade Center in Metro Manila and charges a relatively steep entrance fee of Php 500. One Filipino company that started with Manila Fame and has gained a global following is Interior Crafts of the Islands, a furniture company in Cebu that has only one brand, Kenneth Cobonpue, named after an award-winning Filipino furniture designer whose beds and other creations have been bought by celebrities like Brad Pitt and many others (Santiago and Lopez 2017: 134–38).

Besides Manila Fame, there are two other upscale crafts fairs. One is MaARTe, a privately-run event, which is very exclusive both in its select exhibitors and well-heeled buyers (soapsudsandstuff.com) and also in its venue, the luxury 5-star Manila Peninsula in Makati, the country's premier financial district. Maritess Pineda, one of the founding organizers, has

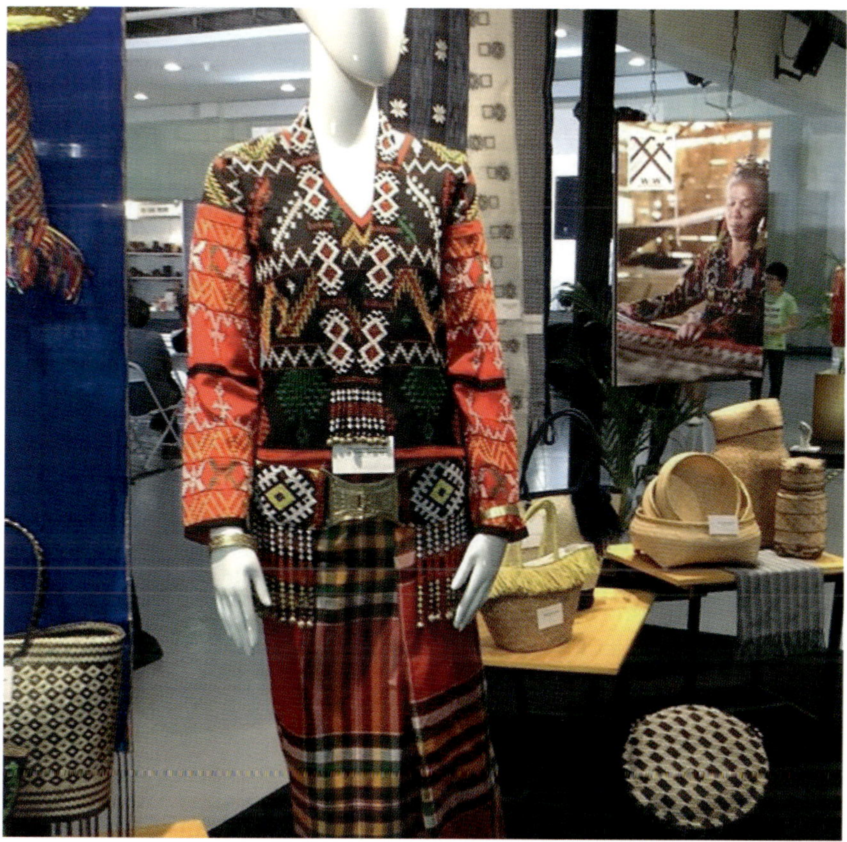

Figure 3. Display at the 2017 Sikat Pinoy National Arts and Crafts Fair.
(Photo © J. Sedfrey S. Santiago)

been quoted as saying: "as you know, we showcase only locally made products. There are arts and crafts we are trying to preserve by giving them a market in MaArte. It will encourage even the artisan's children to do weaving and embroidery" (Tiosejo 2015).

MaArte started as a fundraiser for the Museum Foundation of the Philippines (Lazatin 2018). From being a "simple private-sector initiative to raise funds for the National Museum," MaArte has been transformed "into a community-driven enterprise" serving as a "platform for upcoming micro-entrepreneurs and a showcase of world-class Filipino craftsmanship" (Fortuna 2018).

The other fair is ArteFino, whose founders are the same as MaARTe (soapsudsandstuff.com). Artefino describes itself as "a movement that celebrates the Modern Filipino and the Artist Entrepreneur" and "provides an avenue for people to discover modern applications of Philippine indigenous materials and connect with innovative artisans from different industries" (artefinoph.com). Artefino, which runs for four days and has more exhibitors than MaArte, seeks to "introduce a new ecosystem that empowers artisans and supports sustainable livelihood for communities" (artefinoph.com). This fair seeks to achieve its goals for the local communities through the HeArteFino Development Program, which for 2018, was focused on "efforts to supporting living traditions that may be lost as the generations that follow these living artists decide to devote their careers to modern-day living" (Tibajia 2018). ArteFino is held in a condominium building in Rockwell, Makati, an elite property development, which used to be the venue for MaArte.

MaArte and ArteFino, with their different and overlapping objectives, take place within weeks of each other and both enjoy corporate sponsorship, a measure of the organizers' extensive and high-value network.

In addition to the foregoing fairs which are "general" in the sense that they include different arts and crafts, there are fairs focused solely on traditional hand-woven textiles made with either back-strap or upright pedal-frame looms (Respicio 2014: 58). Foremost of these is Likhang Habi, organized by HABI, The Philippine Textile Council, a non-profit organization which "is designed to showcase the artistry of the country's indigenous weavers" (Sorilla IV 2018). HABI, co-founded by Maribel Ongpin, a well-known art advocate, promotes "the uplifting of the country's indigenous weavers" "by convincing them to use natural fabrics" that HABI says "will improve quality, increase the value of their works, lower their carbon footprint, and enhance the sustainability of their livelihood" (Sorilla IV 2018).

Sorilla IV also writes the following:

> The fair is held each year to provide a major venue for the local weavers to present their wares. It offers them the opportunity to tap Metro Manila's consumer market by giving them free space in the show. It also allows them to deal directly with wholesale buyers, foreign buyers, and stores. "This way, the middlemen, who had been buying the products from them at lower rates and

selling them at much higher prices, are eliminated," said Ms. Ongpin.

The organizers earn a percentage of the sales generated by exhibitors. Likhang Habi, which takes place for three days in the Ayala-owned Glorietta Mall in Makati, has increased the number of exhibitors over the years and in 2018 included for the first time exhibitors from the ASEAN region (Sorilla IV 2018).

Fine arts

The business of fine arts, especially visual arts, is presently experiencing an unprecedented market surge in the Philippines. The phenomenon is felt mainly by those who have interest in the arts (also called stakeholders), including artists, collectors, art galleries and dealers, art critics, curators, art writers, and certainly auction houses, whose activities provide visibility to the art trading scene (Beckert and Rössel 2013; Greenfeld 1988).

Filipino artists today are in a better situation than their worthy predecessors, a select few of whom have ascended to the lofty status of "National Artist." In the past, painters had to work mainly as illustrators or sign painters and sculptors as tombstone makers in order to make a living and support their art-making (Kalaw-Ledesma and Guerrero 1974: 7). Today in-demand living artists can devote their time fully to their art just after graduation from school. A random "survey" of the usual posts of relatively young artists in their instagram accounts shows them on trips to the art capitals of the world like New York, Paris, London, and Tokyo. The Philippine market, which can be divided into primary and secondary sectors, much like the art market of other countries, has recently experienced developments that have contributed to the ascent of the market. In the primary sector, there is the institutionalization of art fairs, and in the secondary market, the robust activities of the auction houses.

Art in the fairs

There are three known art fairs that are held in Metro Manila. The oldest is Art in the Park whose tagline is "affordable art," where the most expensive items do not exceed Php 50,000 (Php 30,000 at the fair's inception twelve years ago). Held at a park of Salcedo Village in Makati, the day-long art fair is organized by the same group that runs MaArte, and the exhibitors normally include "galleries, art collectives, independent art spaces, and student groups (some of them first-time participants)" (ph.asiatatler.com). The event serves as a fundraiser for the National Museum. The second art fair is ManilArt, which is organized by a group of art dealers belonging to the Bonafide Art Gallery Organization. It usually runs for three days in October (the 10th anniversary fair in 2018 edition lasted five days), charges an entrance fee, and is held in a mall located in Bonifacio Global City. ManilArt is supported by the National Commission for Culture and the Arts which provides financial subsidy.

The youngest and biggest art fair in the Philippines today is ArtFair Philippines, which is held for three days in February, in the time between Art Basel Hong Kong and Art Stage Singapore, the two most popular art fairs in the region in terms of visitor attendance (Editors of ARTnews 2015). ArtFair Philippines claims to be the "premier platform for exhibiting and selling the best in modern and contemporary Philippine visual art" (artfairphilippines.com). Starting with just two floors in The Link, a parking structure in Makati, which is temporarily air-conditioned during the event, ArtFair Philippines has since expanded to six floors that are packed with visitors during its entire run. The presence of top-calibre artists and A-list art galleries, as well as known collectors, has contributed to the prestige of the event, which is supported by top corporations. In addition there are special projects mounted by select artists and talks by invited speakers like Sarah Thornton, author of the best-selling book *Seven Days in the Art World*.

Auctioning art

One factor that has contributed to the visibility of activities in the Philippine art market is the robust operations of local auction houses. Presently, there are six auction houses that are all based in Metro Manila, plus one art gallery that occasionally conducts its own auctions. One auction house among the six has become inactive. Four of the remaining—Leon, Salcedo, Casa Memoria, and Harrington's—conduct live auctions, while Avant Auctions does purely online auctions. In 2017, Leon, which is also an art gallery but is now more well-known as an auction house because of its dominant market performance, decided also to conduct online auctions. Thus, while all local auction houses usually conduct four selling sessions in a year (every quarter), Leon conducts around eight auction sales annually, evenly divided between live and online. Salcedo conducts its auctions on two successive days, Saturday and Sunday, because of its extensive range of offerings that include ethnological artifacts like *bululs* (wooden rice god figures) of the Ifugaos in the Cordilleras, and luxury fashion accessories such as branded timepieces and pricey jewelry, as well as vintage cars. Leon used to sell mainly fine arts with a sprinkling of antique furniture belonging to prominent families and personalities, but since its foray into online auctions now also offers cultural artifacts. Avant Auctions remains the only local auction house that conducts business mainly online, although its founder also operates an art gallery. This means that lots unsold online may be sold privately.

The visibility of art auctions can be traced to their well-publicized activities, including auction results that are available in their website, specifically Leon and Avant, and also in other websites which also operate as intermediaries in auctions worldwide like invaluable.com.

The Philippine art scene is mainly directed by private interests. In fact, there is relative absence of government participation except perhaps for the National Commission for Culture and the Arts's subsidy of ManilArt, There are also no media reports of taxation issues concerning the billions of pesos that regularly exchange hands in auction sales keeping the Bureau of Internal Revenue at bay. This does not mean though that there are no issues at all for in truth there are, and they are discussed below.

The value of fairs and festivals

In sum, what has been shown are the different ways by which entrepreneurship can help preserve and even enrich cultural heritage. Entrepreneurial activities involve different stakeholders, with each playing different roles and in varying degrees depending on the industry concerned.

Private entities—mainly artisans from the community and dealers of art and culture—carry out entrepreneurial activities. The market, especially consumers of cultural goods and services, contribute to the sustainability of such cultural enterprises. Non-governmental organizations provide support in various forms, one of which is the conduct of fairs and festivals, either by themselves or in partnership with other sectors like government. The public sector, as represented by the government, does not only manage the regulatory framework (Santiago and Lopez 2017: 16–17) but can also contribute to the production and marketing of cultural goods and services through specific measures like granting funding support, mounting fairs and festivals, providing design assistance, and a host of other out-of-the-box mechanisms. The Center for International Trade Expositions and Missions shows how government can also think and act entrepreneurially and how innovative government programs can help creative industries pursue the international market with success and contribute to the country's economy.

Public events in the form of fairs and festivals held in malls, parks, cultural centers, and other venues publicize what are normally private transactions, thus allowing others to witness such transactions and possibly be influenced in their consumption of cultural goods and services. In addition to being the platforms of cultural enterprises for penetrating the market (both old and new), fairs and festivals have informative value through their education programs, and serve as opportunity for entrepreneurs to build and strengthen their social and network capital (Morgner 2014; Yogev and Grund 2012: 24–27; Pickernell et al. 2007: 4–9). Entrepreneurs can meet other entrepreneurs who may become partners in future ventures. Artists and artisans can be introduced to curators and art and design critics who can help in the innovation of products and services. Outstanding or unique artworks may thus find their way to museums, where exposure can lead to coverage by lifestyle influencers through media, and many other possibilities. In addition, the network created among firms "can offer stable information sources about market relationships that entrepreneurs can then utilize for competitive advantage generally (Klang et al. 2002) with the most successful being those that can utilize the information and its sources most efficiently (Petch 2000)" (Pickernell et al. 2007: 6).

The decisions and actions of stakeholders, whether coordinated or independent, affect the state of the country's cultural heritage. In general, cultural goods, whether products and services, are promoted by cultural entrepreneurs with a basic objective to enhance the value of such goods and services and thus better the economic lot of the creators to encourage continued production and the perpetuation of the tradition.

POSSIBLE PITFALLS

But the world of business is not perfect because it is run by human beings who are not perfect, to use a cliché. The objective of making money can turn into an obsession with maximizing profits at all cost. Commodification is the term given by some writers to this phenomenon. Creators of art and their agents may become so intent on profit-making that they may resort to illegal or unethical practices such as manipulating prices through shilling, especially in the case of art auctions, or short-selling the buyers with the use of materials that are of inferior quality. Commodification of culture has triggered a response from contemporary artists like Rocky Cajigan, himself a member of the indigenous peoples in the Cordilleras. The curatorial statement of his recent exhibit entitled

"Collective Memories" reads in part: "as in previous exhibitions, Cajigan calls attention to the interplay of Cordilleran indigenousness and the prevailing culture of commodification into which it has been thrust."

In connection with commodification, "social justice principles are often violated when cultural heritage values are alienated or destroyed by the destruction, redevelopment, overuse or over-commercialization of heritage assets" (du Cros et al. 2008: 3). Disrespect and disregard for the "social, aesthetic, and other values of cultural heritage" may prove to be counterproductive in the end (Loulanski 2006: 65).

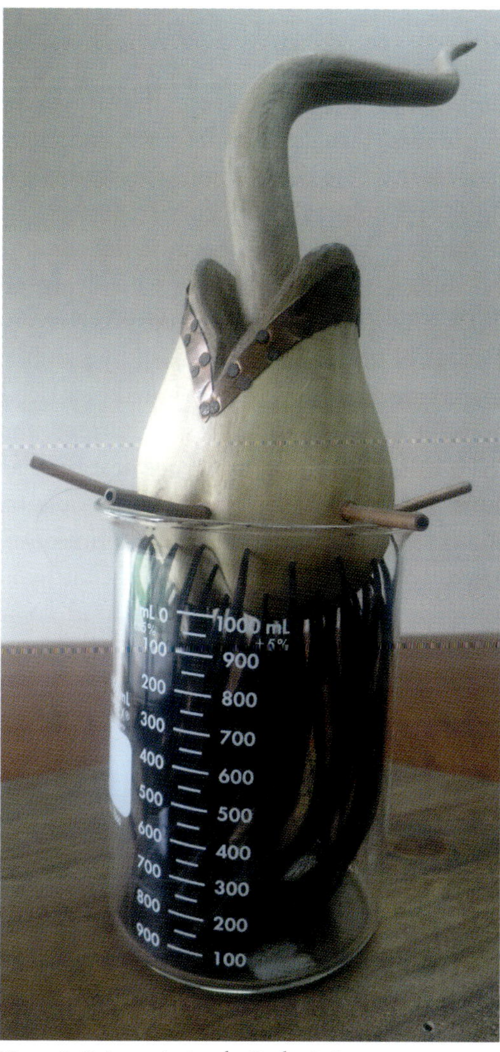

Figure 5. Statement piece by Rocky Cajigan.
(Photo © J. Sedfrey S. Santiago)

The issue of commodification, however, is not really new, As early as 1988, Manta (1988: 22) stated the following in relation to Maranao art:

> Commercialism has threatened the authenticity and integrity of traditional crafts. This has been brought about by mass production and the present high demand for exportation. As a result of modernization and progress, the so-called traditional arts and crafts have changed in style, color and even function, particularly in commercial crafts.

IN THE END

Entrepreneurship can help preserve cultural heritage but it is not a panacea as consumers' taste and preferences can change and market demand can wane as part of the economic cycle. By the time market preference again favors cultural products and services, the tradition or custom concerned may have been lost because the community practicing them may have shifted to other income-generating activities in the meantime. Perhaps a more viable way to ensure the sustainability and preservation of cultural heritage, as proposed by Rambie Katrina Lim, a Filipino cultural entrepreneur, is the continued practice by present and future generations of their communities' traditions and customs, not because they are profitable activities but because they are part of their culture. Traditions and customs are means for people to trace the way to their roots and find their true selves, to paraphrase Andrei Tarkovsky (Obrist with Raza 2014). And it is this true self that makes a person *sui generis,* capable of making a unique contribution to an increasingly globalized society that is a composite of different cultures and peoples bound by commonalities, foremost of which is being human, and consequently we hope, being humane.

References

Acabado, S. B. 2015. *Antiquity, Archaeological Processes, and Highland Adaptation, The Ifugao Rice Terraces*. Quezon City: Ateneo de Manila University Press.

Bachmann, I. and Scheuing, R. 1998. *Material Matters, The Art and Culture of Contemporary Textiles*. Canada: YYZBooks.

Beckert, J. and Rössel, J. 2013. "The Price of Art, Uncertainty and Reputation in the Art Field." *European Societies* 15, 2: 178–95.

Constantine, M. and Reuter, L.1997. *Whole Cloth*. New York: The Monacelli Press.

de Ocampo, N. 2018. "Celebrating Philippine Cinema's 100th year with an exhibit." July 11. bworldonline.com.

de Vera, K. 2018. "Why we're looking forward to Summer Komikon 2018." April 13. rappler.com.

du Cros, H., Bauer, T., Lo, C., and Rui, S. 2005. "Cultural Heritage Assets in China as Sustainable Tourism Products: Case Studies of the Hutongs and the Huanghua Section of the Great Wall." *Journal of Sustainable Tourism*, 13, 2: 171–94, doi:10.1080/09669580508668484.

Editors of ARTnews. 2015. "Which International Art Fairs Have the Highest Attendance?" February 28. www.artnews.com/2015/02/28/which-international-art-fairs-have-thelargest-attendance.

Fernandez, D. 2004. "In Focus: Philippine Theater in English." December 6. ncca.gov.ph.

Fortuna, C. n.d.. "The MaArte Fair is not just for the ladies-who-lunch; there's a lot here for the men, too." rogue.ph.

Gatbonton, J, Javelosa J., and Loa, R. eds. 1992. *Art Philippines*. Pasig: The Crucible Workshop.

Gloria, A. 2018. The Inside Story Behind Christian Louboutin's Manila-Inspired Bags in townandcountry.ph, May 10.

Greenfeld, L. 1988. "Professional Ideologies and Patterns of "Gatekeeping": Evaluation and Judgment Within Two Art Worlds." *Social Forces*, 66, 4: 903–25.

Hamilton, R. 2012. *Weavers' Stories from Island Southeast Asia*. Seattle: University of Washington Press.

Hamilton, R. and Milgram, B. L. 2007. *Material Choices: Refashioning Bast and Leaf Fibers in Asia And The Pacific*. Los Angeles: Fowler Museum at UCLA.

Javier, J. J., Punsalan, C.L., and Tejada, J. A. 2016. "*Tempest de Aelurus* of Philippine Indie Films." *Ateneo Student Business Review* 10: 11–21.

Kalaw-Ledesma, P. 1987. *The Biggest Little Room*. Manila: Kalaw-Ledesma Art Foundation.

Kalaw-Ledesma, P. and Guerrero, A. M. 1974. *The Struggle for Philippine Art*. Manila: Purita Kalaw Ledesma.

Kyung, A. and Cerasi, J. 2017. *Who is Afraid of Contemporary Art?* New York: Thames and Hudson.

Lazatin, H. 2018. "16 Things That Will Get You Excited for MaArte Fair 2018." August 9. townandcountry.ph.

Loulanski, T. 2006. "Cultural Heritage in Socio-Economic Development: Local and Global Perspectives." *Environments Journal* 34, 2: 50–69.

Manta, B. J. 1988. "Maranao Ornamental Designs in Two-Dimensional Art." *Spafa Digest* IX, 2: 19–22.

Maxwell, R. 2003. *Textiles of Southeast Asia: Traditions, Trade and Transformations*. Tokyo: Tuttle.

Mejia, J. 2013. "The so-called maindie movement." September 3. theguidon.com.

Morgner, C. 2014. "The Art Fair as Network." *The Journal of Arts Management, Law, and Society*, 44: 33–46.

Obrist, H. U. with Raza, A. 2014. *Ways of Curating*. New York: Farrar, Straus and Giroux.

Ocultо, E.A., Paulo, G. M., and Santos, J.G. 2016. "The Art of Freedom: The Pinoy Indie Film Scene and Sari Dalena." *Ateneo Student Business Review* 10: 30–39.

Paterno, E., ed. 2001. *Dreamweavers*. Makati: Bookmark.

Pickernell, D., O'Sullivan, D., Senyard, J. M., and Keast, R. L. 2007. "Social Capital and Network Building for Enterprise in Rural Areas: Can Festivals and Special Events Contribute?" In *Proceedings 30th Institute for Small Business and Entrepreneurship Conference*, pp. 1–18.

Respicio, N. 2014. *Journey of a Thousand Shuttles, The Philippine Weave*. Manila: National Commission for Culture and the Arts.

Samson, L., Fajardo, B., Garrucho, C., Labad, L. and Santos-Cabangon, M.G. 2008. *A Continuing Narrative on Philippine Theater: The Story of PETA*. Quezon City: Philippine Theater Educational Association.

Santiago, J. S. and Lopez, C., eds. 2017. *Stewards of Art and Culture. Stories of the Filipino as a Cultural Entrepreneur*. Quezon City: New Day Publishers.

Sorilla IV, F. 2018. "Habi Fair to Showcase the Stunning Craftsmanship of Filipino Weavers." September 28. asiatatler.com.

Tariman, P. 2018. "'Works of the heart': New plays, new voices at Virgin Labfest." June 2. lifestyle.inquirer.net.

Tariman, P. 2018. "These Christian Louboutin bags are inspired by Manila." Posted May 3, 2018. news.abs-cbn.com/life/05/03/18/these-christian-louboutin-bags-are-inspired-by-manila.

Tibajia, C. 2018. "ArteFino returns with artisan crafts for the modern Filipino." August 1. philstar.com.

Tiosejo, M. 2015. "MaArte 2015: Home is where the art is." August 15. philstar.com.

UNESCO 2008. *Impact. The Effects of Tourism on Culture and the Environment in Asia and the Pacific: Sustainable Tourism and the Preservation of the World Heritage of the Ifugao Rice Terraces Philippines*. Bangkok: UNESCO.

Valisno, J. 2011. "Begging and borrowing: how indie films are made." July 15. bworldonline.com.

Vecco, M. 2010. "A definition of cultural heritage: From the tangible to the intangible." *Journal of Cultural Heritage* 11, 3: 321–24. doi.org/10.1016/j.culher.2010.01.006.

Villaraza, L. B. 2007 " PETA and the Articulation of Nationalism, our own voice." oovrag.com.

Yogev, T. and Grund, T. 2012. "Network Dynamics and Market Structure: The Case of Art Fairs." *Sociological Focus*, 45: 23–40.

Protecting Traditional Industrial Heritage in China

Weimin Que and Min Xu

In the UNESCO World Heritage List, industrial heritage is a particular type of cultural heritage. Research on industrial heritage started in the West since the 1950s, especially in Ironbridge, a gorge on the River Severn, UK, where the Industrial Revolution was born. Since 1993, industrial heritage has been emphasized in the UNESCO World Heritage Global Strategy and was an important research theme of the ICOMOS International Cultural Heritage Day on April 18, 2006.

Based on research and exchanges conducted since the 1980s in the international industrial heritage academic field, there is a consensus that industrial heritage can be divided into modern industrial heritage and traditional industrial heritage, either side of the Industrial Revolution. The definition of industrial heritage in *The Nizhny Tagil Charter* runs: "The historical period of principal interest extends forward from the beginning of the Industrial Revolution in the second half of the eighteenth century up to and including the present day, while also examining its earlier pre-industrial and proto-industrial roots. In addition it draws on the study of work and working techniques encompassed by the history of technology."

China is becoming a key country for the protection and reuse of industrial heritage. Traditional industrial heritage is the main part of industrial heritage in China, with the same role and position in the evaluation of heritage as in the West, but with Chinese characteristics. The values of many traditional industrial heritage properties in China surpass those in the West. Therefore, these projects should be prioritized in the selection of projects for protection.

INTRODUCTION

China is becoming a key country for protection and reuse of industrial heritage. Four conference documents have been issued on industrial heritage conservation: *Wuxi Recommendation* (2006), *Wuhan Recommendation* (2010), *Beijing Proposal* (2010), and *Hangzhou Recommendation* (2012). But some serious problems remain in industrial heritage management in China, with no satisfactory plans for reusing industrial heritage according to its special character. Research in China since 2012 has focused mainly on the heritage dating after the Industrial Revolution, with little on earlier sites. This paper concentrates on traditional industrial heritage, from before the Industrial Revolution, stressing the inner value and national specialty of this industrial heritage in China.

DEFINITION OF INDUSTRIAL HERITAGE AND TRADITIONAL INDUSTRIAL HERITAGE

Issued in 2003, *The Nizhny Tagil Charter for Industrial Heritage,*[1] contained the following definitions of industrial heritage, industrial archaeology, and historical period:

> Industrial heritage consists of the remains of industrial culture which are of historical, technological, social, architectural or scientific value. These remains consist of buildings and machinery, workshops, mills and factories, mines and sites for processing and refining, warehouses and stores, places where energy is generated, transmitted and used, transport and all its infrastructure, as well as places used for social activities related to industry such as housing, religious worship or education.
>
> Industrial archaeology is an interdisciplinary method of studying all the evidence, material and immaterial, of documents, artefacts, stratigraphy and structures, human settlements and natural and urban landscapes, created for or by industrial processes. It makes use of those methods of investigation that are most suitable to increase understanding of the industrial past and present.
>
> The historical period of principal interest extends forward from the beginning of the Industrial Revolution in the second half of the eighteenth century up to and including the present day, *while also examining its earlier pre-industrial and proto-industrial roots. In addition it draws on the study of work and working techniques encompassed by the history of technology.*

1. *The Nizhny Tagil Charter for Industrial Heritage* (July, 2003)

Under historical period, the "earlier pre-industrial and proto-industrial roots" can be understood as traditional industry in the times of agrarian culture, and proto-industry in the times of hunting culture, before the Industrial Revolution. The heritage from these periods can thus be called traditional industrial heritage and proto-industrial heritage.

INTERNATIONAL RECOGNITION OF TRADITIONAL INDUSTRIAL HERITAGE

After years of research and academic exchange, the academic circle has reached a consensus recently that traditional industrial heritage is an integral part of industrial heritage.

Research on industrial heritage conservation started in the 1950s. The first paper on industrial heritage was perhaps, "The reconstruction of the Brooklyn Bridge" by an American researcher in 1952.[2] The term "industrial archaeology" was proposed by a UK scholar in 1955.[3] The first society on industrial heritage conservation was set up in London in 1968.[4] The International Committee for Conservation of the Industrial Heritage (TICCIH) was set up in 1978. Since 1993, industrial heritage has been emphasized in the UNESCO World Heritage Global Strategy, and was an important research theme of the ICOMOS International Cultural Heritage Day on April 18, 2006.

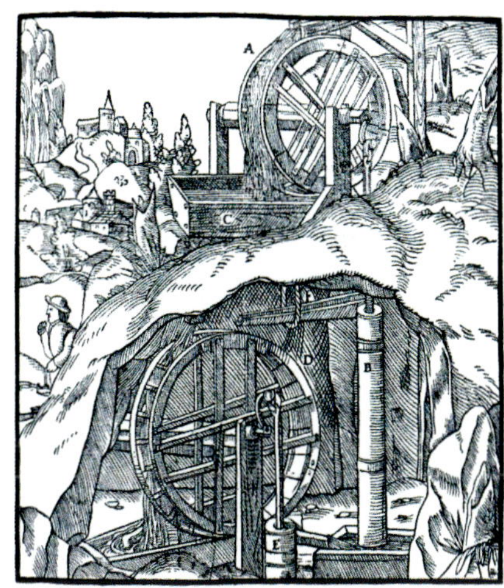

Figure 1. Illustration from Georgius Agricola, *De Re Metallica*, first Latin edition, 1556.

Sources on industrial heritage include encyclopedias of trade and industry since 1763,[5] histories of industry in the early agrarian era,[6] in

2. D. B. Steinman, "The reconstruction of the Brooklyn Bridge," *Columbia Engineering Quarterly*, 1952: 3–90.

3. Michael M. Rix, "Industrial Archaeology," *The Amateur Historian* 2, 8 (1955): 225–29.

4. The Greater London Industrial Archaeology Society; www.glias.org.uk.

5. Denis Diderot, *L'Encyclopedie, ou Dictionnaire Raisonne des Sciences, des Arts et des Metiers* (Paris, 1763), Edited with Introduction and Notes by Charles Coulston Gillispie, New York: Dover Publications Inc., 1959.Vol I: 1–208; Vol II: 209–485.

6. Michael Partridge, *Early Agricultural Machinery* (London: Hugh Evelyn Limited, 1969).

Tudor and Stuart England,[7] and in Scotland;[8] as well as work on traditional industry, such as metalwork (see Figure 1),[9] quarrying,[10] clay industry,[11] ceramic art,[12] coal mining,[13] and rural industry.[14]

Many properties listed in the UNESCO World Heritage List are traditional industrial heritage. The earliest is a neolithic flint mine at Spiennes (Mons)[15] dating to the 20th century BCE. Others include a mill network at Kinderdijk-Elshout and the Aflaj irrigation systems of Oman dating to the 6th century CE; the mining area of the Great Copper Mountain in Falun, and the Wieliczka and Bochnia royal salt mines dating to the 13th century; the Iwami Ginzan silver mine and its cultural landscape and the mines of Rammelsberg, the historic town of Goslar and Upper Harz water management system dating to the 16th century; and the Canal du Midi, Engelsberg Ironworks, and Røros mining town from the 17th century.

Among the most famous sites of traditional industrial heritage is Ironbridge Gorge in the UK:

> Ironbridge is known throughout the world as the symbol of the Industrial Revolution. It contains all the elements of progress that contributed to the rapid development of this industrial region in the 18th century, from the mines themselves to the railway lines. Nearby, the blast furnace of Coalbrookdale, built in 1708, is a reminder of the discovery of coke. The bridge at Ironbridge, the world's first bridge constructed of iron, had a considerable influence on developments in the fields of technology and architecture.[16]

---

7. D.C. Coleman, *Industry in Tudor and Stuart England* (London: Macmillan, 1975).

8. Geoffrey D. Hay and Geoffrey P. Stell, *Monuments of Industry, The Royal Commission on the Ancient and Historical Monuments of Scotland* (Edinburgh: HMSO Bookshops, 1986).

9. Georgius Agricola, *De Re Metallica*, first Latin edition, 1556, Englished translation by Herbert Clark Hoover and Lou Henry Hoover (New York: Dover Publications, 1950).

10. R.J. Saville, *A Langton Quarryman's Apprentice 1826–1837* (Ironbridge Gorge Museum Trust, 1989).

11. John Randall, *The Clay Industry* (Madeley, Salop: Salopian and West-Midland Office, 1877).

12. Llewellynn Jewitt, *The Ceramic Art of Great Britain* (London: J. S. Virture, 1877).

13. Barrie Trinder and Jeff Cox, *Yeomen and Colliers in Telford: Probate Inventories for Dawley, Lilleshall, Wellington and Wrockwardine, 1660–1750* (London, Phillimore, 1980).

14. Michael Zell, *Industry in the Countryside: Welden Society in the Sixteenth Century* (Cambridge: Cambridge University Press, 1994).

15. UNESCO World Heritage Centre official website, whc.unesco.org/en/list/1006. For the other sites in this paragraph, see these numbers on the list: 818, 1207, 1027, 32, 1246, 623, 770, 556, and 55.

16. whc.unesco.org/en/list/371

The two principal sites are the Ironbridge in the Ironbridge Gorge and the blast furnace in Coalbrookdale, but there are several other sites in the buffer zone, mainly clay industries, including the China Museum, Clay Tobacco Pipe Museum, and Jackfield Title Museum. The Victorian town at Blists Hill has sites including an iron foundry, butcher, slaughterhouse, machine shop, locksmith, mine, brick and tile works, candlemaker, baker, and printer.

LITERATURE ON TRADITIONAL INDUSTRIAL HERITAGE IN CHINA

Literature on traditional industrial heritage in China can be classified into historical literature and academic research literature.

The historical literature includes the following classic books on traditional industry:

- *Nong-Zheng-Quan-Shu (Agriculture Encyclopedia in China)*, edited by Qu Guangqi (1562–1633), first printed in 1639, has sixty volumes on agricultural history, agricultural seasons, agricultural irrigation, agricultural tools, planting trees, planting rice and vegetables,

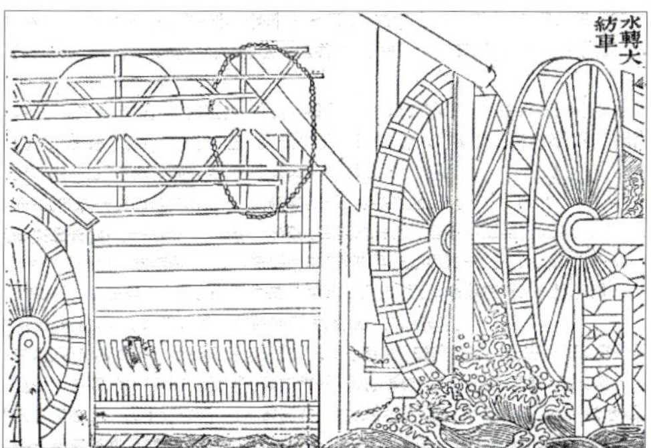

Figure 2. Hydraulic spinning wheel from *Nong-Zheng-Quan-Shu* (*Agriculture Encyclopaedia in China*).

food-making, and preparing against famine years. The volumes on agricultural irrigation and tools have information on traditional handcraft industry. For example, Volume 18 on "Water Conservancy" deals with: air-blower, water-mill (hydraulically driven mill), triplicate watermill, multi-gears watermill, hydraulic hit sifter, hydraulic rice huller, hydraulic roller, toss-pole, toss-roller and toss-mill, water hulling, hydraulic trough hulling, and hydraulic spinning wheel (Figure 2).

- *Tian-Gong-Kai-Wu (Industry Encyclopedia in China)*, with three volumes and eighteen chapters, edited by Song Yingxing (1587–?), first printed in 1637, is an encyclopedia on technology and production in agriculture and handicraft industries such as metallurgy, ceramics, metals, and paper making (Figure 3).

The academic research literature on traditional industrial heritage includes general histories of industry,[17] histories of industrial techniques,[18] industrial business history,[19] and industrial economic history.[20]

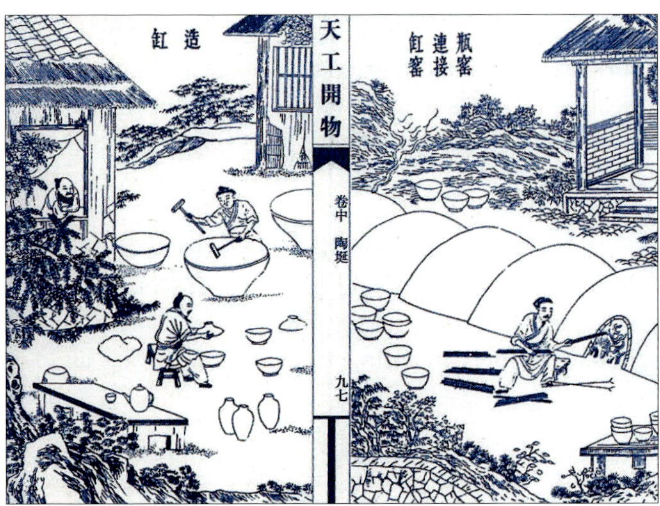

Figure 3. From *Tian-Gong-Kai-Wu* (*Encyclopedia of Industry in China*),Vol. 2, Ceramics.

17. Liu Guoliang, *History of China's Industry, Ancient Volume* (Jiangsu Scientific-Technology Press, 1990); Liu Guoliang, *History of China's Industry, Modern Volume* (Jiangsu Scientific-Technology Press, 1992); Liu Guoliang, *History of China's Industry, Contemporary Volume* (Jiangsu Scientific-Technology Press, 2003); Zhu Cishou, *Ancient History of China's Industry* (Beijing: Xuelin Press, 1998); Zhu Cishou, *Modern History of China's Industry* (Chongqing: Chongqing Press, 1989); Zhu Cishou, *Contemporary History of China's Industry* (Chongqing: Chongqing Press, 1990).

18. Lu Jingyan and Hua Juemin, ed., *Scientific Technological History: Machine Volume* (Science Press: 2000); Jiang Lirong, ed., *Scientific Technological History: Literature Index Volume* (Science Press, 2002); Joseph Needham, *Science and Civilisation in China*, 7 vols. (Cambridge University Press, 1954–); Chinese translation by Sun Yanming (Science Press and Shanghai People's Press, 1990).

19. Tong Yeshu, *The History of Handcraft Industrial Business Development in China* (Chinese Press, 2005).

20. Li Shaoqiang and Xu Jianqing, *History of Handcraft Industrial Economy in China: Ming and Qing Dynasties* (Fujian People's Press, 2004); Wei Mingkong, *History of Handcraft Industrial Economy in China: Wei, Jin, S-N, Sui, Tang and Five Dynasties* (Fujian People's Press, 2004); Hu Xiaopeng, *History of Handcraft Industrial Economy in China: Song and Yuan Dynasties* (Fujian People's Press, 2004).

Among China's fifty-three World Heritage properties, there are four of traditional industrial heritage:[21] Mount Qingcheng and the Dujiangyan System from the 3rd century CE; the Grand Canal from the 5th century BCE (and mainly 7th century); Yin Xu, an ancient capital city of the late Shang Dynasty (1300–1046 BCE); and Fujian Tulou, a property of forty-six buildings constructed between the 15th and 20th centuries in the south-west of Fujian province, over 120 km inland from the Taiwan Strait (Figure 4).

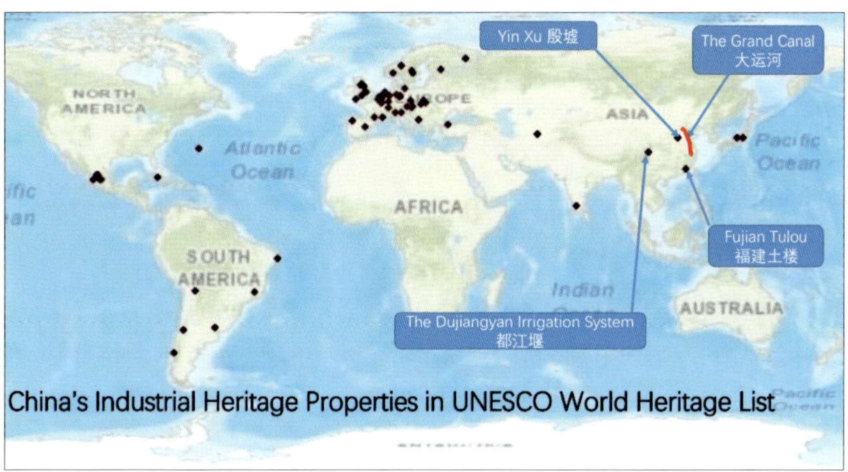

Figure 4. China's industrial heritage properties on the UNESCO World Heritage List.

Among China's fifty-nine properties on the World Heritage Tentative List, there are five of traditional industrial heritage:[22] Ancient Porcelain Kiln Site in China; Ancient Tea Plantations of Jingmai Mountain in Pu'er; Imperial Kiln Sites of Jingdezhen; Lingqu Canal; and Sites for Liquor Making (Figure 5).

Besides those appearing on the UNESCO World Heritage lists, there are many other traditional industrial heritage sites in China with unique characteristics. Since 1949, the government has paid attention to industrial heritage, and has established a three-tier system (state, province, and city-county) for protecting historical monuments and sites. The authorities have issued seven editions of the *List of Chinese National Protected Monuments and Sites*. On the first six of these, there are about 160

21. In the UNESCO list (see above), numbers 1001, 1443, 1114, and 113 respectively.
22. In the UNESCO list (see above), numbers 5806, 5810, 6265, 5814, and 5320 respectively.

properties of industrial heritage among the total of 2377 properties (Table 1 and Table 2).

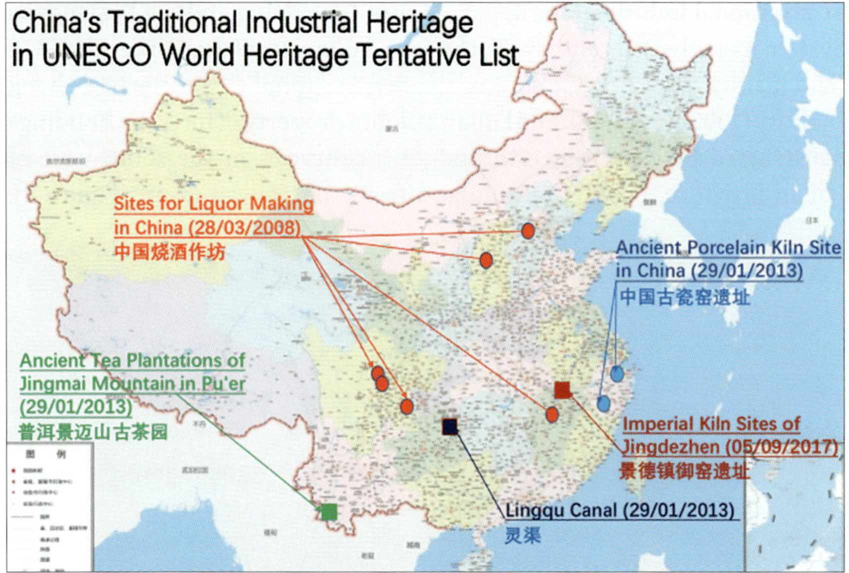

Figure 5. China's traditional industrial heritage properties in UNESCO World Heritage Tentative List.

Table 1. The Number of Industrial Heritage Properties in the List of Chinese National Protected Monuments and Sites

List No.	Date of Announcement	Total Number	Industrial Heritage	Percent
1	03/04/1961	179	11	6.15
2	02/24/1982	62	7	1.13
3	01/13/1988	285	20	7.02
4	11/20/1996	250	18	7.20
5	06/25/2001	521	37	7.10
6	06/02/2006	1,080	68	6.30
Total		**2,377**	**161**	**6.77**

Table 2. Industrial Heritage Properties in the List of Chinese National Protected Monuments and Sites by type

	List I	List II	List III	List IV	List V	List VI	Total
Wine-making	0	0	0	1	1	3	5
Textile	0	0	1	0	0	0	1
Oil	0	0	0	0	1	0	1
Nuclear	0	0	0	0	1	0	1
Beer-making	0	0	0	0	0	1	1
Power station	0	0	0	0	0	1	1
Military	0	1	1	2	0	3	7
Mine site	1	1	0	2	4	2	10
Bridge	6	1	3	2	8	23	43
Handicrafts	0	0	0	0	0	1	1
Irrigation project	0	1	4	1	3	6	15
Water traffic	0	0	0	1	3	3	7
Pottery-making	0	1	9	4	11	16	41
Observatory	0	0	0	1	0	0	1
Railway	0	0	0	0	1	2	3
Metal casting	3	2	2	0	0	1	8
Salt-making	0	0	0	0	0	1	1
Metallurgy	1	0	0	1	2	4	8
Post	0	0	0	1	0	0	1
Ship-making	0	0	0	1	0	0	1
Paper-making	0	0	0	1	2	1	4
Total	**11**	7	**22**	**18**	**37**	**68**	**161**

Besides the industrial heritage under the government systems of protection, there are also some private museums and local factory museums maintained by local enterprise and private parties.

CASE STUDY OF TRADITIONAL INDUSTRIAL HERITAGE: SALT MINING IN ZIGONG CITY

Salt has played an important role in Chinese history, not only as an essential item in daily life, but also a key to financial security for emperors.

In the interior of China, most salt comes from salt wells. The largest well-salt production base is at Zigong City, once called "The essence of Sichuan province" or the "Capital of well salt," and much richer than any other place in Sichuan. Zigong's technology of salt-making is unique, including drilling methods that were later adapted for modern oil and natural gas wells. These technologies are a great contribution to human civilization. Several academic papers have been written on Zigong City and its economic development. Here I will summarize this research, and make suggestions for conservation of the rich industrial heritage of Zigong's salt industry.

Salt production in Zigong can be traced back to the reign of Emperor Zhang (76–88 CE) during the Eastern Han Dynasty. Zigong gradually grew to become a city because of the salt economy. A salt monopoly was in force during the Han Dynasty. An ancient book, *Bo Tu Lun*, mentions "salt from Jiang Yang," an ancient name for Fushun County, the site of Zigong City today. In the reign of Emperor Wu (561–578 CE) of the Northern Zhou Dynasty, salt wells at Fushi and Dagong were producing on a comparatively large scale, resulting in these two places becoming the earliest administrative units in Zigong area.

The salt industry developed steadily during the Tang and Song Dynasties, with many new salt wells and increasing productivity. During the Kai Yuan period of the Tang dynasty, Fuyi (the new name of Fushi) and Rongzhou shared the first place in salt output in middle Sichuan. By the early Song Dynasty, the output of Fushun (the new name of Fuyi) and Gongshen (the new name of Dagong) was a tenth of the total in Sichuan.

Due to unrest in the Yuan Dynasty, Zigong's salt production stagnated until the early Ming era. During the Jiajing period of the Ming Dynasty, new sources were found and new wells drilled, resulting in unprecedented economic prosperity for Zigong.

As production cost for well salt was higher than sea salt, the market for Zigong salt was confined to Sichuan, except at two times when the coastal regions were at war, and Zigong's salt spread nationwide, resulting in the city being dubbed the "Salt Capital."

Zigong pioneered techniques for drilling boreholes and purifying the salt. During the Eastern Han Dynasty, Li Bing, the governor of Sichuan, oversaw drilling of the first salt well in China at Guangdu. During the Northern Song Dynasty (1041–1048 CE), the shock-type drilling method was invented at the Zhoutong Well, four centuries earlier than similar techniques in Europe. In 1835, the Shenhai Well became the deepest drilled borehole in the world at 1,001.42 meters. It is sometimes called the "father of well drilling" or "China's fifth-largest invention." At Zigong, soy milk was used to remove impurities to improve the quality of the salt.

Natural gas was discovered in wells drilled for salt production and initially used to boil brine. From the early 17th century, the gas was produced in significant quantitites. Around the turn of the 19th century, a new form of well head known as *kang pen* was invented to solve problems in recovering the natural gas. As a result, wells were able to output thousands of cubic meters of low-pressure natural gas each day.

Ever since the Ming Dynasty (1368–1644 CE), Zigong pioneered techniques for improving the safety of drilling and extracting operations. Some of those skills are still used in modern oil exploitation.

Zigong City developed from the salt economy, not as a military or political center. The early population was settled around the salt wells, with no city planning and no walls. As population expanded, markets appeared for cloth, food, timber, and other materials. Today, the names of many streets and blocks still record the salt industry in the past. Until 1939, the city's four main zones were known as Salt Well, Salt Range, Salt Field, and Salt Workshop. The city's culture is also influenced by salt.

The story of Zigong's salt has been recognized in the international academic world. The British scholar Joseph Needham listed twenty techniques from Zigong's salt industry in the volumes on chemistry in his monumental *Science and Civilization in China*. In 1993, Hans Ulrich Vogel described the drilling techniques from Zigong in an article in *Scientific American*, calling the deep Shenhai Well "The Great Well of China." Mark Kurlansky, an American writer, devoted a section of his book, *Salt: A World History*, to Zigong's history, technology, economy, and cuisine.

In China, specialized works on the history of salt have appeared since the early 20th century. Chen Ran's *Index of Works on the Chinese Salt History* lists almost a thousand books or articles published between 1911 and 1989. More have appeared since. However, this academic literature focuses on the history rather than the heritage.

HERITAGE SITES OF ZIGONG

At the time of writing, Zigong has five sites listed as National Protected Cultural Heritage, fifteen as Provincial Protected Cultural Heritage, and seventy-one as Civic Protected Cultural Heritage. Most of these sites are salt mines, salt wells, or otherwise associated with salt, and most are within the present built-up area of the city (Figure 6).

Table 3. Salt-related Protected Cultural Heritage Sites in Zigong

	Name	Location	Brief Introduction
National	Shenhai Well	Daan District	salt well, the first ultra-deep well
	Xiqin Guild Hall	Artesian Well District	Shanxi guildhall of salt merchants
Provincial	Salt Mill Site of Jicheng Well	Daan District	salt well
	Chastity and Filial Stone Archways of Lianggao Mountain	Daan District	stone archway of famous salt merchants' wives
	Chen's Ancestral Temple	Gong Well District	ancestral temple of Chen family
	Dongyuan Well	Gong Well District	salt well
	Huanhou Guild Hall	Artesian Well District	guildhall of hired laborers
	Highness Temple	Artesian Well District	guildhall of boat people
Civic	Li's Ancestral Temple	Daan District	ancestral temple of Li family
	Hele Ancestral Temple	Daan District	bank premises
	Wanshou Hall	Daan District	Jiangxi guildhall of salt merchants
	Highness Temple	Daan District	ancestral temple of Zhong fmily
	Zhonghehao Ancestral Temple	Daan District	Boat people raising funds
	Site of Sanduo Village	Daan District	site of an ancient village of salt merchants
	Shuangcheng Well	Daan District	salt well
	Yuantong Well	Daan District	salt well
	Site of Dagong Well	Gong Well District	site of a salt well
	Guizhou Guild Hall	Gong Well District	Guizhou guildhall f salt merchants
	Jinliu Well	Gong Well District	salt well
	Longwang Well	Gong Well District	salt well
	Nanhua Guild Hall	Gong Well District	Guangdong guildhall of salt merchants

	Name	Location	Brief Introduction
Civic	Pingkang Bridge and Water Gate	Gong Well District	the ancient salt waterway
	Tianlu Hall	Gong Well District	house of a salt merchant
	Yuyong Well	Gong Well District	salt well
	Yuanfeng Well	Gong Well District	salt well
	Yunzheng Well	Gong Well District	salt well
	Zhong Bridge and Water Gate	Gong Well District	ancient salt waterway
	Yonger Well	Yantan District	salt well
	Yuchangong Clan Hall	Yantan District	ancestral temple of Wang family (richest in Zigong)
	Site of Baolong Well	Artesian Well District	site of a salt well
	Chuanzhu Clan Hall	Artesian Well District	Sichuan guildhall of salt merchants
	Huicaikou Salt-Pass	Artesian Well District	ancient salt road
	Leshan Stele	Artesian Well District	erected by salt merchants
	Tonghong Well	Artesian Well District	salt well
	Xiaoqiao Well	Artesian Well District	salt well
	Xinshuangsheng Well	Artesian Well District	salt well
	Yandi Hall	Artesian Well District	guildhall of laborers

Salt mines and salt wells

Around 13,000 salt wells were sunk over Zigong's history. In the region of Dafengbao, there are 198 wells distributed over an area of 1.2 square kilometers,[23] roughly one well per 600 square meters, the densest distribution found in China, and possibly even in the world (Figure 7).[24]

23. Ma Zongyao and Nie Chengxun, "Ziliuwell Dafengpu Rock Salt Development Status and Its History," *Well Salt History Communication,* 1 (1983) (in Chinese)

24. Song Liangxi, "Techniques from openwell to Zuotong well, 1987; Song Liangxi, *Proceedings of salt history* (Chengdu: Sichuan People Press, 2008) (in Chinese).

Wooden derricks of a distinct shape over the salt wells, locally known as *tianche*, have become the symbol of the city, celebrated in songs and poems. By 2009, eighteen had been listed as Civic Protected Cultural Heritage Sites, however, ten of these have since been abandoned.

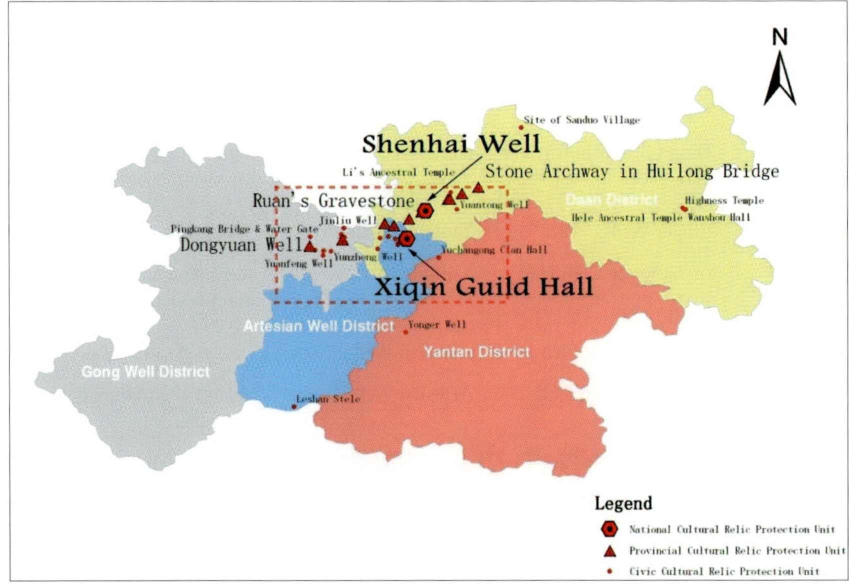

Figure 6. Distribution of salt relevant Cultural Relics Protection Units in Zigong.

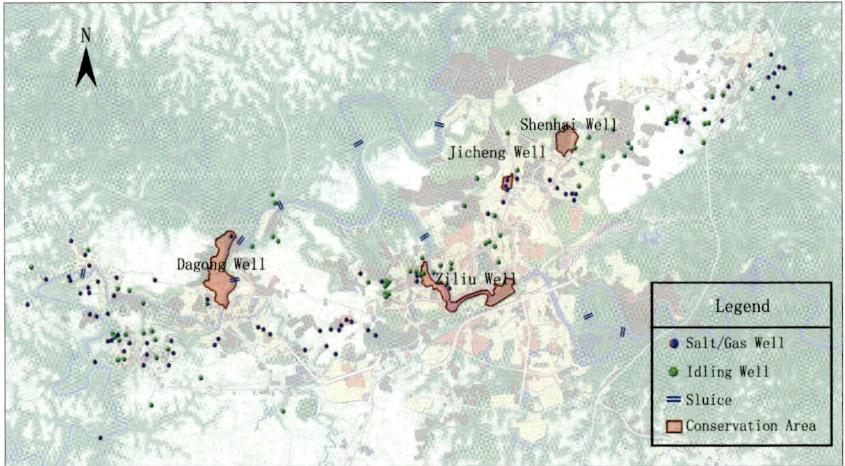

Figure 7. Distribution of salt wells in Zigong, according to *Zigong Urban Master Planning* (2001) and *Investigation of salt mines and wells* (2004).

Table 4. Partial list of salt guildhalls in Zigong

Type	Name	Builder
merchants' hall	Wuhuang Hall (五皇殿)	salt traders of all provinces
	West Qinling Guildhall (西秦会馆)	salt traders from Shanxi Province
	Nanhua Hall (南华宫)	salt traders from Guangdong Province
	Qiyun Hall (霁云宫)	salt traders from Guizhou Province
	Tianshang Hall (天上宫)	salt traders from Fujian Province
	Jiangxi Temple (江西庙)	salt traders from Jiangxi Province
	Huimin Hall (惠民宫)	salt traders from Sichuan Province
trades union hall	Jingshen Temple (井神祠)	salt miners
	Ziyun Hall (紫云宫)	salt traders
	Caishen Temple (财神庙)	bankers
	Wangye Temple (王爷庙)	boatmen
	Henghou Hall (桓侯宫)	cattle traders
	Laojun Temple (老君庙)	blacksmiths

Guildhalls became important during the Ming and Qing eras.[25] Most were built by merchants and laborers from outside the locality, for the purpose of "Greeting the gods and keeping in touch with Yingshenma (迎神麻), Lianjiahui (联嘉会), Xiangxiju (襄义举), and Duxiangqing (笃乡情)."[26] Salt guildhalls appeared in Zigong during the Yongzheng and Qianlong reigns of the Qing Dynasty. The earliest, West Qinling Hall, was

25. Wang Rigeng, "Gradual progress of guildhalls in Ming and Qing," *Historical Research*, 4 (1994) (in Chinese)

26. Jiangsu Provincial Museum, *A record of guildhall in Chaozhou and Collections of cave stone inscriptions of Jiangsu Province since Ming and Qing Dynasty* (Beijing: Joint Publishing, 1959) (in Chinese).

built between 1736 and 1752,[27] and now houses the Zigong Salt History Museum, listed as a National Protected Cultural Heritage Site. Many others were subsequently built by merchants from many provinces, varying greatly in size and style, reflecting different customs and religious beliefs. Although these guildhalls have lost their original function, their distinctive architectural forms are an integral part of the heritage of the salt industry.

Salt mines among industrial heritage

The study of industrial heritage began in the 1850s. As old industrial facilities fell out of use, the public began to recognize the value of industrial heritage, leading to research, conservation, and redevelopment. In 2005, TICCIH was listed as a consulting organization of UNESCO, showing that industrial heritage was gaining more attention.

Industrial heritage includes sites and artefacts with historical, technological, social, or scientific value. They include buildings, machinery, workshops, factories, mines, refineries, warehouses, energy sources, and transport facilities.[28] In 2006 there were forty-three industrial heritage sites on the UNESCO World Heritage List, ranging in time from the 20th century BCE to the 20th century CE, and distributed across twenty-three countries. Three of these are related to salt, all in Europe.

Table 5. Salt-related sites on the UNESCO World Heritage List

ID	Country	Year	Name	From Century	To Century
806	Austria	1997	Salzkammergut Cultural Landscape	2nd BCE	20th
818	Poland	1978	Wieliczka Salt Mine	13th	13th
203	France	1982	Royal Saltworks of Arc-et-Senans	18th	18th

The Salzkammergut Cultural Landscape was a site of salt ore mining from the early 2nd century BCE.[29] The rock salt mine at Wieliczka Salt Mine, which was established in the 13th century, has 300 kilometers of

27. Song Liangxi, *The rise and social function of Zigong guildhalls* (2001); Song Liangxi, *Proceedings of salt history* (Chengdu Sichuan People Press, 2008) (in Chinese).

28. Que Weimin, "Chinese traditional industrial heritage in the scope of world heritage," *Economic geography*, 6 (2008) (in Chinese).

29. whc.unesco.org/en/list/806

tunnels on nine levels, decorated with carvings of artworks and altars.[30] Construction of the Royal Salt Works at Arc-et-Senans began in 1775 during the reign of Louis XVI. In keeping with the spirit of the Enlightenment, the massive salt works was designed in a semicircular complex, inspired by the concept of an ideal city.[31]

The Zigong site also has a long history of 1900 years and a record of technological achievements, and hence measures up to the criterion for World Heritage listing.[32]

Table 6. Comparison of salt heritage sites under the World Cultural Heritage evaluation criteria

World Cultural Heritage Evaluation Criteria	i	ii	iii	iv	v	vi
Salzkammergut Cultural Landscape			x	x		
Wieliczka Salt Mine				x		
Royal Saltworks of Arc-et-Senans	x	x		x		
Salt Heritage in Zigong				x	x	x

Besides Zigong, three other cities have grown from the salt industry. They are Yancheng, Yuncheng and Golmud. At these sites, salt was produced from the sea of lakes, using the natural forces of the sun and wind.

Zigong is unique among these cities in producing from salt wells, and thus having developed drilling technology. Zigong also remains a center of salt production, while sea salt production at Yencheng has declined because of environmental change.

30. whc.unesco.org/en/list/32

31. whc.unesco.org/en/list/203

32. The criteria are: i. to represent a masterpiece of human creative genius; ii. to exhibit an important interchange of human values, over a span of time or within a cultural area of the world, on developments in architecture or technology, monumental arts, town-planning or landscape design; iii. to bear a unique or at least exceptional testimony to a cultural tradition or to a civilization which is living or which has disappeared; iv. to be an outstanding example of a type of building, architectural or technological ensemble or landscape which illustrates (a) significant stage(s) in human history; v; to be an outstanding example of a traditional human settlement, land-use, or sea-use which is representative of a culture (or cultures), or human interaction with the environment especially when it has become vulnerable under the impact of irreversible change; vi.to be directly or tangibly associated with events or living traditions, with ideas, or with beliefs, with artistic and literary works of outstanding universal significance. (The Committee considers that this criterion should preferably be used in conjunction with other criteria). whc.unesco.org/en/criteria/

Table 7. Comparison of salt cities

City	Nicknames	Geographic Location	Dynasty	Name Origin	Salt industry Status
Zigong	Capital of Salt	Southern Sichuan	Northern Zhou Dynasty (561–578 A.D.)	Collective term for Artesian Well and Gong Well	The center of well salt production in China
Yuncheng	Post-secondary Salt City	Southern Shanxi	Built at the end of the Yuan Dynasty (1206–1368)	Location of the Salt Administration during the Yuan Dynasty	Provincial chemical raw materials base
Yancheng	Capital of Lakes	Northern Jiangsu	Fourth year of Yuanshou in Wudi period (119 BC)	Saltworks all over the city	Sharing leading position on salt production at Huai area
Golmud	Salt Lake City of China	Eastern Qinghai	Belongs to Tu yuhun during the Western Jin Dynasty (265–316)	A district with most rivers and lakes	Richest salt comprehensive deposits in the world

Table 8. Comparison between salt cities

City	Type	Salt Manufacturing Techniques	Distinguishing Feature	Salt and City Development
Zigong	Well salt	Inject water in wells to dissolve salt, then boil the brine pumped from wells	The Shenhai Well is the first ultra-km deep well drilling by artificial	Develop salt culture tourism
Yuncheng	Lake salt	Using natural power, collected by the artificial	Yuncheng Salt Lake is one of the world's three major inland salt lakes in sulfate type	Develop the salt lake into "Floating Baths"
Yancheng	Sea salt	Evaporate brine in the sun to make salt	It's one of Chinese eight significant sea salt production bases	Develop salt and chemical industry
Golmud	Lake salt	Collect natural crystal of minerals by the artificial	Qarhan Salt Lake is a large multiple salt deposits with the primary composition of potassium and magnesium brines	Develop salt lake sightseeing

Current status of Zigong's salt heritage protection

Because the remains of the industrial heritage at Zigong are scattered over a wide area, it will be difficult to provide protection using the conventional approach of declaring a bounded conservation area or zone.

Zigong is already designated as a Historic and Cultural City with a system of zoning. Most of the salt sites lie within an area called the Zigong World Geopark. As noted above, the Shenhai Well and West Qinling Hall are listed as national heritage conservation sites, and several other sites are listed as provincial or civic heritage sites. These listings show the commitment to heritage conservation at Zigong. However, at present there is no integrated plan for the area. All the conservation plans emphasize the importance of architectural heritage, instead of industrial heritage.

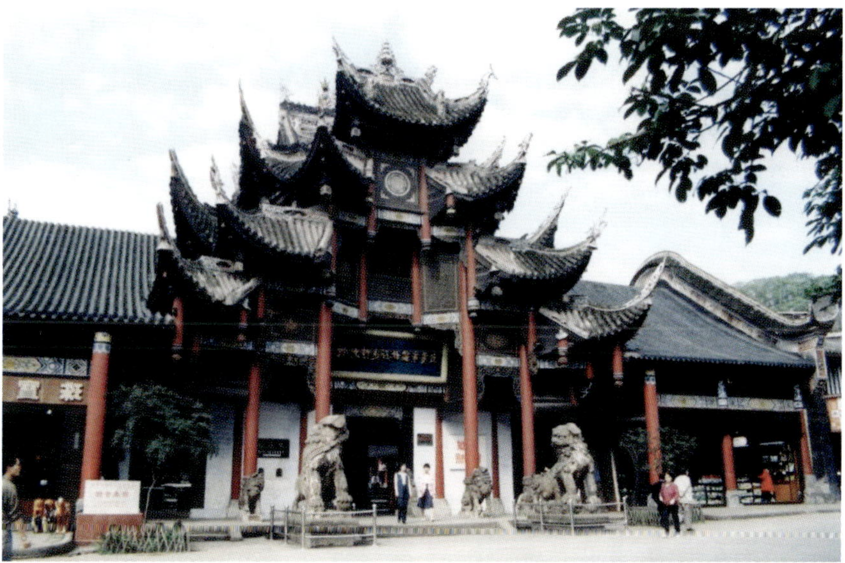

Figure 8. Xiqin Guild Hall, Zigong Salt Mining Industry Museum.

As with other types of heritage, industrial heritage has both physical form and social significance. The physical form includes the buildings, equipment, and the work processes.[33] These can be conserved in several ways including protection of the original fabric, and simulation of the operations. At the Salt History Museum, housed in the former West Qinling Hall, there are displays which fully demonstrate the process of salt manufacturing. At the Shenhai Well, the original equipment has been

33. Kou Huaiyun, *The study on the protection of the technology value of Industrial Heritage* (Shanghai-Fudan University, 2007) (in Chinese).

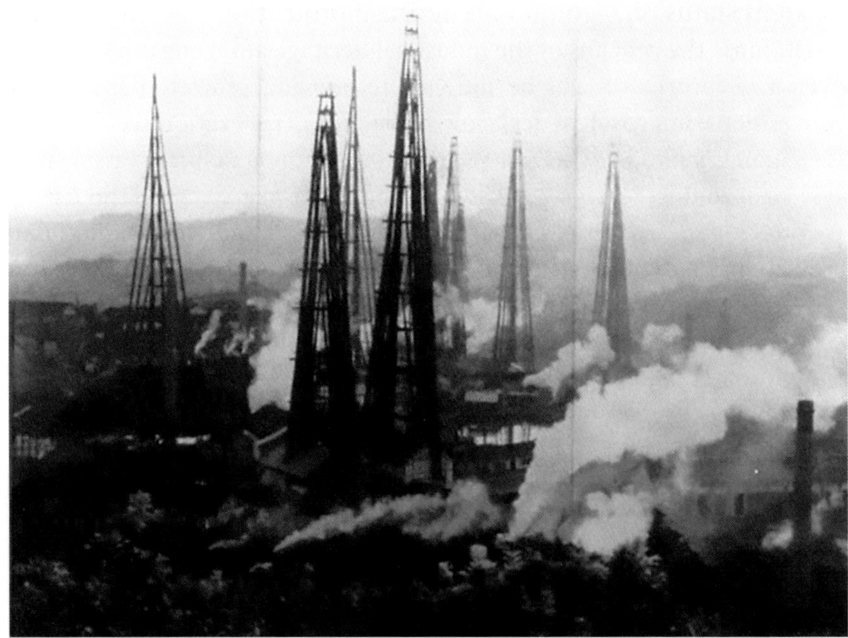
Figure 9. Zigong salt wells in the past. (Wiki Commons)

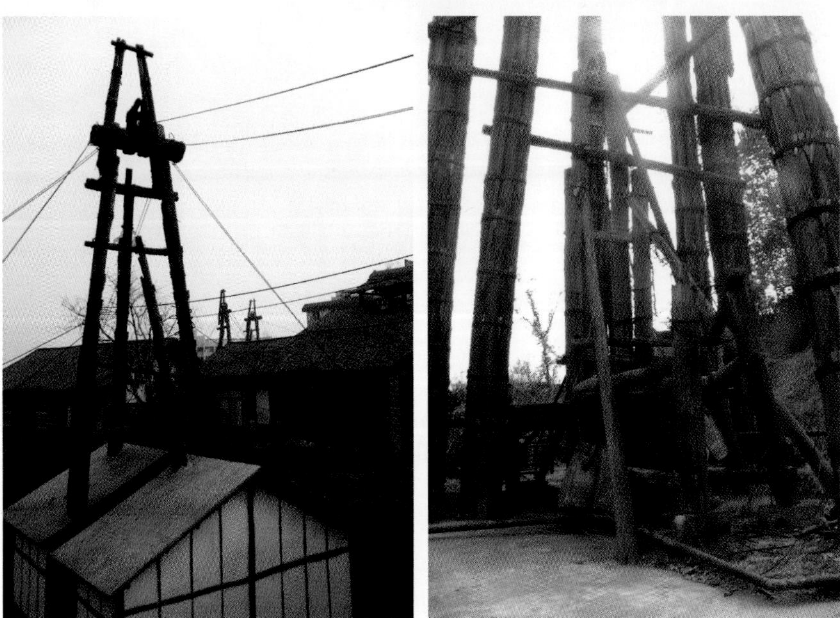
Figure 10. Ji-cheng salt wells. (Photos © Weimin Que, Dec. 26, 2010)

restored, and specialized workers are employed there to produce salt in the traditional way.

At present the social significance of the salt industry is less well-conserved and displayed at Zigong. The industry has clearly had an enormous impact on urban space, transport, economic life, folk culture, and so on. For the future, the whole city of Zigong should be conceived as a museum of salt heritage. Within that overall concept, various aspects of the salt heritage can be conserved and displayed in a series of museums, theme parks, and exhibits (Table 9).

Table 9. Proposal for Zigong salt heritage protection

Heritage Type	Retained Resources	Protection Form	Protection Mode	Materials Selected From
Operation skills	Personnel allocation, production mode, etc.	-	Static, open	Texts, images@museum
Industrial equipment	Production tools, auxiliary equipment, etc.	spot	Static, closed	Texts, images /in-kind exhibition@museum
Process flows	Technology, step process, etc.	line	Dynamic, open	Texts, in-kind exhibition @museum
Industrial works	Equipment layout, factory buildings, etc.	surface	Static, closed	In-kind display @conservation area; Texts, images /in-kind exhibition@museum
Urban space	Street forms, geographical names, etc.	line	Static, open	Texts, images /in-kind exhibition@museum; Textual description@street
Transportation	Courier routes, wharfs, etc.	line	Static, open	Texts, images @museum; in-kind display @conservation area
Economic life	Halls, dwellings, arch, ancestral temples, etc.	spot	Static, open	Texts, in-kind exhibition
Folk culture	Salt workers' food, poetry, etc.	-	Dynamic, open	In-kind experience and texts@theme park/block

THE SIGNIFICANCE OF TRADITIONAL INDUSTRIAL HERITAGE TO CHINA

Industrial heritage, especial traditional industrial heritage, has important significance to China.

First, research on both tangible and intangible cultural heritage should be combined in a field of Chinese traditional industrial heritage research.

Second, the study of Chinese traditional industrial heritage will promote the renewal, utilization, and development of traditional industries in all parts of China, delivering both economic benefits as well as social and cultural benefits. Renewal and transformation of traditional industries in cities and towns and environmental renovation of mining remains in rural areas will have a positive impact on the development of a harmonious society and new rural areas.

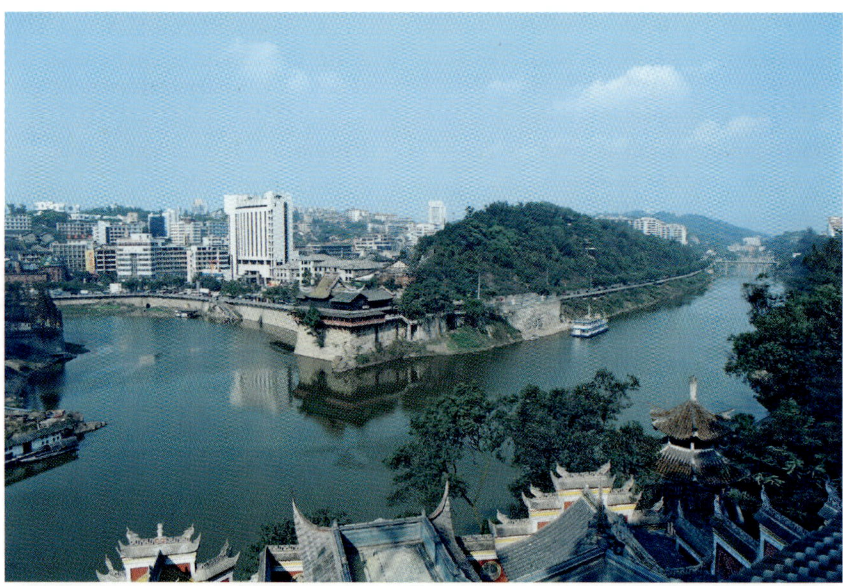

Figure 11. Zigong in 2010. (Photo © Weimin Que)

Third, the study of Chinese traditional industrial heritage will further the general cause of conserving China's cultural heritage. Before interest arose in industrial heritage, scholars and administrators who engaged in the research and management of cultural heritage came mainly from the academic fields of culture and archaeology or from government departments. Since the study of industrial heritage, especially traditional industrial heritage, has become an important part of cultural heritage research, the impact of cultural heritage and archaeological research has begun to penetrate into more and more areas of the national economy. The numbers engaged in cultural heritage research has rapidly expanded, and the social atmosphere for protecting cultural heritage has improved.

Fourth, the study of Chinese traditional industrial heritage will help to vitalize the economic development of the Western region, the rise of the central region, and the economic revival of the northeast. China's traditional industrial heritage is distributed across the different cultural regions, hence the social benefits from the protection and utilization of traditional industrial heritage will be well-balanced across the region. The Western, central, and northeastern regions will enjoy the same opportunities, challenges, and benefits as the southeastern coastal areas in terms of resource protection, cultural development, rational utilization of traditional industrial heritage, and the social and economic benefits.

China's traditional industrial heritage is industrial heritage with Chinese characteristics. Its heritage value is similar to the traditional industrial heritage in the West, with some sites having exceptional value. Therefore, traditional industrial heritage sites should have priority in the selection of properties for nomination to the World Heritage List.

Contributors

Catrini Pratihari Kubontubuh, Chairperson of Indonesian Heritage Trust, Republic of Indonesia

Frances Rudgard, Managing Director at Cambodian Living Arts, Kingdom of Cambodia

Gour Mohan Kapur, State Convenor of the West Bengal and Calcutta Regional Chapters of The Indian National Trust for Art and Cultural Heritage, Republic of India

Hu Xinyu, Trustee of Beijing Cultural Heritage Protection Center, People's Republic of China

Jean-Baptiste Phou, Head of Creative Programs at The Cambodian Living Arts, Kingdom of Cambodia

Joseph Sedfrey Santiago, Associate Professor at The John Gokongwei School of Management, Ateneo de Manila University, Republic of the Philippines

Kai Brennert, Institutional Partnerships Coordinator at Cambodian Living Arts, Kingdom of Cambodia

Khoo Salma Nasution, Vice-President of Penang Heritage Trust, Malaysia

Min Xu, College of Architecture and Urban Planning, Qingdao University of Technology, People's Republic of China

Piriya Krairiksh, Senior Research Scholar at The Thailand Research Fund, and Founder of The Piriya Krairiksh Foundation, Kingdom of Thailand

Que Weimin, Professor at The College of Urban and Environment Sciences, World Heritage Research Center, Peking University, People's Republic of China

Sujeong Lee, Senior Researcher at The Cultural Heritage Administration of Korea, Republic of Korea

Veomanee Douangdala, Co-Founder of Ock Pop Tok Weaving Center, Lao People's Democratic Republic

Yin Myo Su, Founder of Inle Heritage Foundation, Republic of the Union of Myanmar

Yongtanit Pimonsathean, Visiting Associate Professor at The Faculty of Architecture, Thammasat University, Kingdom of Thailand

Johannes Widodo and Tara Gujadhur acted as discussants and rapporteurs at the conference.

The conference organizing committee included Pikulkeaw Krairiksh, President of the Siam Society, Anna Fulgham, Danielle Schwaar, Euayporn Kerdchouay, Eileen Deeley, Jarunee Khongswasdi, Jenjira Van Der Linden, James Stent, Kanitha Kasina-Ubol, Kulathida Sivayathorn, Pimpraphai Bisalputra, Thomas Vitayakul, and Thweep Rittinaphakorn. Chris Baker oversaw the publication.

The Siam Society is grateful to the Ministry of Culture, the Tourism Authority of Thailand, and PTT Global Chemical Public Company Limited for their support for the conference where these papers were originally presented.